D1025019

Psychotherapy Tradecraft

THE TECHNIQUE AND STYLE OF DOING THERAPY

By

Theodore H. Blau, Ph.D.

BRUNNER/MAZEL, *Publishers* • New York

Library of Congress Cataloging-in-Publication Data

Blau, Theodore H.
    Psychotherapy tradecraft.

    Bibliography: p. 291
    Includes index.
    1. Psychotherapy. I. Title. [DNLM: 1. Psychotherapy
—methods. WM 420 B6435]
RC480.B56 1988   616.89'14   87-21786
ISBN 0-87630-479-X

Copyright © 1988 by Theodore H. Blau

Published by
BRUNNER/MAZEL, INC.
19 Union Square
New York, New York 10003

All rights reserved. No part of this book may be reproduced by
any process whatsoever without the written permission of the
copyright owner.

MANUFACTURED IN THE UNITED STATES OF AMERICA

10 9 8 7 6 5 4 3 2 1

Contents

PART III. RENEWAL

Tables and Figures

Acknowledgments

Efforts will be made to attribute ideas and procedures cited to available sources, where appropriate. Some procedures and techniques are original with the author. A great many more are the result of good mentors, general exposure to the literature and, most significantly, to talented and often gracious colleagues. Should the influence of anyone not be cited, the omission is unintentional and regretted.

Of those who influenced much of my thinking, practice technique, and style as a result of personal contact, I wish to especially acknowledge and thank the following: Bruno Bettelheim, Albert Ellis, Norman Farberow, Jerome Frank, Anna Freud, Herbert Freudenberger, Alfred Friedman, Robert Harper, Samuel Ingalls, Don Jackson, Sidney Jourard, Bertram Karon, Ogdon Lindsley, Abraham Maslow, Wendell Muncie, Fritz Perls, Carl Rogers, John Shlien, Edwin Shneidman, W.U. Snyder, and Hans Strupp.

Listening, arguing, learning, testing, modifying, counseling and sometimes imposing, I have used and appreciated my mentors, colleagues, and friends as well as I can. I would hope that the following pages reflect faithfully their influence upon my style of therapeutic tradecraft.

Introduction

My entrance into the mental health profession was accidental. While awaiting my call to service during the second World War, I sought a job to earn spending money and to pass the weeks of nervous waiting. Answering an advertisement for a "clerk-male" (no affirmative action in those days), I was hired to work in the psychology department of the Elmira Penitentiary. Elmira was a maximum security prison in the New York State Correctional System.

My boss, a young master's level psychologist, Raymond Corsini, created an excitement about things psychological. I spent only three months at Elmira before I was called up. In that time, I discovered the excitement of studying human behavior, an excitement that has lasted over 40 years.

While working with Corsini, I stumbled across the term "psychotherapy." Since I had been a chemistry and physics major during my one year of college, the term meant little. In response to my question of "What is it?", Corsini neatly defined it as "treatment for mental disorders." My curiosity aroused, I asked Corsini how one did psychotherapy. When I questioned him about interviewing, intelligence testing, and personality testing during my early weeks as his clerk, he was always explicit in explaining and demonstrating. I had an opportunity to see the origins of the great teaching style that was later to characterize Corsini's work. When I posed the "How is it done?" question regarding psychotherapy, the response was uncharacteristically vague and unspecific. I recall the dialogue as follows:

Blau: Can you treat any kind of mental disorder with psychotherapy?

Corsini: Well, that depends on a lot of things.

Blau: Like what?

Corsini: It's very complicated.

Blau: Well what do you do?

Corsini: What do you mean?

Blau: I mean—how do you *do* psychotherapy?

Corsini: Well, you don't exactly *do* it.

Blau: You must *do* something!

Corsini: Not necessarily. Sometimes the most important thing is to do *nothing*?

Blau: Do *nothing*?

Corsini: Yes . . . The patient has to do it.

Blau: Do what?

Corsini: Do the psychotherapy.

Blau: Well . . . Do you *teach* the patient how to do psychotherapy?

Corsini: No. That wouldn't work. He has to sort of discover how to do psychotherapy by himself.

Blau: You mean, like, the patient guesses what to do, then you tell him he's done right or wrong?

Corsini: No. You never tell the patient he is right or wrong.

Blau: Well—what do *you* do?

Corsini: The psychotherapist mostly listens.

Blau: To what?

Corsini: To the patient.

Blau: How does this cure mental disorders?

Corsini: Sometimes it doesn't.

Blau: I can appreciate that.

I was thoroughly confused. I had always been pragmatic and mechanically inclined. I tried to make a mental picture of the process, the persons involved, and the dialogue, but I was at a loss.

After the war, as I began to study psychology, the puzzle remained. Corsini had accurately reflected the vagueness concerning process and technique extant in the field of psychotherapy. Much later I found there were reasons—good and bad—to avoid excessive focus on technique. There remains, however, an imbalance between available information about the theoretical aspects of psychotherapy and the session-by-session tradecraft necessary for the conduct of effective psychotherapy.

Despite grave questions concerning treatment, efficacy, quality, outcomes, and ethics, psychotherapy has developed and grown not only as a professional tool, but as a highly desirable experience sought by troubled people at almost every social level.

Although the history of psychotherapy began in Europe, there is no question that this treatment method reached its zenith in the United States. America welcomed and nourished psychotherapy.

The history is long, interesting, and puzzling. This genesis is described and reviewed in Chapter 1. During the hundred years of psychotherapy's development, a wide range of theoretical foci have emerged. Few have disappeared. Even the most esoteric theories and concepts, long rejected by most teachers and practitioners, still attract some adherents.

The literature of psychotherapy is heavily weighted on the side of theory. There is an almost complete absence of *tradecraft*—what to do, when to do it, and how to do it.

Tradecraft refers to the specific techniques used by experienced and skillful psychotherapists to create the therapeutic setting; to invite and maintain a therapeutic alliance; to enhance the patient's progress; and, finally, to allow the patient to integrate and complete the process of psychotherapy. A search of psychoanalytic literature reveals an enormous amount of theory and speculation, countertheory and counterspeculation, but little tradecraft.

Psychotherapists have been battling about the question of "outcomes," "iatrogenic results," and other knotty issues. At this point in time, it is probably unrealistic to consider waiting for some quantum of additional proof before we train psychotherapists. The meta-analyses that have been reported by Smith & Glass (1977) and others demonstrate the worth of psychotherapy for the relief of emotional discomfort and the development of an improved view of self-worth.

There are a number of "schools" that require a very formal kind of preparation for the practice of psychotherapy. Most of the adherents to such schools, to a larger or lesser degree, discount practitioners of other schools. The internecine warfare among psychotherapists has a long and sometimes humorous history, but in most respects is without real significance.

Cultism in training abounds. Students seem to take on the style, the language and the concepts of their gurus. Such behavior is strikingly similar to religious fervor. The research is fairly clear that no one particular method or school clearly outweighs the others in terms of outcomes (Fiedler, 1951; Frank, 1979; Strupp & Hadley, 1977). Patients themselves sometimes "attach" themselves to a school. One sees "cultist" patients who are products (or victims?) of very intense and long-range psychoanalytic, Jungian, or Adlerian methods. Others may become part of briefer therapeutic-like ventures where a special language has developed, or where special procedures and group interactions are required (Gestalt, EST, Primal Scream, and so forth).

The processes by which one becomes a psychotherapist are explored in Chapters 2 through 4. Psychotherapy training is offered in many styles and settings. Some require a very formal preparation, while others require a variety of therapeutic participations after which the applicant is considered ready to practice. Both formalistic and experiential professional preparation will be explored in some detail in this volume.

There are probably some very good people conducting psychotherapy in every therapeutic school or style. There are a number of qualities necessary for a therapist to be effective and helpful. Personal qualities of sensitivity, empathy, and preparation to "give of self" require more specification. There are some skills or abilities that should receive considerable attention. These include a broad understanding of culture as it is today, and of the various regional, religious, family, and ethnic backgrounds from which patients have emerged.

The effective psychotherapist should have a great capacity to tolerate hostility, resentment, rejection and aggression. Reasons for this kind of tolerance will be presented. Much is to be said for Slavson's maxim that the really fine psychotherapist is someone who has suffered inordinately and has in some way overcome this successfully (Slavson, 1943). It is unlikely that a truly capable and sensitive therapist has never had any real emotional troubles.

The capacity to be aware of one's own faults and one's blind spots is critical. Tradecraft procedures and guidelines will be presented to help emerging therapists develop self-analytical skills. There will be a discussion of limitations, burnout and renewal.

Rarely can patients articulate clearly to the therapist where they expect to go or what they seek to accomplish. Vague generalities in the form of achievement ("happiness," "actualization," and other descriptors) are often discussed and too rarely explicated.

"Relief" is a general conceptual goal expressed by patients when they first come for psychotherapy. They seek the end of long depressive periods, grieving, resentment, failure-arranging, and other negative life circumstances. Beyond these usually lie deeper, hidden goals. Ensuring the maintenance of inadequate relationships, expending much energy for little return, and other neurotic styles characterize the lives that patients have lived up to the beginning of therapy.

A strong case will be made for a very thorough psychological assessment before therapy in order to identify some of the key conflict situations with which the patient will deal, assets available for the therapeutic process, and critical foci for discussion.

The experienced psychotherapist understands that the unspoken goals of the neurotic who approaches therapy include searching for mastery, justice, vengeance, punishment, and magic. Particulars of these expectations will be considered, as well as how such unrealistic expectancies can be channelized into productive insight.

It will be proposed in Chapter 5 that the first session of psychotherapy and possibly the second are critical in establishing the ground rules for the joint venture between the therapist and patient. The value of psychological assessment will be presented in the discussion of starting therapy. Suggestions will be made as to how to identify the therapist's responsibilities and the patient's accountabilities.

A great deal of attention will be paid to structuring. Techniques will be presented for patients to use in identifying the quality and level of their own progress. The purpose of the structuring of the therapy will be to place clearly in the patient's hands the responsibility for conducting the process as efficiently as possible with an awareness that the therapist will create a sanctuary wherein this can take place.

Chapters 6 through 8 on in-process tradecraft will include "acid tests," reflection, attitudes of acceptance, building of expectancy, interpretation, analysis of fantasy and dream content, maintaining the safety of the therapeutic session, and ensuring the patient's continued participation. Goals, expectancies, forms and procedures, files, breaking barriers, risk-taking, denying, comfort and success, and talking in two languages will be explored.

Chapter 9 on special issues will pursue in detail the requirements for dealing with patients suffering character disorders and borderline states. This section will also deal with such issues as the obsessional patient, the self-destructive patient, the interfering spouse, parent or child, and ancillary family issues.

Special attention will be directed to the joint responsibility of therapist and patient to focus on the issue of termination as early as possible in the therapy (Chapter 10). Signs, symptoms, opportunities, and "testing the water" procedures will be described.

The issues of transference and resistance and how they can enhance termination of therapy will be reviewed in terms of technique. Questions about the return to therapy by patients who later encounter troubles will be addressed.

Renewal needs and burnout as expected barriers to the continuance of effective therapy will be reviewed in Chapter 11 and resolutions suggested.

Throughout, the focus will be on technique and tradecraft.

PART I

On Becoming a Therapist

CHAPTER 1

The Origins of Psychotherapy Tradecraft

There has always been a need for help by suffering humans. We can assume that as long as *homo sapiens* has had language and tribal ritual, some of these needs have been spiritual and emotional. Witch doctors, shamans, priests, wise men, earth mothers, and other tribal dignitaries, formally designated or self-appointed, developed rituals and responses to deal with the pains and fears of their people. The origins of these forms of "psychotherapy" are only partly documented. Specifically designated tribal practitioners have clearly been available for millenia to resolve pain and conflict (Fabrikant, 1984).

It is probable that a kind of psychotherapeutic relationship existed between rulers (kings, emperors, pharoah, popes, war leaders, etc.) and their personal advisors (chamberlains, court counselors, consigliori, philosophers, ministers, secretaries, retainers, soothsayers, witch doctors, medicine men, augurs, and courtesans). Thus, the availability of psychotherapy to the well-to-do and the powerful has existed from the origins of the interaction to the present. An exhaustive study of the development of psychotherapy in the 20th century is beyond the scope of this book, but a brief review of the modern antecedents of psychotherapy today follows.

THE PSYCHOANALYTIC CONTRIBUTION

Freud and his colleagues would be credited by most psychotherapists as the pioneers of modern psychotherapy. Fundamental concepts of psychoanalytic theory continue to influence almost all forms of dynamic psychotherapy nearly a century after Freud first explicated his ideas concerning mental aberrations and their cure or resolution.

The cardinal concepts developed within the psychoanalytic framework by Freud and his many distinguished colleagues and students which continue to influence most dynamic psychotherapists include:

Freud's Topographic Concept of Mental Phenomena

Freud divided human mental phenomena into three major areas or sources of influence. Briefly described, they are:

- *The ego.* The "self" and the human's awareness of self.
- *The id.* Primitive urges, survival-oriented, within all human beings.
- *The super-ego.* Human conscience developed through experience with society's expectations.

Levels of Consciousness

A second concept crucial to the psychoanalytic theory of personality development, in respect to balance and imbalance, suggests that all humans have several levels of awareness. These include:

- *The conscious.* Those perceptions and cognitions about which the person is clearly aware of at any point in time.
- *The pre-conscious.* This level consists of memories, ideas, or thoughts which can easily be brought into conscious awareness.
- *The unconscious.* Excitations, ideas, or experiences that were pushed into the unconscious, away from the direct awareness of the conscious or the retrieval capacity of the preconscious. These are thought to be "unacceptable" ideas or excitations in psychoanalytic theory. They are "pushed" into the unconscious by the ego in order to protect the individual from threatening ideas or memories.

Neurotic Conflicts

Freud and his colleagues conducted psychotherapy within the framework of a theory which proposed that neurotic personal conflicts were battles between life drives and self-destructive impulses, as well as between pleasure drives and reality.

Stages of Personality Development

The psychoanalysts suggested that all civilized persons grow from birth to full maturity by passing through stages of personality development. Each stage poses opportunities for growth and power, but also for conflict. If a person resolves the conflicts, often with the help of parents, teachers, and social expectancies, the values of that stage are integrated and the person goes on to the next developmental stage, finally reaching full, functional maturity.

Disruptions, impoverished or missed experiences, and traumas during any of these stages may lead to serious negative consequences for the stability and strength of the personality in later life. Those who pass through various stages of development from birth to maturity without acquiring experience or models, who experience significant trauma, or who do not resolve unrealisitic fears and expectancies tend to become what psychoanalysts view as neurotics, unprepared to live their adult lives happily or effectively.

Defense Mechanisms

This concept emerged in psychoanalytic theory to describe the ways in which children and adults protect themselves from anxiety. Some anxiety is considered to be realistic (normal). Anxieties without a fairly direct connection to commonly stressful circumstances are considered unrealistic (neurotic).

A teenager who loses a girlfriend and is disappointed in this loss may deal with his anxiety (the disappointment) by a variety of defense mechanisms such as *displacement* (intense and aggressive activity on the football field) or *rationalization* ("I really didn't like her that much"). Such defense mechanisms are considered useful or "normal" for relieving stress.

Neurotic defense mechanisms may be distinctly abnormal, such as *delusional thinking* ("my opponent sneaked a drug into my coffee this morning to make me lose"). There may be neurotic extensions of ordinary defense mechanisms such as *displacement* (after breaking up with his girl, John began practicing blocking and tackling for three and four hours a day *after* regular football practice). A neurotic extension of *rationalization* might be: "I didn't *really* like Betty. If she hadn't broken up with me, I'd have broken off with her. I really only went out with her because I felt sorry for her. She's really pretty bad."

Treatment Methods

Once Freud had conceptualized personality structure and neurotic defenses, he proposed a system of treatment which became known as psychoanalysis. The formal structure of traditional psychoanalytic therapy includes the following:

- *Frequency.* Generally, three to five sessions per week over an extended period of time. The classic psychoanalytic session lasts 50 minutes.
- *Place.* Psychoanalysis takes place in the analyst's office, with the patient (or analysand) lying on a couch while the psychoanalyst sits in a chair during the session
- *Procedures.* The analyst is generally fairly inactive, preferring that the patient choose topics and do most of the talking. The patient's random expressions are termed *free associations.* When there is a free flow of very emotional responses, *catharsis* is said to have taken place. The analyst makes *interpretations* in an effort to aid the patient in discovering his or her own neurotic behavior. It is expected that the patient will learn more about himself or herself as the sessions proceed. As self-awareness increases, neurotic mechanisms of defense become less necessary. When this happens, the patient can expect to feel better.

Psychoanalysts of the first half of the 20th century intensified their focus on social role and environmental influences in the development of neurotic life-styles. This movement, sometimes referred to as *neoanalysis,* emphasized the importance of cultural expectancies and pressures on both family life and individual development.

This has been a very condensed and limited presentation of the theory and technique of psychoanalysis. It serves to illustrate the important influences of psychoanalytic theory and psychotherapy on the development of other 20th century dynamic psychotherapies (Bernstein, 1965; Martin, 1971; Fabrikant, 1984).

REVISIONS OF PSYCHOANALYSIS

Efforts to modify or modernize psychoanalytic theory and style continue. With some regularity, psychoanalysts are accused of adhering to ideas which have never been sufficiently explored scientifically. Recent neuropsychological research lends support to Freud's ideas on the biology of the unconscious (Harper, 1975).

MID-CENTURY DEVELOPMENTS

Rogerian Therapy

Following the development of psychoanalysis, a variety of derivatives and modifications of Freud's pioneer work emerged. Rogers (1942, 1951,

1961) introduced and developed *non-directive* or *client-centered* psychotherapy. Rogers proposed a universal need for *positive regard*. In the therapeutic setting, such regard is to be given *unconditionally*, according to the Rogerian position. Therapists must develop a deep, sensitive resonance to *clients'* needs, which Rogers called *empathy*. Rogers and his students emphasized the importance of *congruence* (outer expressions matching inner feelings). Congruence must be first modeled by the psychotherapist if the client is to respond in kind. In Roger's conceptualization, the patient will respond to unconditional positive regard and congruence, and *actualize* their potential.

The Humanistic Therapies

Following the Rogerian movement, and to some extent a development by Rogers' students, proponents of a *humanistic* approach to psychotherapy emerged in the 1950s. Labeled *Phenomenological* psychotherapy, *Existential* psychotherapy, *Gestalt* psychotherapy, and a host of other permutations, they were often called "now" therapies. Little attention was given to detailed evaluation of background, family, or social influences. Focus was on the patient and his or her interaction with the environment in the here and now (Martin, 1971).

Nondynamic Therapies

Nondynamic *behaviorally*-oriented psychotherapies were proposed and developed at mid-century. Attempting to utilize psychological research and theory in the areas of basic reinforcement principles and social learning, these therapies focused primarily on inappropriate, disturbing, or inefficient behavior. Patients or *subjects* were helped to identify and chart or record their own behavior patterns. The subject would then decelerate, shape, or mold the behavior toward selected goals, using rewards or, in some cases, aversive or punishment responses (Wolpe, 1958; Bandura, 1969; Dollard & Miller, 1950; Sherman, 1973). These therapies have challenged traditional psychotherapy as the primary treatment of choice for many disorders.

Crisis Consultation

In recent years, mental health professionals have developed shorter, more specific interventions to deal with very impelling problems. Suicidal ventures, tragic death, rape, sudden and intense marital conflict, divorce sequelae, and child custody battles tend to create stress reactions which are addressed by mental health workers using the crisis consultation method. In this method, a series of supportive contacts between the psychotherapist and the client/patient/victim are scheduled until the immediate stress is relieved. Dynamic or analytic psychotherapeutic methods are rarely used. Contacts may be several times daily. The contacts are considered by some to be primarily *counseling* rather than psychotherapy.

The dividing line between counseling and psychotherapy is not clear. Counseling, more than dynamic psychotherapy, is characterized by the following:

- A shorter series of contacts than in psychotherapy.
- Less regularly spaced than a psychotherapeutic sequence.
- The counselor usually attempts to direct the patient or client to focus on what are considered the most pressing problems.
- Counselors are usually active in suggesting solutions and achieving specific goals.
- Counseling procedures all but ignore the dynamic structural systems which may underlie the clients' nonenhancing behavior.
- The counselor usually expresses clear approval or, occasionally, disapproval of behavior which meets the counselor's preconceived notions of what is good or bad for the client.
- Counselors, as a group, have considerably less training in personality theory, family systems, developmental psychology, and abnormal psychology than psychotherapists.
- Counseling tends to be more repressive of inner dynamics, focusing more on behavior believed to make the client more functional.

The counseling environment is generally less accepting of unusual ideas, tangential emotional states, and open exploration of feelings than dynamic psychotherapy. Psychotherapists tend to consider and explore and analyze client behavior which might generally be labeled "irrational," "peculiar," or even "insane." Counselors tend to see such behavior as beyond their role and counterproductive to the counseling task.

Some counselors do explore deeply and some psychotherapists counsel. The variety of styles and mixes is unknown but probably very extensive (Budman & Gurman, 1983).

Behavioral Medicine and Biofeedback

Although relatively recent as a "movement," the concept of seeking relief of symptoms and developing feelings of wellness through brain-behavior linkages is not new. During the early 1930s, some psychotherapists began to use exercises, passive concentration, and other means of inducing shifts in the patient's psychophysiological state. Such methods became known as "autogenic training" (Harper, 1975). Biofeedback is a method of controlling a physiological/behavioral system by reinserting past performance into the patient's awareness. To accomplish this, monitoring instruments are used to detect and amplify the patient's internal physiological response to pain, anxiety, fear, tranquility, and other states. The measurements may include skin temperature, skin conductivity, heart rate, or brain waves. The measured information is fed back to the individual on a visual display or an auditory signal, allowing the patient to modify the body processes (usually heart rate, body temperature, muscular stimulation, or brain waves). The modification of these body states by the patient may then reduce or eliminate a wide range of symptoms (Stern & Ray, 1977).

Biofeedback has been successfully used to alleviate anxiety, reduce high blood pressure, and relieve migraine headaches. Some researchers report success in reducing hallucinations in hospitalized schizophrenics. Promising research suggests such techniques may be used in rehabilitative neurotraining with the brain-damaged patient (Brown, 1975).

This short chapter cannot serve as a thorough review of the development of psychotherapeutic methods. All therapists should be aware of the origins of their tradecraft as well as alternate opportunities for patients to seek resolution of pain and distress. References which would be helpful in developing a deeper appreciation of the century of development which lies behind current psychotherapy are starred (*).

OUTCOME RESEARCH

Major problems face psychotherapy practitioners in choosing among the many conceptual and methodological approaches that make up the field of psychotherapy. Many distinguished researchers feel that outcome research will eventually help guide the development of more efficient and broadly applicable therapeutic methods (Harvey & Parks, 1982).

There has been much criticism of dynamic psychotherapy (Stuart, 1970; Telch, 1981; Eysenck, 1978). On the other hand, a number of distinguished researchers support the significance and efficacy of dynamic and behavioral psychotherapeutic methods (Fiedler, 1951; Strupp & Hadley, 1977; Smith & Glass, 1977; Frank, 1979; Glass & Kiegl, 1983; Lambert, Christensen & DeJulio, 1983).

At this writing, most researchers in psychotherapy agree to some extent on the following conclusions about the process:

1. No one form of psychotherapy seems significantly more effective than any other form in terms of the proportion of patients who show positive change.
2. More patients gain from their psychotherapy experience than not.
3. Almost all of those who engage in psychotherapy experience some degree of fear or anxiety reduction, increase in self-esteem, and improved adjustment in productivity (school or work).

CHAPTER 2

The Essence of the Psychotherapeutic Process

In 1909 Muensterberg observed, "That which binds all psychotherapeutic efforts together into unity is the method of treatment." In a more modern view, Frank (1961) suggested three criteria for a psychotherapeutic relationship: (1) A trained, socially sanctioned healer whose healing skills are accepted by the sufferer; (2) A sufferer who to seek relief comes to the healer; (3) A fairly circumscribed and structured series of contacts between healer and sufferer, individually or group shared. The changes in the sufferer's life are brought about primarily with words, acts, or rituals in which the sufferer and the healer participate jointly.

Before the tradecraft can be presented with clarity and effect, certain information and assumptions concerning the process and product of psychotherapy should be clarified. Following the general assumptions presented in this chapter, roles, procedures and behaviors of all concerned in the process will be explored in greater detail in later chapters. Illustrations of particular aspects of tradecraft and technique will be offered.

THE PARTICIPANTS

The Patient

The person who seeks service, relief, or change may be called "patient," "client," "analysand," or any one of several other labels. Throughout this work, the reference will remain "patient," with little or no im-

11

plication of "illness" other then the generic bad feelings most patients report on seeking psychotherapeutic services.

Patients are sufferers. Very few who feel good and are positive about themselves seek psychotherapy. Relief, understanding, or a new style of behavior is requested or required. Almost all who seek psychotherapy have tried other methods, without sufficient satisfaction in the product or results. Most are frightened, angry, depressed, or perturbed.

It is probable that more people who want or need psychotherapy do not come for help than those who do make appointments with psychotherapists. Shame, fear of revelation, and expectancy of failure plague all patients to some degree. Such intense feelings may prevent large numbers of potential patients from ever seeking help. Most people who do seek psychotherapeutic services will tell their therapist that the decision to make an appointment was a painful process of resolving ambivalence and finally, after many delays, taking the risk of making the appointment.

There are those sufferers who enter therapy, find the setting too stimulating or frightening, and quickly leave. After five to ten sessions they may decide that psychotherapy "doesn't work" or that the therapist is giving them too little advice and direction. Some patients experience a *flight into health,* proclaiming insistently that the therapist is wonderful and has "cured" the problem in half a dozen sessions. Such frightened patients may return at some future time when they feel more able to bear the emotional strains they fear are associated with self-exploration.

Some patients may enter psychotherapy, establish a routine of regular sessions in their lives, and show no inclination to ever leave. The psychotherapy becomes real life to them, rather than a preparation to live real life more effectively and comfortably. Although all patients who commit themselves to the therapeutic process tend to become somewhat dependent and needful of the therapeutic sessions, some seem willing to settle for the occasional peace and safety of the regular psychotherapeutic session. They avoid the steps necessary to expand their capacity to incorporate broader and deeper experiences into their lives and to become their own therapists.

The Psychotherapist

The essential role of the psychotherapist is that of healer. This role may be played in many ways. It is a role that goes far beyond being present, talking, and listening.

The psychotherapist is a professional person who has received training at a basic level in one of the helping professions (psychology, social work, medicine, education, mental health services), and then proceeds to more advanced training, supervision, and qualification in one or more styles of psychotherapy. The student of psychotherapy is not a psychotherapist. Experience and supervision should follow didactic training before students present themselves as qualified healers, available to sufferers.

In addition to the formal training requirements for status as a psychotherapist, certain personal traits have been found to be helpful in some instances, essential in others. By the time trainees present themselves to the public as ready and qualified to treat patients, they should be able to demonstrate to themselves, to their supervisors, and to their trainers that they can perform their role with intelligence and sensitivity. The competent psychotherapist must be committed to the process with a reasonable degree of confidence in the process and an expectancy that there will be positive results.

The competent therapist must be realistic without excessive rigidity. Awareness of the complexities and stresses of the real world is essential. The most competent therapists are usually very experienced about life as a result of having worked through challenges, failure, success, and perturbation of their own. The very best therapists may be those who have experienced, faced, and resolved complex life circumstances and interpersonal conflict.

The competent and skillful therapist is willing to relinquish power and prestige in the eyes of his or her patient as the patient gains understanding, insight, confidence, and self-esteem. To complete psychotherapy successfully, a patient must gain in power and responsibility with the tacit acceptance of the therapist.

Therapists must develop and maintain appropriate role orientation in order to create a productive and successful therapeutic setting. Such a setting must be safe: a sanctuary, where the patient may risk viewing forbidden or frightening ideas. Role orientation, together with structuring and verbalization, forms a triumvirate of what psychotherapists "do" (Proctor & Rosen, 1983).

The therapist must, above all, be willing to commit himself or herself to the process of enhancing the patient's potential for self-help. This should include a consistent, relatively energetic, thoughtful, and flexible exercise of the best psychotherapeutic tradecraft the therapist can command.

THE PROCESS

The psychotherapeutic process has been viewed in widely divergent ways. O'Connell (1983) has proposed that success in psychotherapy is essentially a *placebo effect*. He characterizes the process as one in which the therapist and patient are two "believers." They form a complementary but unequal relationship. The therapist defines and explains, while the patient accepts and digests this information. The therapist inspires confidence in the process and an expectancy of success. Some have argued that a *placebo effect* is a powerful psychological process, not to be disdained (Wilkins, 1984).

In order for the process of psychotherapy to move forward with success, the patient must be active. In a variety of ways, the patient begins to tolerate random events without overreactions. The patient learns to experience a flexibility of wants and needs. Plans can be made, as well as sacrifices, without undue stress or pain. The patient begins to generalize tolerance and, hopefully, finds that this is, firstly, safe, and then even satisfying. Dynamic psychotherapies differ from other forms of psychotherapy in expecting and working toward very broad generalization and application of efforts and gains.

The Nature of Neuroses

To a large extent, psychotherapy is guided, at least initially, by the symptoms, stresses, behaviors, and mechanisms of defense brought to the treatment setting by the patient. Some of the commonest themes or lifestyles brought to psychotherapy for modification include:

Illness. Many patients simply *hurt*. Headaches, stomachaches, bowel disturbances, sleep disruption, eating disorders, general malaise, and specific body pain or discomfort are common to many patients.

Poor productivity. Neurotic life adjustments are frequently characterized by enormous energy devoted to limited or even infinitesimal personal productivity.

The repetition of familiar patterns. In almost all dynamic psychotherapy, one sees simple and complex repetitive patterns of poor adjustment in many important aspects of the patient's behavior. Sometimes these patterns of maladjustment emulate the behavior of parents or even grandparents as though to maintain a familial tradition of neurosis.

Waiting for Godot. In Nobel Laureate Samuel Beckett's play *Waiting for Godot*, the two main characters consider a variety of the world's ills, arguing solutions pro and con. In no case do they make a decision, ending each sequence with an agreement to wait until their mentor Godot arrives to help make the decision. Godot never arrives. So it appears with many psychotherapy patients. Painful problems and conflicts seem to hang suspended. The patient seems constrained to avoid taking action in his or her best interest—as though waiting for Godot.

The Peter Pan fantasy. Sir James Matthew Barrie dramatized brilliantly the conflicts surrounding emergence from childhood into the often painful realities of maturity. In his *Peter Pan*, a somewhat asexual male character, *Peter* (always played by a female) with intelligence, courage, idealism, and considerable magical power, teaches, leads, and protects a host of admiring children. Yet, when the chips are down, he (she?) needs a "Wendy mother" to meet childish but powerful dependency needs. Many patients dream of and work toward power and success but seem able to maintain such drive only when supported by a powerful mother figure, ever present to meet unresolved dependency needs and fears of abandonment. The powerful individual unable to function in work or social interaction without an infantile, demanding, and often mutually destructive relationship with a superficially nurturing figure is a common neurotic theme.

The Sisyphus reaction. In Greek mythology, Sisyphus is condemned to roll a boulder up a hill until the top is almost successfully reached. At that point, Sisyphus is unable to achieve the last effort which will bring success, and the stone rolls down the hill. Sisyphus is forced to strive for but never quite reach success. Experienced psychotherapists see many variations of this neurotic theme of striving but never quite winning (usually because of unconscious guilt). Fear of success leads to self-sabotage (Pappo, 1983). As the psychotherapeutic process proceeds, the manner in which the patient tends to spoil success is frequently revealed and constitutes a major step toward resolution.

Anhedonia. People who are seen in psychotherapeutic settings generally have little fun. Their lives seem focused on problems, conflicts, responsibilities, guilt, and self-recrimination. In its extreme forms, this lack of pleasurable experience is called *anhedonia* and represents a symptom of very severe maladjustment. Many patients, particularly in the earlier stages of psychotherapy, seem fearful of seeking or even discussing pleasure.

The Hamlet ambivalence. Shakespeare's tortured character laments "to be or not to be," neither able to face life boldly nor able to end it. Such responses are so frequently found among patients in psychotherapy that it may be that all patients who explore the self with any degree of thoroughness must face their mixed feelings about continuing to battle a seemingly endless series of problems and frustrations. Depression, feelings of hopelessness and thoughts of terminating one's life may be a part of living, seen frequently, poignantly, and insistently in psychotherapy. The patient who believes that life is too painful, yet death is too frightening, presents a figure of extreme confusion and unhappiness. Indecision about the value of one's life can be an important starting point for therapeutic exploration of the sources of such painful feelings, as well as of alternate and more satisfying life choices.

Secret doubts. Many superficially successful, powerful, self-assured people seek psychotherapy. By usual and customary standards, they are high achievers, admired and envied by others. Such outstanding persons can be very unsure and doubtful within themselves. They may see themselves as "Fakes," "Lucky," "Undeserving," etc. Such secret self-doubts eventually produce painful symptoms.

Dutch boy reactions. In the classic child's fable, the Dutch boy must keep his finger in the dike to prevent the awesome power of the sea from breaking through and destroying the community. Many patients maintain their neurotic balance by "holding in." The idea of "letting go" is too frightening. To let go, talk freely or express feelings spontaneously is perceived as inviting disaster. Although the patient may intellectually accept the value of free association of thoughts, allowing oneself to let go is too terrifying. Early in the psychotherapeutic course, the patient becomes aware of the necessity and value of letting go, but, as in real life, is usually unable to act in his or her own best interest. The inability to let loose, to share, to experience in the therapeutic setting reflects the patient's customary constricted life-style.

By no means do the above simplifications represent the full scope of problems, symptoms, or neurotic defenses characteristic of those who seek help in psychotherapy. They are representative and illustrative. That some may be characterized in classic literature suggests that humans have suffered emotional distress and inner confusion throughout the history of civilization.

The patient's initial or *presenting* complaints rarely represent the most important or target issues which eventually become the major focus of psychotherapy (Sorenson, Gorsuch & Mintz, 1985). Experienced therapists learn that complaints or problems first presented by patients are frequently modified or replaced as therapy proceeds.

The Psychotherapist's Activity

Although dynamic psychotherapists may say little during the therapeutic session, a great deal goes on (or should go on) internally. Acquiring and utilizing a variety of special professional evaluative and structural skills are vital to effective conduct of psychotherapy. Significant elements of the therapist's activity during psychotherapy include:

Clear procedures. The effective psychotherapist avoids unnecessary stress and unsureness by establishing clear and reasonable ground rules regarding fee, time, sequence, and procedures in the psychotherapeutic contract between patient and therapist.

Establishing a sanctuary. Essential to successful psychotherapy is a setting perceived by the patient as safe. Such safety is demonstrated superficially by closed doors, a soundproofed office, and confidential records. Of equal or greater significance is the quality of interactional safety created by the experienced therapist. This aura of security enables and encourages the patient to speak of painful thoughts, explore frightening experiences and fantasies, and consider openly the risks of abandoning neurotic behavior.

Consistency. Progress comes from changes in the patient's perceptions and awareness. Changes by the therapist can easily disrupt and extend the psychotherapeutic process. The therapists style, office decor, manner of approach, and verbal expression must be relatively known to and predictable by the patient. This plays an essential part in establishing the therapeutic setting as a sanctuary.

An aura of encouragement. Direct expressions of support and encouragement by the dynamic psychotherapist may do more harm than good. The essence of encouragement is the experienced psychotherapist's consistent presence, attention to the details of the patient's expressions, and tolerance for the patient's various emotional responses. Judgments of progress, supportive statements, and encouragement by helpful hints suggest that the patient is in some way without potential for the essential self-qualities necessary to direct, support, and govern his or her own behavior.

Tolerance. Although no one aspect of the psychotherapist's attitude or personality can be considered solely responsible for the success or failure of the psychotherapeutic process, tolerance may be a principal factor.

Tolerance must be viewed in two ways: first in respect to individual value judgments, and then with regard to the inherent pressures and demands of the practice of psychotherapy.

The psychotherapist must be capable of allowing free expression of ideas, thoughts, fantasies, and fears. The patient must be free to hold, explore, or reject any view or belief. A preference for ideas or practices which differ from those of the psychotherapist must be permitted and respected. The therapist may not agree or sympathize with such practices or beliefs, but must allow and endure discussion of anything by the patient during the psychotherapy session.

In addition to the tolerance noted above, the effective psychotherapist must be able to endure or tolerate sequences of sessions involving apparently tangential and sometimes unpleasant responses on the part of the patient. These may include long silences, violent hostility toward others (including the therapist), manipulation, limit-testing, fawning dependency, evasion, and innumerable other face-to-face demonstrations of the patient's propensity to interfere with his or her own opportunities to live effectively and happily.

Few psychotherapists have this quality of tolerance early in their careers. It seems to develop as experience demonstrates the power of such acceptance to enhance the psychotherapeutic process.

Focus. The psychotherapist must become prepared, by training and experience, to sense the emergence of a word, a phrase, a memory, or a description that is of greater significance than meets the eye (or ear) when first expressed by the patient. The first clues a patient gives to deep, disturbing, causal experiences is likely to be subtle, disguised or tangential to what the patient seems to be saying. The experienced therapist senses such potentially important information and encourages the patient to first focus attention on what has been said. The goal is for the patient to follow the focusing with further exploration, then to *experience* the emotion connected with the emerging, previously hidden or misunderstood material (Gendlin, 1971).

Clarification of roles. Few patients begin psychotherapy with clear ideas as to what they are going to "do" during the process. Most patients expect that the therapist will conduct, direct, or govern the process. In spite of careful early structuring by the psychotherapist, patients tend to continue to be unsure of the parts they might best play during the therapy session. They continue to have a wide range of realistic and unrealistic expectancies as to the psychotherapists's responsibilities in the session in spite of repeated structuring. This is to be expected. The patient is likely to demonstrate the expectancies, confusion, and demands of his or her life-style during psychotherapy sessions. The therapist, by style and attitude, must consistently help the patient to be aware that choice of topic, exploration of feelings, maintaining congruence and weighing of values are tasks best performed by the patient. Ensuring the consistency and stability of the session is a vital role of the psychotherapist.

Avoiding judgments. Almost all those who seek psychotherapy feel empty, limited, undervalued, or simply "bad." They may seek a variety of expectations, decisions, directions, or judgments from the psychotherapist. To judge or evaluate a patient is to tacitly proclaim that he or she is not capable of self-determination. The competent psychotherapist avoids weighing or judging the patient's values. Every effort is made to have the patient evaluate himself or herself as part of the therapeutic process of attaining control of one's own life. It is tempting to respond to the patient's pleas for the therapist's wise judgment or opinion. The wise and emotionally secure psychotherapist considers respect for the patient's potential for self-evalutation to be of much greater value than any demonstration of therapeutic wisdom.

The refusal of advice. In spite of structuring to the contrary, most patients expect specific directions and suggestions concerning the best way to deal with their conflicts. Although this may be a major aspect of various kinds of counseling, advice in dynamic psychotherapy should be regarded as usually unhelpful. Advice-giving tells the patient that the therapist accepts the patient's incompetence, confusion, and poor judgment. Advice-giving postpones or undermines the patient's risk-taking, self-evaluation, and independence.

Expectation of fluctuations. All psychotherapists and patients experience "good" sessions and "bad" sessions. For some patients, a very productive session is almost inevitably followed by one or more sessions characterized by evasion, long silences, and tangential discussion. Patients can become fearful of self-revelation and too-rapid development of understanding. They seem compelled to create the security of a slow-down in the process of psychotherapy. The competent psychotherapist understands such fluctuations and tolerates "plateaus" where the patient seeks reassurance against loss-of-control anxieties by slowing or stopping the self-exploration process.

The surrender of leadership. Some of the satisfactions sought by those who train to become psychotherapists involve feelings of power and security associated with authoritarian and leadership roles. Indeed, many patients seek or prefer an authoritarian psychotherapist during periods of despair and confusion. An authoritarian role played by the psychotherapist is probably somewhat helpful very early in the process of psychotherapy. Unless the therapist is willing to abdicate this role and surrender the leadership and control of the focus of the therapy session, independence for the patient is unlikely to be achieved.

The style and speed of the exchange of focus of control from the psychotherapist to the patient will vary in each case. The movement of power from the psychotherapist to the patient is likely to be erratic but must occur if the patient is to be successful in his or her psychotherapeutic venture.

Reality-testing. In view of the strong warnings to the therapist about interfering with the patient's exploration, evaluation, and control, some might view the therapist's role as close to passive. Such is not the case. The psychotherapist's skill in processing of information and communicating with the patient represents the essence of progress in psychotherapy. The effective psychotherapist must learn to sense the quality of reality in what the patient says.

In the early stages of therapy, the things which the patient discusses may be bland and at least superficially realistic. As the patient becomes sufficiently comfortable in the sanctuary created by the psychotherapist, details of the patient's unrealistic view of self, family environment, and society emerge. When this begins to happen, inexperienced psychotherapists may become concerned, seeing episodes of *decompensation* as a negative sign. With experience, the psychotherapist will discover that regression may occur as patients hesitantly and tentatively begin to explore the unrealistic principles and compulsive values of their lives. Only when the patients can perceive and experience their own barriers to well-being will change occur. The experienced psychotherapist learns to tolerate and accept episodes of irrational thinking.

This stage of therapy requires the most flexible skill and sensitivity on the part of the therapist. The therapist must first help the patient hear what he or she has said. The patient must then connect the unrealistic habit, perception, or behavior to the important stresses and disappointments the patient has brought out in previous sessions. This type of *focusing* in turn eventually leads to the patient's awareness of the unrealistic nature of neurotic perceptions. As patterns of unrealistic thinking, choice-making, and behavior are explored in greater depth, the patient begins to take over the reality-testing role from the therapist.

Prochaska and DiClemente (1983) have pointed out that contemplation, not catharsis, leads to action by the patient. Although catharsis is often an important antecedent, cognitive-effective reevaluation by the patient leads to progress. This is the essence of reality-testing.

In Chapter 7, the content and application of therapist responses will be presented in detail.

The Patient's Activity

Much of patients' activity in psychotherapy represents their neurotic life-style. Psychotherapy is a structured situation where patients' reactions to stress, fear, opportunity, and inner strivings are similar to ways they respond in their everyday lives. Few patients maintain for very long a presentation of self very different from their usual pattern. Once the patient decides to remain in psychotherapy past the first few sessions, the living style of the patient usually emerges. The more frightened the patient, the longer it may take for a full disclosure of fears, doubts, defenses, and prejudices.

Even the most carefully defended obsessional patient or the terrified schizophrenic will eventually reveal the operational self if he or she continues sessions with a competent psychotherapist. Psychotherapy sessions are miniatures of real life where a patient can safely observe his or her own responses, experience neurotic adjustment, and become comfortable enough to take risks in exploring more adaptive ideas and behavior.

The psychotherapeutic process moves forward in direct proportion to the degree to which the patient allows communication. It must be made clear from the beginning that psychotherapy will progress in response to the patient's active participation. If the patient is unable to talk about himself or herself, the therapist is unable to respond. The patient cannot analyze and understand his or her neurotic responses to life until these are brought out. Therapy will proceed when the patient is able to do the following:

Take leadership in choosing topics. The patient should choose the topic during the psychotherapeutic session. When the therapist suggests topics for discussion, a number of things occur which are counterproductive to successful therapy:

- The therapist implies that he or she knows better than the patient what is important in the patient's life.
- The patient is encouraged to be dependent.
- Important areas of the patient's life may remain hidden.

Although many patients seem reluctant to express themselves spontaneously early in the psychotherapeutic process, the therapist must not become restless and deprive the patient of the topic-choosing role.

Increase responsibility for exploration. Choosing topics and initiating communication are first steps for patients in proceeding through psychotherapy. Once the patient becomes comfortable in selecting topics, expressing thoughts, and describing experiences, the therapist must encourage the patient to explore chosen topics in depth. During early stages of psychotherapy most patients describe their behavior in fairly superficial ways. Only by exploring in depth can the patient become aware of the causes and effects of their neurotic styles of coping with life.

At first, the psychotherapist will respond frequently with "Tell me more about that." As the psychotherapeutic process develops, the patient learns to probe and explore thoughts, recollections, and emotions in depth. The psychotherapist, in turn, encourages such explorations less frequently, moving the power and responsibility to the patient.

Accept the burden of judgment. Few patients enter psychotherapy able to make comfortable evaluations of their own worth. One goal of psychotherapy is for the patient to become realistically and effectively self-evaluating.

During the early stages of the psychotherapy process, patients frequently ask the therapist to evaluate progress or to judge the patient's values, experiences, and behavior. An essential element of what many refer to as "growth" in psychotherapy is for the patient to begin to judge his or her own values and behaviors. In the beginning, the psychotherapist can expect patients to demonstrate a good bit of resistance to accepting the role of self-judgment. The effective psychotherapist uses a variety of techniques to encourage the patient to engage in self-judgment. These will be explored extensively in later chapters. As the ritual of expecting the patient to judge his or her own performance becomes a constant theme in the psychotherapeutic session, the patient begins to experiment with self-judgment. The process eventually becomes automatic and comfortable for the patient.

In order to be successful in psychotherapy, the patient must unlearn many of the constraints taught by family, school, and society in general. All civilized adults have learned to live effectively with some degree of constraint, control, or "holding in." We are all products of such childhood maxims as, "If you can't say something nice, say nothing," or "Let sleeping dogs lie," or "Why stir up muddy waters?" or "You'll catch more flies with honey than with vinegar."

At a fairly early age, most children in our culture are taught to control, suppress, and repress impulses. This training is often focused on the child's spontaneous expressions of creativity, anger, or sensuality. "Holding in" is a reasonable part of developmental training and allows for an orderly society where the members agree on rituals regarding acceptable and unacceptable behavior. Too much or too little restraint training can have unfortunate consequences in later life.

Almost all patients in psychotherapy suffer from an excess of constraint. Even those whose behavior is at times unrestrained and impulsive may be "acting-out" after long periods of holding in. Patients, particularly in the earlier stages of psychotherapy, struggle to "let go." No matter how much the psychotherapist encourages the patient to associate freely, express ideas, experience feelings, and reexperience early emotional responses, the patient must first deal with the long-ingrained fear of "letting go." Guilt and/or punishment is the expected outcome should the controls be loosened.

A considerable number of sessions may pass before patients are aware of their inner constraints and the price they pay to maintain these constraints. The patient is then faced with the risk of experimenting with "letting go" during the therapeutic session. Even after the patient has some early success with experiencing strong emotion during a session of psychotherapy, the experienced psychotherapist is not surprised to find that the patient becomes fearful of the successful "letting go" experience. This usually results in one or more sessions where the patient avoids further emotionality by focusing on bland or safe topics during the session. Bugental and Bugental (1984) described the patient's fear of changing as a response to the imperiling of the patient's life structures.

By "letting go" and experiencing conflicts underlying an unsatisfactory life-style, the patient can gradually tolerate change.

Rosenbaum and Horowitz (1983) found that a patient's ability to engage successfully in psychotherapy depended on such factors as active engagement, psychological-mindedness, incentive-mediated willingness to sacrifice, and positive valuation of psychotherapy.

THE CONTENT AND FOCUS OF PSYCHOTHERAPY

What is to be discussed in psychotherapy? The answer is simply "anything." Much of the content of the patient's deliberation during a psychotherapeutic session is skeletal. It forms a relatively unemotional framework upon which the more significant ideas, recollections, and emotional experiences of the patient can be positioned or seen in perspective.

Details of the patient's early growth and development, family life, cultural background, education, mating, work, political beliefs, and social habits all constitute information necessary for the psychotherapist to know and appreciate.

Only after acquiring a thorough knowledge of the patient's individual and unique life and times can the psychotherapist select appropriate psychotherapeutic tradecraft to best serve that patient. Once the psychotherapist (and often the patient, for the first time in his or her life) is aware of the patient's autobiography, the process of psychotherapy can go forth. Each patient and each therapeutic course is unique, but attention focused on certain general areas and topics tends to move the psychotherapeutic process forward in a productive and positive manner.

Emotionally-tinged issues, experiences, and thoughts. Anything that patients relate about their feelings is likely to lead to progress in psychotherapy. The patient may discuss frightening experiences. Those thoughts, which the patient says evoke guilt, pain, rage, anxiety, or panic, are invaluable contributions to the process. The more the patient *experiences* the emotion being described, the more progress is likely to occur. The emotion can be associated with the patient's past, current conflicts, the psychotherapeutic relationship itself, or the future. The topic is secondary to the amount and quality of affect experienced by the patient.

Closely held false beliefs. Almost all patients have a superabundance of beliefs, prejudices, decision styles, formulae, maxims, and rules for living which are, in fact, false or self-destructive. Sometimes these beliefs which govern the patient's behavior and experience are cultural. Frequently they serve a dynamic defensive purpose. Such attitudes may range from relatively common prejudices such as "All politicians are crooks" to very personalized and systematic conceptions that border on or even become delusional (i.e., "Everyone in my family and at work is against me and dislikes me"). The more a patient will talk about closely held false beliefs, the greater the opportunity for reality-testing. The patient may speak quite comfortably about such notions. Questions or probing will at first be rejected. The psychotherapist must tolerate such rejections and continue to expect the patient to explore.

Unacceptable or painful realities. Akin to closely held false beliefs are a series of ideas, concepts, occurrences, or expectations which are unacceptable to patients. To understand, to accept, and to act on such realities are not only painful but sometimes terrifying to the patient.

As psychotherapy progresses, the patient is more likely to risk looking more closely at unacceptable or painful realities and to consider whether these can be explored. With exploration, acceptance becomes possible. Following this, the patient may begin to view and interact with life more realistically and with greater satisfaction. When the therapist brings such issues to the fore, the patient may ignore, avoid, or plead confusion in response. Some common themes which are frequently unacceptable or painful to patients whose emotional lives are based on denial or avoidance of reality include:

- One can spoil one's own success.
- I have been a victim of my own loved ones.
- My parents failed to fulfill many promises.
- My parents and teachers lied to me.
- The rules and values of childhood frequently don't work in the real world.
- I am not as bad as I believe myself to be.
- There will be a certain amount of injustice in everyone's life about which nothing can be done.
- Godot will never come.
- Nothing is forever.
- Love does not conquer all
- Many of my anxieties and obsessions have been groundless.
- I often arrange the painful experiences in my life.

Anhedonia. Few patients report that they are able to enjoy themselves with any regularity. Having fun is almost precluded in a neurotic adjustment. Anything the patient has to say about pleasure or the avoidance of pleasure is important and is material for the application of psychotherapeutic tradecraft. Sometimes patients will describe *relief* as pleasure or fun. This evasion can be an important defense against pleasure and is worthy of attention during psychotherapy.

The prediction of tomorrow from the behavior of yesterday. Etched in stone on the lintel of The Archives of the United States in Washington, D.C. is the adage, "The Past is the Prologue." So it may be with the most significant of the patient's behavior patterns and response styles. Most of the psychotherapeutic process focuses first on identifying patterns of behavior which interfere with the patient's quality of life. (Quality of life is here defined as the satisfactions gained from working, earning, socializing, loving, using leisure time, parenting, using the environment, eating, sleeping, and accepting the self. This will be discussed later in more detail.) Once the neurotic patterns are identified, it is important for the patient to discover that these non-adaptive occurrences tend to be repeated over and over. The self-defeating patterns may appear in family life, the workplace, school, socializing, or any other part of the patient's life.

As the psychotherapy proceeds, the therapist will glean enough information to begin to help the patient to identify and, later, to anticipate the occurrence of old patterns. This growing ability to anticipate situations can become an opportunity for patients to first predict, then to control their own behavior. Most of these topics emerge at first incidentally or tangentially. An important part of the psychotherapist's tradecraft is the sensitivity to identify the particular content of the patient's associations on which to focus.

At first the psychotherapist can expect most patients to deny or avoid the significance or even the existence of these painful response patterns. Much of the skill of the psychotherapist lies in the ability to help the patient to first consider, then resolve these unhelpful or destructive patterns, in spite of negative affects associated with revelation and experiencing.

THE PRODUCT

Change is the goal of psychotherapy. Although the effects of psychotherapy differ for each patient, certain categories of change may be anticipated.

Change in Old Behaviors

As the patterns of self-defeating behavior emerge, the patient has the opportunity to eliminate those things which interfere with fulfillment. The most commonly seen changes in old behavior patterns after successful psychotherapy include the following:

A decrease in willingness to sacrifice for unworthwhile reasons. As psychotherapy proceeds, the patient usually begins to value himself or herself in a growing number of situations involving work, family, health, creativity, and social interaction. Giving up, giving in, withdrawal, useless frenetic behavior, and inappropriate compliance or rebellion tend to lessen or disappear. There are fewer "I don't count" self-evaluations and behaviors.

A lessening of the experience that pain must precede, accompany, or follow pleasure. Many patients maintain a balance between their natural drives for pleasure and their guilt by arranging to suffer in any number of creative ways. As patients become aware of their patterns of response and as internal values are experienced more frequently, the compulsion to suffer tends to occur less frequently.

A decrease in self-destructive ways. With the insight and self-awareness which can be expected in successful psychotherapy, a consequent lessening in the patient's self depriving and hindering usually takes place. Most therapists find that reports of failure, loss, and frustration become rarer as psychotherapy proceeds.

Desensitization to unrealistic expectancies for justice or vengeance. As patients move toward the completion of their therapeutic course, emphasis tends to shift from the past to the present, and then to the future. As the patient focuses more on the opportunities to live life successfully in the future, there is usually much less seeking of unrealistic or impossible reparations for emotional debts from the past.

New Perceptions

As psychotherapy progresses, the patient's deliberations tend to include, with increasing frequency, such statements as, "I never thought of it that way" and "I never noticed that I did that." The essence of self-awareness is the ability to see oneself, clearly, as others see one, and within the context of hopes, fears, aspirations, and responsibilities.

A developing ability to analyze. A specific outcome for the psychotherapeutic process is for the patient to become his or her own therapist. As therapy proceeds, patients usually demonstrate an increasing willingness and ability to review and analyze their own responses for common themes or patterns, attitudes harmful to self and others, and tendencies to avoid opportunities for success and fulfillment. The more effective the psychotherapy, the greater will be the patient's participation and leadership.

The capacity to think about tomorrow. Focusing on the past is a common element of psychotherapy, more so in the earlier than in the later stages of the process. As the patient gains awareness, confidence, and energy from an understanding of the past, an increased focus on the future can be expected. As patients develop increased self-awareness, more attention to the opportunities for self-fulfillment today and tomorrow can be expected. Realistic and comfortable planning is one outcome which can be expected from successful psychotherapy.

Awareness of self-worth. Almost all patients experience a growth in self-respect concomitant with progress in psychotherapy. More statements reflecting positive attitudes toward the self can be expected toward the end of therapy than are found in the early stages of the process. As patients pass through the often painful experiences of learning to know themselves, one product is inevitably a series of sometimes surprised but pleased acknowledgements of self-respect.

New Behaviors

External observable changes accompany successful psychotherapy. These behaviors may be dramatic in some cases. For example, a previously passive, anxiety-ridden, dependent person may take a realistic and successful stand against manipulative and domineering figures in the home or workplace. In other instances, the behaviors may be of a more subtle nature, as when a driven, compulsive, depressed patient begins activating and enjoying recreational opportunities. Some kinds of "new" behavior following successful psychotherapy include:

Improved communication. As patients move toward success in psychotherapy, their language seems to become clearer. They report fewer instances where they are misunderstood or where they misunderstand others. There tends to be a decrease in rambling, tangential, and defensive expressions and an improvement in the ability to express the self clearly and at the appropriate time.

Increased congruence. Together with clearer communication, patients successful in psychotherapy seem better able to express ideas which reflect more accurately their inner thoughts and values. There is a lessening of the anxiety previously associated with saying things which match inner convictions. As the patient develops and uses congruent communication, anxiety tends to lessen in general and self-esteem builds.

Growing ability to risk and win. Except for the narcissistic and borderline disorders which are treated by some psychotherapists (to be explored in Chapter 9), most patients fear taking chances. This is particularly true when risks require that patients know and count on their own intelligence and judgment. Shakespeare's admonition, "There comes a time in the tide of man which taken on the flood leads on to fortune," is either ignored or is the source of paralyzing anxiety and ambivalence for most neurotic persons.

At the beginning of psychotherapy most patients continue to repeat patterns of constraint, overcontrol, suspicion, evasion and denial in their daily lives. Opportunities for change, for success, or for pleasure are consistently denied, spoiled, or avoided. As Freud noted, even before he developed the psychoanalytic method, "I am astounded by the number of intelligent patients who spoil their own success" (Jones, 1953).

As patients move forward in psychotherapy, they tend to very slowly identify and then gradually begin to withhold their self-defeating fear responses. This major step in therapy is ordinarily followed by cautious risk-taking with new ideas during the therapy sessions. Later, patients identify and take some risks in their everyday life. As this risk-taking is reviewed and integrated in the therapy sessions, the patient begins to build skill and confidence in identifying and participating in those risks likely to enhance his or her quality of life.

Knowing when to hold fast. One of the reasons that neurotic patients fail in life situations is their tendency to become flooded with anxiety when the unexpected occurs. The experienced psychotherapist finds that most patients overreact to new situations with an expectancy of failure, pain, or embarrassment. This overreaction can include a variety of defensive responses such as withdrawal, evasion, or denial. In social and work situations, this can mean that the neurotic patient avoids opportunities which could lead to pleasure or success. Instead, the patient leaves the scene of opportunity.

Among the new behaviors which can be expected to appear as the patient moves toward success in psychotherapy is a growing ability to "hold fast" during stressful times, fighting and overcoming what was previously an absolute sureness that "things won't work out." With increasing self-awareness, the patient's inner voice of doom becomes muted and is replaced by a growing willingness to stay and see what happens.

The inability of many patients to "hold fast" is illustrated by the following example: The patient, a 27-year-old unmarried accountant, reports during his seventh session of psychotherapy:

Patient: I finally went to an office party but I might as well have not.
Therapist: You were disappointed.
Patient: Not really, I knew I'd have a hard time—feel I didn't belong—and that's what happened. As soon as I walked in, I knew it was a mistake. Even though I knew almost everyone there, I felt like a fool.
Therapist: Like you didn't belong.
Patient: Exactly! Even though I work with these people, it was

different. They were talking, laughing—all the things I can't do with people—so I left. I shouldn't have gone in the first place.

Another patient, a 29-year-old computer programmer, reported as follows in his 67th session, having learned much about himself in therapy:

Patient: I had a good time, I'm really surprised. I accepted the invitation to Charley's birthday party but . . . I almost cancelled half-a-dozen times. One part of me wanted to go and see my friends and coworkers in a fun setting . . . (*long pause*) . . . I guess I was scared of them seeing me.

Therapist: One part of you wanted to go but the old fears were strong.

Patient: Yeah. . . . I've turned down a lot of invitations but the most important part was after I got to the party. I was very uncomfortable. After the first "hellos," nobody was talking to me. I decided to leave. Then I remembered about how we discovered that this is what I always do—start something I wanted, then quit at the first sign of tension or rejection or anything.

Therapist: Something was different this time?

Patient: Yeah. . . . I actually thought, "If you leave now, you'll feel worse about it later and you'll be stuck with facing this again . . . over and over," so I decided to stick it out.

Therapist: How did you do that?

Patient: I gritted my teeth and started wandering around, and I'd say "Hi" to people when they looked at me or said "Hi" to me. It's funny—I used to give a little smile and turn away when people said "Hi." They would leave me alone when I did that and I did feel rejected. This time, though, when I looked at people they would start talking to me.

Therapist: Did that feel better?

Patient: Not at first. I actually got more nervous. I still thought about leaving but I decided I *had* to try staying. After a little while, I found myself talking to people. I even told a joke to one group.

Therapist: You never thought you'd be able to do that.

Patient: You betcha! I used to think that I would stutter or forget the punch line or something. This time though, I hung in.

Therapist: It seems to have paid off.

Patient: It sure did. After the party one group invited me to go out with them for pizza. We talked and drank coffee until 1:00 A.M. I was a little scared, but . . . I was glad I hung in.

This was the first step in a series of situations in which the patient chose to "hold fast" and was rewarded and encouraged by the results.

Experiencing rather than defining significant events. When patients speak of themselves and their lives in the early phases of psychotherapy, they tend to present descriptions, definitions, comparisons, and value judgments which are primarily intellectual. Only limited segments of what the patient says early in therapy reflect a depth of feeling or experience. As the psychotherapy progresses and the patient becomes more comfortable as well as skillful in self-evaluation, the psychotherapist is likely to see facial expressions and gestures, as well as to hear phrases and vocal tones reflecting a growing ability by the patient to feel, to experience, and even to savor and appreciate what is happening within.

Early in his psychotherapy, a sophisticated, well-educated man of 38 described a visit to his rather elderly father as follows:

Patient: I try to visit the old man at least once a week, but it's difficult with all I have to do.
Therapist: It's really an inconvenience.
Patient: It is definitely an inconvenience . . . and old people are picky and demanding. Nothing you can do is right. . . . They could find something to complain about in a hundred dollar bill. It's a real chore . . . uh . . . I'm sure he's pretty unhappy at the nursing home, but what am I supposed to do? Don't I have a life to lead?
Therapist: Perhaps you sometimes worry about whether you are doing the right thing.
Patient: . . . (*pause*) Yeah . . . I suppose that's the guilt trip most people feel about older parents. . . . But they forget, they're sloppy, they're childish. It's a mess! But what can I do?

A little more than a year later, the same patient spoke of his father again. In the year since the earlier session, the patient had resolved a good bit of guilt and rage. He had risked confronting the father about various items of unfinished business involving conflicts that were long-standing between them. The following was one of the last discussions the patient had about his father during his psychotherapy:

Patient: I was thinking about my father when I got up this morning—it's amazing! He struggles to maintain a kind of dignity. . . . I never realized that without the advantages of education or money he has always been a dignified person. I remember once when I was a kid I talked my father down to a girlfriend. She looked at me in a funny way and said, "You don't know. Your Dad's a gem." That was over 20 years ago and suddenly this morning I see what she meant. (*patient weeps softly*) Instead of going to lunch today, I visited him. I didn't shake hands like I usually do. . . . I kissed him. He was surprised. Then he smiled . . . and kissed my hand. I know now that he has always done the best he could . . . and it was a lot better than I ever gave him credit for . . . I feel.

Therapist: It's like a weight lifted from you.

Patient: Yes . . . but more than that . . . it's like a pleasure, or joy or even some fun that I almost missed in my life.

Measurable rewards. Success in psychotherapy should lead to success in the patient's everyday life. For some it may be a new ability to be productive—to work and to earn commensurate with ability and skill. It has been demonstrated that success in psychotherapy results in a significant and attributable increase in income (Riess, 1967). For other patients, the most important rewards may be an improvement in social experience, creativity, or ability to have fun.

CHAPTER 3

The Psychotherapist

Psychotherapy is a technique practiced by a variety of mental health professionals. It is rarely the only clinical activity of psychologists, mental health and family counselors, social workers, or psychiatrists, the professionals who are America's primary practicing psychotherapists. Most mental health professionals engage in diagnosis, teaching, consulting, training, or other activities in addition to conducting psychotherapy.

In 1975 over two-thirds of America's 72,000 psychotherapists were psychiatrists and clinical psychologists. Clinical social workers accounted for about 18% of practicing therapists, with marriage and family counselors making up the remaining 8%. Today, a decade later, there are approximately 160,000 psychotherapists in America. Clinical social workers represent about 38% of all psychotherapists, psychiatrists 23%, clinical psychologists approximately 21%. Marriage and family counselors account for the remaining 18%.

The distribution has changed significantly over the past 10 years and may continue to change. These changes have been accompanied by considerable differences of opinion among the various mental health professions as to technical, political, and financial territoriality. The avowed and actual differences among psychotherapists belonging to different professions are particularly bewildering to the consumer who is ordinarily left with limited guidance to help in choice-making (Goleman, 1985c). This issue will be explored in some detail in Chapter 4.

EDUCATIONAL PREPARATION

The educational preparations of the mental health professionals who become psychotherapists differ considerably. Although the psychoanalytic method of psychotherapy originated among physicians, Freud did not consider psychoanalysis a medical specialty. Much to the chagrin of some of his medical colleagues, the father of modern psychotherapy suggested that psychoanalysis dealt with psychological, not medical disorders (Jones, 1953).

Clinical Psychologists

Most psychologists who practice psychotherapy have taken a four-year undergraduate degree majoring in psychology. Subject matter varies, but in general the program includes experimental psychology, general psychology, psychometric methods, abnormal psychology, social psychology, personality, aging, physiological psychology, and survey courses in diagnostic and treatment procedures in mental health. In addition, courses in other areas of human behavior such as sociology and anthropology are taken, as well as a variety of liberal arts studies.

Following the bachelor's degree, the master's and the doctorate are taken over a four- to six-year period leading to the Doctor of Philosophy degree. Traditional graduate programs emphasize advanced studies in the areas first encountered at the undergraduate level, plus practicum placements in a variety of mental health settings where the clinical psychologist receives direct experience with patients in various forms of diagnosis, psychotherapy, and other intervention methods. Before receiving the doctorate, the candidate in clinical psychology must accrue a minimum of 2,000 hours of acceptable supervised clinical experience. Most programs require the candidate to produce a dissertation research project of original, publishable quality before the doctorate is granted. The newer Psy. D. or *professional* programs in psychology include a heavier schedule of clinical courses and practice, at the expense of some of the traditional research training.

The doctorate is considered the *journeyman* or basic level of preparation for practice. The master's degree in psychology is no longer considered sufficient for independent clinical practice.

Course content may vary from school to school, but most graduate programs in clinical psychology strive to receive accreditation from the American Psychological Association. This accreditation includes stringent requirements for courses, content, and supervision.

In order to be licensed, clinical psychologists must spend one year (approximately 2,000 clinical hours) in an approved postdoctoral training setting. Psychologists are licensed or certified in all 50 states.

Clinical Social Workers

Those who receive an undergraduate, or bachelor's degree in social work generally study a variety of subjects similar to those taken by psychologists, with a stronger emphasis on social institutions and processes. Accreditation as a clinical social worker (formerly often called *psychiatric social worker*) requires a master's degree. This is considered the basic level of preparation for practice. A modest amount of training in psychotherapeutic methods is usually included in the program. Approximately 35 states license social workers at this time. Clinical social workers employ their training in help-giving systems. Using their knowledge of cultural diversity and their commitment to the under-class, they work with individuals, families, and small groups (Tolson, 1984).

Marriage and Family Counselors

Undergraduate requirements for admission to special master's level programs in marriage and family counseling or mental health specialist vary much more than the requirement for clinical psychology or clinical social work. The graduate program is usually two years in length, concentrating almost exclusively on practical aspects of mental health services delivery. Training in psychotherapy is usually very specific and reflects the treatment philosophy of the senior staff of the program. Marriage and family counselors are licensed in only nine states at this writing.

Psychiatrists

The psychiatrist usually has taken a bachelor's degree in the "hard" sciences (physics, chemistry, biology, zoology, mathematics, etc.) with little opportunity to study human behavior or social institutions. Medical school offers an opportunity for a brief rotation in psychiatry, usually limited to diagnostic classification methods, chemotherapy, and clinical observation of patients. Following the medical degree, the physician usually takes a residency program of three to four years to study psychiatric diagnosis, treatment, and mental hospital practice under close supervision in various clinical facilities. The resident usually receives some training and supervision in psychotherapeutic methods. The style, depth, intensity, and quality of psychotherapy training vary considerably among the many residency programs. All psychiatrists are licensed to practice medicine. Some states certify specialization in psychiatry.

At the completion of formalized training, mental health professionals are unlikely to be skilled psychotherapists. Psychotherapy training differs from one education or clinical setting to another. In order to become skilled in psychotherapy, it is usually necessary to go on to advanced training and supervision. This is not always done and many mental health professionals begin to practice psychotherapy without training beyond the requirements for certification or licensing in their respective professions.

TRAINING IN PSYCHOTHERAPY

Most psychologists, psychiatrists, clinical social workers and other mental health professionals receive some specific training and supervision in psychotherapy during their formal training programs or residencies. Such training usually occurs in field placements. These placements may be at mental health clinics, psychiatric hospitals, university counseling centers, or medical school clinics. Supervision may be received from senior psychotherapists whose professional background is in clinical social work, psychiatry, or clinical psychology. The comprehensiveness of such training varies considerably from program to program.

There are a number of ways in which mental health professionals may seek advanced training in psychotherapeutic methods. The principal ways of acquiring such training are reviewed briefly below.

Psychoanalytic Training

Classically, the expected training for the practice of psychoanalysis consists of a personal analysis, followed by a training analysis in which the aspiring psychoanalyst reviews his or her work with patients under the careful scrutiny and control of a senior psychoanalyst. On completion of training, the analyst usually seeks membership in one of the psychoanalytic societies. Attendance at seminars and completion of certain educational sequences are usually required. These criteria vary from "school" to "school." Training ordinarily takes several years. Supervision is individual and usually quite exacting. At some major psychoanalytic centers, prescribed courses, symposia, and lectures make for a very full program of instruction and experience.

University Centers for Postgraduate Training

A number of universities sponsor programs for advanced training in psychotherapy. Such centers combine didactic offerings such as seminars, colloquia, and visiting speakers together with well-structured supervision by senior and adjunct faculty.

Treatment Facility Postgraduate Training

Throughout the United States there are treatment facilities which offer, in addition to their usual patient services, advanced training in psychotherapy. The training may be as limited as a series of evening lectures by senior mental health clinicians, or as extensive as a fellowship requiring several years of staff membership in the sponsoring institution.

Workshops, Retreats and Seminars

Sponsored by professional organizations, treatment facilities, educational centers, and individuals, relatively brief training opportunities are continually available for studying psychotherapeutic methods and applications. Well-known psychotherapists of most recognized "schools" of psychotherapy present their methods and case material for colleagues and students. Although most of such presentations are didactic and instructional, films, videotapes and, in some instances, participant interaction allow students to experience some nuances of psychotherapeutic interaction.

Individual and Group Supervision

Large numbers of graduate mental health professionals acquire or extend their psychotherapeutic knowledge and skills through formal or informal arrangements for supervision by senior psychotherapists in their community. Such arrangements vary considerably in terms of regularity, frequency, and fee arrangement. In a group practice or agency, younger clinicians may meet at a regular psychotherapy colloquium conducted by senior clinicians focusing on the work being done with patients in that agency. Clinicians who practice independently are sometimes invited or allowed to participate in these psychotherapy learning experiences. Individual mental health practitioners may select a senior, well-regarded psychotherapist who is willing to supervise the clinician's psychotherapeutic activity on a regular basis for a private fee. Social workers have a long-established tradition of case supervision which can lend itself to supervision of the therapeutic activities of inexperienced psychotherapists.

It has been suggested that there is a *developmental model of supervision* which tends to follow key issues which emerge during the supervision sessions. Friedlander, Dye, Costello and Kobos (1984) propose that supervision progresses from the trainer developing a great deal of tolerance of ambiguity, proceeding then to recognition of the limits of psychotherapy, and then later to the discovery that the psychotherapeutic process involves the deepest form of human communication. Supervision reaches the final developmental stage when the therapist-in-training accepts the existence and value of models and styles of intervention which meet the varying needs of patients and situations.

There is little disagreement that supervision plays a vital role in psychotherapy training (Garfield & Kurtz, 1976). Quality and appropriateness of supervision is another matter. Yogev and Pion (1984) found that much supervision in therapy is presented at a beginning-student level by supervisors, regardless of the background and experience of the traineee being supervised.

A survey of 151 predoctoral internship programs accredited by the American Psychological Association (Hess & Hess, 1983) indicated that for each three hours of psychotherapy provided to patients by interns one hour of supervision was received. Supervisors were psychologists, psychiatrists, and social workers. The predominant style was one-on-one. One-third of the training settings taught interns to be supervisors. Some facilities carefully evaluated and monitored the quality of supervision for trainees, residents, or interns. Almost one-half of facilities which provided psychotherapy supervision maintained no formal ongoing training for supervisors. About one-fourth of facilities arranged for a senior staff member to supervise the psychotherapy supervisor. Over 50% of the facilities which were studied provided psychotherapy supervision for mental health professionals other than psychologists.

There is a style of supervision which Robertson (1984) calls *didactic teaching*. He suggests that this type of supervision tends to emphasize style or focus, teaching students such specific modalities as individual psychotherapy, dynamic group therapy, marital therapy, family therapy, etc. Although no substitute for a supervised practicum, this type of supervison can bridge the gap between classroom study of psychotherapy and individual supervision of the performance of student psychotherapists.

PSYCHOTHERAPEUTIC SETTINGS

Psychotherapy may take place in a variety of settings. The tone, character, style, and efficiency of the process may differ from setting to setting. Recent studies of various treatment facilities and the therapists who serve patients in these settings are beginning to clarify different ways that psychotherapists offer services.

Most psychotherapists work in either institutional or private clinical facilities. They may practice alone, with groups of colleagues of the same professional identification, or in groups where a variety of mental health professions are represented. In such mixed groups, psychiatrists have, in the past, been the senior partners of the groups with clinical social workers, clinical psychologists, and other mental health professionals serving as salaried staff or junior partners. There are some situations now where all the mental health professionals participate equally in a group practice.

Institutional settings include psychiatric hospitals, general hospitals, rehabilitation centers, residential treatment facilities, crisis consultation centers, university clinics, prisons, military facilities, police departments, and other places where mental health services are required and provided. Quality, intensity, style, and cost of psychotherapy are likely to vary more in institutional settings than in independent settings. In spite of common belief to the contrary, the cost of psychotherapeutic services in a large or bureaucratic setting may exceed the cost of private services (Adams & Orgel, 1975).

Psychotherapists who work in an independent setting have been compared with colleagues who provide psychotherapeutic services in the institutional setting. Results suggest that those who practice in an institutional setting or in a "split" practice (part institutional, part private) are more likely to feel stressed and to experience less of a sense of personal accomplishment than psychotherapists practicing privately. Institutional working conditions and pressures tend to be more onerous and inimical to quality clinical work than conditions in private settings. Those psychotherapists practicing privately report a more positive sense of community and collegial contact than do institutional psychotherapists (Farber, 1985). Settings and sources of referral will be considered in greater detail in the next chapter.

THE NATURE AND STYLE OF PSYCHOTHERAPISTS

The backgrounds, mean age, work settings, and training of psychotherapists are changing rapidly. These changes may reflect modified requirements for practice, current consumer availability and expectancies, new styles of mental health service delivery, and other factors. Recent research has begun to illuminate these previously little-known factors.

Demographics

Studies conducted in 1982 (Norcross & Prochaska) noted that 79% of the sample of psychotherapists were male. Prochaska and Norcross reported in 1983 that a subsequent survey showed that 27% of a sample of contemporary psychotherapists were female. By 1985, Farber reported that 63% of his sample of 314 psychotherapists were male and 37% were female. Psychotherapy is no longer a mental health service offered primarily by males.

Farber's sample of senior psychotherapists (1985) was 99% white. Seventy-one percent of the 314 psychotherapists in his sample were married, while 29% were single, divorced, or widowed. The average age of the sample was 51 years. Sixty-five percent were in private settings, 7% offered psychotherapy in an institutional setting only, while 28% split their time between offering psychotherapy privately and in the institutional setting. The average experience as a psychotherapist for Farber's sample was 19.6 years. Psychotherapists in this "senior" sampling averaged 27.6 hours of psychotherapy per week. Ninety-four percent of these psychotherapists reported that professional satisfaction with their work exceeded stress. Ninety-five percent reported that they felt their work was effective.

Preferences and Style

Prochaska and Norcross (1983), in a national study of contemporary psychotherapists, found a very wide rage of orientations.

Orientation (or "School")	Percent
Eclectic	30.2
Psychodynamic	18.0
Psychoanalytic	8.5
Cognitive	8.3
Behavioral	5.6
Existential	4.4
Humanistic	4.1
Systems	3.4
Gestalt	3.4
Adlerian	1.5
Sullivanian	1.2
Communications	1.0
Other	8.1

Nothing in these data indicates whether differences in the avowed orientation reflected clear differences in psychotherapeutic style and procedure.

Brenner (1982) reported that the psychotherapists in his sample preferred to work with young, attractive, verbal, intelligent and successful patients. This preference has come to be known as the YAVIS patient.

The preferred age range of patients was found to be between 20 and 40 years, although Brenner notes a growing trend among psychotherapists to work with children and older adults.

Confirming earlier studies, Prochaska and Norcross (1983) found that psychotherapists spend a little over half their professional working time doing psychotherapy. Sixty-five percent of treatment services offered was individual psychotherapy.

Norcross and Wogan (1983) found that both male and female psychotherapists in their survey reported feeling more effective with female patients. All therapists in the study reported that they felt least effective with older patients and patients suffering organic brain syndromes.

In pursuing the question of what external data influenced psychotherapists, Sergeant and Cohen (1983) found that most psychotherapists were more influenced by experimental or research-based studies in regard to the therapeutic process than by quasi-experimental or anecdotal reports.

Definitive research relating psychotherapist characteristics, attitudes, and practices to patient needs is yet to come. Norcross and Wogan (1983) propose that future research must specify the characteristics and practices of the psychotherapists being studied if the results are to be useful.

Personal Psychotherapy

Freud and his students saw personal analysis as a prerequisite to qualification as a psychoanalyst. Those who still believe that personal psychotherapy is an important experience for the *compleat* psychotherapist are strong in their affirmations, while those who openly oppose this concept are in the minority. Norcross and Wogan (1983) found that among psychologist-psychotherapists the experience of personal psychotherapy was more the rule than the exception. Eight-eight percent of psychotherapists who described their orientation as "Humanistic" reported having had personal psychotherapy. Eight-two percent of psychologists who were members of the Division of Psychotherapy of the American Psychological Association indicated that they had experienced personal psychotherapy.

Whether these data suggest that most psychotherapists believe that personal psychotherapy is an important educational or training prerequisite to psychotherapeutic practice is yet to be determined. The data may mean that psychotherapists, as a group, are people who have required personal psychotherapy. The data may suggest that personal psychotherapy represents a route by which some discover a chosen vocation.

Personal Satisfactions

Although psychotherapeutic work is demanding, most psychotherapists report that satisfactions outweigh stresses (Farber, 1985). Almost
90% of the therapists studied indicated they would again pursue training
as a psychotherapist were they to have the opportunity to start over.

Most psychotherapists in this study (88%) felt their work resulted in
personal growth. Over 50% reported that although their work as a psychotherapist was demanding, they still had time left over for family
and friends.

Farber and Heifetz (1981) also examined the satisfactions experienced
by psychotherapists. They concluded that the most satisfying aspects of
the practice of psychotherapy included promoting growth and change,
achieving intimate involvement in the lives of patients, and feeling professionally respected. Stresses and negative effects of psychotherapeutic
practice will be considered in detail in Chapter 11.

The Skillful or Expert Psychotherapist

Each patient seeks and hopes to find the most experienced and skillful
psychotherapist. Research suggests that such an exploration by the
patient may be very wise. Most of the definitive outcome studies suggest
that orientation or style of practice may be of no importance, but the experience of the psychotherapist is paramount in predicting a successful
outcome (Fiedler, 1951; Frank, 1961, 1979; Wallach & Strupp, 1964; Vanden Bos & Karon, 1971; Smith & Glass, 1977; Dent, 1978). Aside from
measuring this quality of "experience" or "skillfulness" in terms of years
in practice, number of patients seen, or total number of psychotherapeutic hours conducted, most of what has been written is anecdotal.

The views of famous psychotherapists are worth consideration. Freud
(1962) suggested that the skillful psychotherapist functions best as a lis-
tener, and in this role strives to control his or her own unconscious
thoughts. Speaking may give the patient material which influences or dis-
torts communication.

Prinzhorn (1932) claimed that the psychotherapeutic gift was made
up of three things: (1) a wide and sure knowledge of human beings; (2) the
ability to eliminate the private ego (objectivity); and (3) an innate
capacity for leadership demonstrated by "certain aim" of interpretations
(knowing what to say and when).

Wilhelm Reich (1949) stated that although the character of the psychotherapist would affect the choice of patients, a training analysis could

create a plasticity of character allowing the psychotherapist to be more flexible and to deal with a variety of patients.

Jung (1964) proposed that for different kinds of patients different psychotherapeutic approaches are necessary. He suggested that psychological treatment of the mentally ill is based more on a relationship than on the application of a technique. He defined this unique capacity to form a therapeutic relationship as knowing oneself well enough not to destroy the unique values of the patient. Jung proposed that the psychotherapist must conduct treatment with a knowledge and understanding of the patient's background and prejudices.

The impossibility of each psychotherapist treating every kind of personality disorder was emphasized by Fromm-Reichmann (1950) when she wrote that with experience, the psychotherapist will learn which kind of patients respond best to the psychotherapist's personality and style.

After studying psychotherapists of various orientations, Fiedler (1951) concluded:

The most characteristic aspects of the relationship which differentiate experts from non-experts . . . is the greater ability of the expert to understand the feelings of the patient, his greater security in the therapeutic situation, and his capacity to show interest and warmth without becoming overly involved with the patient (p. 442).

Carl Rogers (1954) is best known for his description of the "good psychotherapist" as having *warmth, unconditional positive regard* for the client, and being able to respond with *accurate empathy*. Rogers (1951) further opined that therapists, even when they have resolved many of their own difficulties in a therapeutic relationship, still have conflicts, tendencies to project or unrealistic attitudes on certain matters.

Vanden Bos and Karon (1971) have suggested that ineffective psychotherapists share a general personality characteristic they called *pathogenesis*. Their research, using the Thematic Apperception Test, demonstrated that this negative trait was characterized by the therapist being compelled to classify behavior of the patient pejoratively, as well as from a distance. Pathogenesis clearly correlated negatively with therapeutic effectiveness.

Wallach and Strupp (1964), after studying 313 psychologists and psychiatrists who were practicing psychotherapists, concluded that six factors characterized successful psychotherapeutic practice. Briefly these are:

Factor	Description
I	The maintenance of personal distance.
II	A preference for intensive (analytic, uncovering) therapeutic procedures.
III	Keeping verbal interventions at a minimum.
IV	Flexibility. Psychotherapy more as art than science.
V	Technique is critical.
VI	Countertransference is always a danger with the hostile patient.

In repeating some parts of the investigation of Wallach and Strupp, Wogan and Norcross (1983) reported a study of 136 psychotherapists who were members of the Division of Psychotherapy of the American Psychological Association. Their analysis suggested five factors associated with the expertness of psychotherapists:

Factor	Description
I	Personal distance (emotional uninvolvement).
II	Constrained verbal activity by the psychotherapist.
III	Flexibility (psychotherapy more as art than science).
IV	Therapeutic distance (technique).
V	Preference for goal-oriented psychotherapy.

These studies may indicate that there have been changes over time in knowledge about intervention techniques and psychotherapeutic styles. Continued research will hopefully provide more specific data to be used by those responsible for the education, training, and supervision of psychotherapists.

CHAPTER 4

The Setting and Structure for Psychotherapy

Psychotherapists have traditionally practiced privately or as staff members in health or service institutions. Psychotherapeutic services are becoming more available through the development of new delivery systems. In order to be more accessible to referral sources such as industrial and government Employee Assistance Programs (EAPs), some psychotherapists are joining together in private Independent Practice Associations (IPAs) which are essentially group practices. Health Maintenance Organizations (HMOs) often provide psychotherapeutic services on a contract basis, in conjunction with a wide range of medical services. These are essentially private institutions offering a variety of health services to self-insuring organizations.

Large numbers of public and private nonprofit institutions, usually hospitals, clinics and residential treatment centers, continue to offer psychotherapy services. Although new styles of service delivery are being developed (Cummings & Fernandez, 1985; Vanden Bos, 1980; Inman, 1982), psychotherapists are likely to continue to practice independently or as staff members of institutions.

From the studies available, it would appear that psychotherapists who practice independently suffer less frustration in delivering psychotherapy than do their colleagues who practice as institutional staff members. Farber (1985) reports that those who work in hospitals or clinics are frustrated by administrative red tape in their efforts to help their patients. Sixty percent of those studied felt that their professional skills and efforts had been frustrated by budgetary considerations. The same percentage reported being disheartened by working conditions in their institutional setting. This suggests that institutional settings may create working conditions onerous or inimical to effective clinical work.

SOURCES OF REFERRAL

A distinct advantage enjoyed by psychotherapists in institutional settings is the constant flow of patients referred by the organization's intake system. For a psychotherapist to be successful in a private setting, a fairly reliable flow of patients is required. The need for psychotherapy seems to be growing and referral sources abound. The more common of these will be considered briefly:

Self-Referral—The Telephone Book Yellow Pages

Ethical constraints against advertising which were once imposed on psychotherapists no longer apply. Statutory and regulatory decisions now allow all professionals to advertise. Those psychotherapists who are starting an independent practice should certainly be listed in the local telephone book's yellow pages under "Psychotherapists" and/or their appropriate professional designators (i.e., "Psychologists," "Clinical Social Workers," "M.D.-Psychiatrists," etc.). In the past, patients rarely indicated that they sought help in the yellow pages. More recently, particularly in small to moderate-sized communities, mental health professionals are reporting more referrals from this source.

Referral Services

In many communities, civic organizations, university graduate departments, mental health associations, and ministerial associations maintain a list of available mental health practitioners to whom they can refer calls for help. These services may restrict listing to members of specific professions or to psychotherapists willing to base fees on the patient's capacity to pay. Such services are usually very helpful to the psychotherapist starting an independent practice.

Other Professionals

If a psychotherapist just beginning practice is known to psychotherapists or other professionals in the community as a result of having trained or worked in local mental health treatment centers, senior colleagues may be a source of patient referral. Much will depend on the nature of the relationship the practitioner has had with colleagues and mentors, as well as on their generosity. Some psychotherapists begin independent practice by renting office space from a well-established psychotherapist or other professional. In this case, the landlord/colleague may refer patients.

Civic Groups

In every community there can be found a host of civic organizations, service clubs, church groups, parent/teacher associations, chambers of commerce, and other formally constituted groups of people with similar interests or goals. These groups meet regularly and there is ordinarily a "program" at each meeting, presented by an invited speaker who is likely to educate or entertain the membership. Psychotherapists have been invited to such meetings to speak on topics as specific as "Burnout in High-Stress Occupations" or "Dealing with Depression," and as general as "Living with Stress" or "Tolerating Teenagers." Such talks can lead to referrals from those who hear the presentation.

The Clergy

Many clergymen (and women) have received training in pastoral counseling. All religious leaders deal with troubled people. The resources and skills of the priest, minister, rabbi, or pastor are frequently insufficient to deal with the more complex problems presented. When this happens, the troubled person is often referred to mental health professionals in the community.

Employee Assistance Programs

Many large industrial concerns have become aware of the importance of meeting employees' personal needs in addition to providing attractive wage and benefit packages. In pursuit of improved efficiency and cost-effectiveness, such companies may employ mental health professionals as consultants, with whom troubled employees may schedule one or more sessions. Should the consultant decide that a longer, more traditional intervention such as psychotherapy is indicated, referral is usually made to a mental health practitioner in the community. Most, if not all, of the professional fee is covered by the company's insurance benefit package. Although cost-effectiveness is a matter of some concern in such arrangements, quality of service and patient satisfaction are the primary expectations of such referrals.

Government Agencies and the Courts

When the emotional state of a person who is to be adjudicated is in question, the presiding judge or the adjudicating agency may recommend professional help as part of the disposition of the case. Referral may be made to independent as well as institutional mental health professionals. This has traditionally involved patients who have been identified as compulsive gamblers, drug abusers, child molesters, wife beaters, and others who come to the attention of agencies or the courts because of behavior dangerous to themselves or others. Many psychotherapists are reluctant to work with such patients. Treatment of these patients will be considered in Chapter 9.

With the advent of no-fault divorce, joint custody, and mandatory mediation in family courts, large numbers of troubled husbands, wives, and children with essentially neurotic conflicts are being referred to both independent and institutional practitioners for psychotherapeutic intervention.

A number of government agencies have developed guidelines for human reliability in safety and performance which require that personnel maintain emotional stability (pilots, enforcement officers, nuclear workers, etc.). Referrals from such agencies are becoming more common as administrators are made aware of the value of psychotherapy in maximizing an individual's personal adjustment and effectiveness.

The Legal Profession

Lawyers and judges are more familiar with mental health services than ever before. Most law-school graduates during the past two decades have received a broad liberal arts undergraduate education. They have taken courses in psychology and sociology. They are somewhat familiar with the skills of mental health professionals. In addition, attorneys who work in specialty areas such as criminal law, personal injury, and family law have come to know mental health professionals who have served as expert witnesses. As a result of this exposure, attorneys are a growing source of referral for practicing psychotherapists (Blau, 1984a).

Self-Referral—Former Patients

When the psychotherapist in private practice finds that most new patients are referred by former patients, he or she has become solidly established in the community. This circumstance usually means that the psychotherapeutic services have been of quality and the patients who have received those services are willing to recommend their psychotherapist to others. Although other professionals may hold a high opinion of a psychotherapist because of personal friendship or respect for the therapist's credentials, only the patient who has participated in psychotherapy is likely to know what really goes on in the psychotherapeutic interaction with a specific therapist. Self-referrals constitute the most stable source of patients for the independent practitioner.

THE PSYCHOTHERAPIST'S OFFICES

Since the initial task in psychotherapy is the establishment of a sanctuary where the patient's revelations are as protected and secure as possible, the physical setting where this takes place is a matter of some importance. In a study of the effect of office design on visitor response, Campbell (1979) found that among undergraduate subjects positive attitudes were expressed toward plants and wall posters. Clutter led to negative ratings, while furniture arrangement had little impact one way or another.

During the period of time in which classical psychoanalysis was the predominant psychotherapeutic treatment method, furnishings were purposely stark so as to eliminate the therapist's personality from the treatment setting. The many approaches to psychotherapeutic practice today have given rise to variety in office style, often reflecting the psychotherapist's taste and personality. Some trends in office design that have been observed include:

- The use of windows, plants and aquariums, which symbolize the triumph or ascendancy of *Eros*—the life forces—over *Thanatos,* the hallmark of despondency. The growing plant is seen as a metaphor proclaiming psychotherapy a growth process.
- A growing presence of clocks, which symbolize the value of the time-limited psychotherapeutic session.
- Larger and lighter waiting rooms without secret exits so as to emphasize the value of choosing psychotherapy as a means of "expanding" rather than of guilt-ridden "shrinking."
- Fewer couches for the patient with the psychotherapist hidden in a wing chair. This, together with fewer beards and ashtrays, seems to symbolize greater self-acceptance and health-awareness by modern psychotherapists.
- Furniture which reflects the personal taste and comfort-seeking of the psychotherapist.

Most psychotherapists agree that the patient's spontaneous reactions to the decor of the treatment room are worthy of exploration and analysis as part of the therapeutic process (Dullea, 1983).

The Physical Setting

The traditional psychoanalytic setting of a waiting room, consulting room with couch, therapist's chair and desk, with double doors connecting the rooms, can still be found. Traditional psychoanalytic psychotherapists often follow the consulting office configuration of earlier analysts or of their mentors.

Psychotherapy today is practiced by mental health professionals of diverse social, cultural, and professional backgrounds. The structural and logistical conditions found in psychotherapists' offices reflect this diversity. Few psychotherapists redecorate their offices after they have been in practice for several years. The office decor becomes a presentation of self. Though items are added, drapes and rugs replaced, and furniture refurbished, rarely does one find that experienced psychotherapists will drastically modify the office in which they began full professional practice. The comments and suggestions which follow should be considered guidelines for settings which are unlikely to disrupt effective psychotherapy.

Location and Structure

Patients meet with their psychotherapist one or more times a week. Transportation may pose logistical barriers to a regular schedule of appointments unless the therapist's office is located relatively close to public transportation. Many patients prefer anonymity when consulting a mental health professional and parking facilities which are convenient but not easily associated with the psychotherapist are desirable.

The offices of a psychotherapist should be located in a professional setting, whether as part of a large professional building or an individual office structure. Having an office as part of the home or above the garage is likely to interfere with the development of a successful and effective psychotherapeutic practice.

The size and configuration of the psychotherapist's office are a matter of personal taste. If the psychotherapist offers additional services such as testing, biofeedback, neurotraining, or group psychotherapy, larger quarters will be required than for the professional who offers only individual psychotherapy.

A waiting room is mandatory for professional practice. Patients come early for their appointments. They may be accompanied. Most patients need a place for transition between the outside world and the sanctuary of the therapy room. The waiting room should be a pleasant, comfortable setting where patients can sit and read or contemplate without being disturbed by a flow of traffic. Plants, muted music, and current reading material help create an appropriate and comfortable atmosphere. Clerical staff should not be in the waiting room, since this tends to encourage quasi-therapeutic or personal relationships, which will disrupt the effective psychotherapeutic process. Individual chairs rather than couches or bench seating are likely to please and reassure patients. A small desk and chair is a convenience for patients who wish to work, study, or write while waiting for their appointment.

Offices for clerical staff should be separate from the waiting room yet available to patients for the scheduling of appointments or dealing with fees, billing, insurance, or other matters.

Sound conditioning is essential for the effective practice of psychotherapy. Ambient voices, noise, and other sounds are disruptive to patients. Proper sound conditioning begins with insulated walls and doors which are extra thick and closely fitted. Rubber weatherstripping on the casements of the therapy office doors will enhance sound conditioning. Doors should not have vents or louvers since these readily admit ambient sound.

Poor sound conditioning may allow psychotherapeutic communication to be heard by staff and others in the office, destroying the sanctity and security vital to the proper conduct of psychotherapy. Though initially expensive, a thick rug, a lowered acoustical tile ceiling, and floor-length drapes in the office where psychotherapy takes place are desirable. Sound conditioning can be enhanced by soft background music.

Lighting should be adequate but muted. Darkened offices are not recommended.

Psychotherapists who practice in institutional settings usually have little choice in selecting the location, structure, and furnishings of their consulting rooms.

Furnishings

The traditional psychotherapy setting of early psychoanalytic days consisted of a couch for the patient, an arm chair for the therapist, usually placed outside of the patient's line of sight, and a desk. Bookcases and curio shelves were common. Today, many psychotherapists have lounge chairs, rockers, sling chairs, bean bag chairs, and other forms of contemporary seating for themselves and their patients.

Psychotherapists will spend the greater part of their professional careers in the chair chosen for the consulting room. Few therapists move

from one seating place to another. The most comfortable and ortho-
paedically correct seating possible is strongly recommended in order to
avoid back problems.

Seating for the patient should consider comfort and convenience.
Many experienced psychotherapists furnish their offices with several
seating options for the patient, i.e., a deep, soft chair, a firm chair and
a couch.

Drapes, rugs, furniture style, and decoration should reflect the psychotherapist. The decor should be pleasant and relatively unstimulating. Personal mementos, photographs, and hobby materials or products are likely
to distract and interfere at some point in the psychotherapeutic process. A
pleasant neutrality concordant with the psychotherapist's style and personality is a desirable interior decoration goal for the therapist's office.

Unless bureaucratic constraints forbid it, the institutional psychotherapist can do much to enhance the effectiveness of his or her psychotherapy by individualizing the psychotherapy treatment room in respect
to the ideas and concepts noted above.

PRACTICE MANAGEMENT AND ORGANIZATION

Few psychotherapists are trained or experienced in organizational or
management matters. The degree to which psychotherapeutic activity is
enhanced or disrupted by the everyday business elements of professional
practice can spell success or disaster for both therapist and patient. The
way in which a patient is treated by staff members is bound to influence
the patient's feelings of security and thus the course of therapy.

Clerical contacts, the response of receptionists, billing and collection
procedures, and even the handling of case file material seem to be more
impersonal and less caring within an institutional setting than in the offices of the independent practitioner of psychotherapy. This can make the
psychotherapeutic job more difficult for both patient and therapist. This
situation may to some extent account for the higher "no show" and cancellation rate found in the institutional setting than among individual
practitioners (Adams & Orgel, 1975; Farber, 1985).

There are certain fundamental procedures and principles of practice
management which, when instituted and regularly monitored, can enhance the psychotherapeutic process. These will be considered briefly:

Staff

Psychotherapists may employ a secretary, a receptionist, and a billing
clerk. One person often does a variety of management jobs within the

practice. Institutions and group practices may employ a large number of ancillary staff supervised by an office manager. In some settings, one of the professionals who enjoys organizational tasks may supervise clerical and paraprofessional staff. All staff who come in personal contact or communication with patients are potential helpers or hinderers in the therapeutic process. Staff must be initially selected with this point in mind. Reasonable intelligence, good judgment, a pleasant and straightforward manner, and the ability to avoid conflict are all highly desirable, and perhaps essential, traits for staff in a psychotherapeutic setting. It is extremely difficult to recruit staff who possess all of these qualities. If care is taken to select relatively stable yet flexible assistants (as well as associates and colleagues), training and supervision can result in effective staff development.

Training

Psychotherapists must not only set standards for their staff but must reflect such standards in all professional contacts. An expectancy that staff will treat patients with courtesy and friendliness while maintaining a certain psychological distance must be reinforced by the psychotherapist adhering to these standards.

Informal discussion of patients should not only be discouraged, it should be forbidden. The patient's case folder should be available only to the psychotherapist and the patient. Any information concerning the patient necessary for purposes of billing or appointment scheduling should be available in separate files. Staff having ready access to the patient's file destroys the confidentiality which must be promised to the patient in order for psychotherapy to proceed.

Training should be an on-going activity between the psychotherapist and the staff. Questions should be encouraged and answered in a timely fashion. The psychotherapist should use training procedures to ensure that staff members feel that their contributions to the therapeutic process are important. The essence of staff training is to ensure that the patient sees the psychotherapist and his or her staff as creating a safe, professional setting conducive to psychotherapeutic exploration.

Telephone

It is inconceivable that a psychotherapist today would practice without telephone service. Yet the conveniences of telephone communication are balanced somewhat by potential problems. As with any aspect of psychotherapeutic practice, the telephone should enhance the process.

The patient's first contact with the psychotherapist is almost always by telephone. Some therapists arrange that this contact be made with a secretary or intake worker, while others prefer to speak with the prospective patient at this first contact.

Extensive discussion of the patient's problems over the telephone should be discouraged. Telephone contacts are not sufficiently confidential and are too impersonal to be effectively therapeutic. The primary use of the telephone with patients should be for the scheduling or modifying of appointment times. The use of the telephone with patients should be an important area of training with staff. Whether initial telephone contacts are made between psychotherapist and patient or staff and patient, every effort should be made to ensure that this initial contact is comfortable for the patient.

All experienced psychotherapists are familiar with patients who seem to prefer discussing significant personal issues by telephone, rather than during the therapeutic session. Except in the most unusual situations, discussion of psychotherapeutic issues on the telephone should be discouraged. Special situations where this important rule must be broken will be presented in Chapter 9.

Patients occasionally need to contact their psychotherapist outside of office hours. This is only rarely essential, but the therapist must provide an opportunity for patients to contact the office should this be necessary. It is suggested that the therapist's home telephone number be unlisted. An answering service should be retained to answer calls outside of usual office hours. The answering service operators should be willing to respond to patient's calls with some sensitivity and good manners. It is often helpful for the psychotherapist to discuss this with the answering service supervisors to ensure their awareness and cooperation. With time, most answering services become lax and continual monitoring of the quality of service by the psychotherapist and his or her staff is required.

Some psychotherapists prefer to cover their office phone with an answering machine. This tends to be somewhat impersonal. Should the psychotherapist not pick up calls regularly, an emergency may occur and not come to the psychotherapist's attention. This could create an ethical and/or legal vulnerability.

Emergency Coverage

It is unlikely that a psychotherapist will be available at all times to see patients or answer telephone calls. Because of holidays, vacations, and professional meetings, the psychotherapist will be unavailable at times. It is usual and customary practice to arrange for fellow mental health professionals to "take calls" when the psychotherapist is inaccessible. Some therapists trade off weekends and holidays, sharing the responsibility of being "on call."

It is unnecessary to discuss the patients who are likely to request help from colleagues "on call." Experienced mental health professionals understand that psychotherapy is not advanced by telephone consultations. Crisis consultation, support, and concern are the services which can be rendered until the patient's therapist can be next seen. When a patient calls for help regularly on evenings, weekends, or holidays, this must be dealt with during the psychotherapeutic session. Issues of this nature will be examined in Chapters 8 and 9.

Confidentiality and the Security of Records

Confidentiality is indispensable for a successful psychotherapeutic course. Those who seek to understand themselves and to reconstitute their lives through psychotherapy are often fearful, suspicious, unsure, embarrassed, and in some cases terrified of their ideas, thoughts, dreams and experiences. Early in the course of therapy it becomes evident to the patient that revelation is required in dynamic psychotherapy. Without the confidence that uncomfortable ideas will be kept between the patient and psychotherapist, patients are likely to withhold important or even crucial thoughts. The psychotherapist must take the responsibility for creating a sanctuary where the patient can learn to reveal and experience painful thoughts, memories, dreams, and fears.

Confidentiality rules, constraints, and sanctions are usually put forth by the professional association to which the psychotherapist belongs. Some states have statutory requirements for confidentiality in psychotherapeutic relationships.

There are certain basic procedures which can create this necessary sanctuary. Briefly described, the following procedures should be a part of every psychotherapist's practice.

Files. All clinical material, reports, and progress notes should be kept in a separate folder, clearly identified as the therapeutic file. No one but the psychotherapist and the patient should have access to this folder. Other professional staff, clerical staff, or administrators should never have access to a therapy file. All therapy files should be secured in a locked place between sessions.

Progress notes. The style and extent of progress notes or therapy session narrative vary widely among psychotherapists. Current legal constraints require that such notes be taken in some form as a traditional, usual, or customary form of practice. Although legal situations requiring a psychotherapist to produce progress notes are rare, such situations can occur. These will be reviewed in Chapter 8.

Discussion of cases. No patient should be identified during any professional meeting or consultation without the patient's permission. Certainly, psychotherapists meet in appropriate professional settings and discuss their work. Any extensive consultation which might identify the patient should not take place without the patient's explicit permission. Under no circumstances should a psychotherapist discuss patients in a casual or social setting.

Staff security. All professional, paraprofessional, and clerical staff with whom the psychotherapist is associated must join together to protect the confidentiality promised the patient. When staff are hired by the psychotherapist, the urgency of complete respect for confidentiality procedures must be presented by the psychotherapist. Periodic review and reinforcement are necessary to ensure the continuation of the confidentiality aspect of psychotherapy.

The Issue of Privilege

Privilege is a statutory requirement in most states, to prevent psychotherapists from testifying or providing information about their patients in legal matters. Different states spell out privilege and exclusions to the privilege rule in different ways for a variety of mental health professionals. In most states, a judicial or statutory exception to the privilege rule is made when the patient's mental health is at issue in a suit filed by the patient. In most states, privilege is limited when the patient is indicted for a capital crime (DeKraai & Sales, 1982, 1984). Psychotherapists should contact an attorney friend and ask for a copy of the statutes pertaining to confidentiality and privileges for the state in which the therapist practices. Even the fact that the patient is engaged in psychotherapy may be considered a confidential and privileged matter. Recent court decisions suggest that psychotherapists may have to reveal some details of the patient's attendance in psychotherapy to third party insurance carriers for review purposes.*

McKirdy v. Superior Court of San Francisco. 188 Cal. Rptr. 14 (1982). See also: *Massachusetts v. Korbin* SJC-3671 (1985).

The Psychotherapist's Office Hours

Few mental health professionals restrict their practice to individual, dynamic psychotherapy. Teaching, training, consulting, conducting assessments, group psychotherapy, and forensic testimony are some of the related professional activities of most psychotherapists. Experienced therapists are able to determine the optimum number of hours and types of patients they are able to see comfortably and effectively. Forty or more hours per week seeing patients for individual psychotherapy is the exception rather than the rule.

Some psychotherapists see patients for therapy during the first three days of the week, leaving the end of the week for diagnostic work, teaching, or consulting. Some psychotherapists prefer to see patients only during the afternoon five days a week, leaving morning for family, teaching, writing, or recreating. The psychotherapist's schedule should reflect a pattern that is personally comfortable. An excessive number of patients or too many clinical hours per week will lead to difficulties for both therapist and patient.

Psychotherapeutic appointments should ordinarily be quite regular, whether once, twice, or more times per week. Patients are more likely to make the process an important part of their lives if the psychotherapy experience takes place at the same time each week. Shifting appointments frequently or making appointments *ad lib* may be acceptable for counseling or crisis intervention. In serious, dynamic psychotherapy, such shifts usually create unnecessary resistance and disrupt the therapeutic course.

ASSESSMENT BEFORE THERAPY BEGINS

Divergences of opinion exist among psychotherapists as to whether a diagnostic evaluation is helpful before psychotherapy begins. Most psychotherapists classify or categorize their patients, sometimes behaviorally, sometimes with a psychodynamic formulation and sometimes with reference to standard nomenclature (DSM–III, DSM–III–R, ICDM–9). Several psychotherapeutic schools (psychoanalysis, Rogerian therapy) have proposed that diagnostic activity is of little importance, since the characteristic aspects of the patient's life are likely to become clear as psychotherapy proceeds.

Three styles of evaluation will be presented to illustrate a range of possibilities for the use of assessment prior to beginning psychotherapy. Each is part of the record of the same patient who was seen by different therapists.

Psychiatric Referral

The following referral was made to a psychotherapist who began psychotherapy without further formal evaluation (names and other identifying information are fictitious):

Dear Dr. Smith:
     I take pleasure in referring to you for psychotherapy Miss Jane Doe. I first saw Miss Doe at General Hospital where I was called in consultation by Miss Doe's ObGyn doctor, Sam Jones. Dr. Jones was concerned with Miss Doe's mental status because of several crying episodes reported by floor staff during her recent hospitalization for a fairly routine D & C procedure.
     On examination, I found Miss Doe to be a white, unmarried female, 22 years of age. She was oriented in all three spheres. Neurologic evaluation was negative. Hallucinations and delusions, sometimes related to menses.
     The patient states that she has been depressed more or less consistently since the end of an unhappy love affair about a year ago.
     My impression is that Miss Doe suffers a Dysthymic Disorder (300.40 DSM-III). I have prescribed Elavil for sleep and have referred her to you for psychotherapy.
                                             Sincerely yours,
                                       William A. Brown, M.D.

The issues appeared to be straightforward, and supportive psychotherapy on a weekly basis was begun. After six months (approximately 20 sessions), the patient reported that she was feeling much better and terminated psychotherapy. The value of the simple traditional assessment which is reported above is in its simplicity and cost-effectiveness. The manifest problem was identified and psychotherapy (or counseling) to deal with the uncomfortable and debilitating symptoms was recommended in conjunction with antidepressive medication. The patient's overt satisfaction with the treatment was expressed at termination.

Psychodynamic Evaluation

Approximately two years later, after moving to a college setting, Ms. Doe consulted with the mental health center of her university. She was interviewed by a psychiatrist and a social worker. A staff psychologist administered a Minnesota Multiphasic Personality Inventory. The staff assessment, which led to referral for psychotherapy, was as follows:

MELVILLE STATE UNIVERSITY
MENTAL HEALTH CENTER

STAFF EVALUATION
January 15, 1984

NAME: Doe, Jane B.   ADDRESS: Alpha Dorm
BIRTHDATE: January 14, 1960   AGE: 24
CURRICULUM: Computer Science   EDUCATION: Sophomore

This self-referred student requests services to deal with feelings of lethargy, depression, gastric distress, and poor concentration. She has returned to school after several years in the workforce and is having some difficulty in adapting to academic life.

SOCIAL HISTORY

Ms. Doe is the youngest child and only girl in a family of four children. Her father is a successful physician in the Midwest. Her mother is a supervisor of education in the Chicago school system. The parents have been divorced since she was thirteen. She believes the mother divorced the father because of his illicit love affairs.

Ms. Doe lived with her mother from the time of the divorce until age seventeen. The mother is described as a hardworking, somewhat emotionally labile woman who has recently terminated her third marriage. Ms. Doe feels her three brothers were somewhat favored by both parents. All three brothers entered military service as they turned eighteen.

Ms. Doe went to live with her father at age seventeen, at his request. He wanted her to go to college and felt this would be most economically feasible if she lived with him, worked part-time in his office and attended a local community college. Ms. Doe did this for a year and a half. She found her father to be a domineering, opinionated, and parsimonious person who forced her to work for her college expenses, her room and board at his house and for the use of his second car. After a year of mediocre performance at school, Ms. Doe fell in love with an Air Force officer and moved to California with him. This affair ended unhappily. Ms. Doe received psychiatric evaluation while in the hospital for minor surgery. She was referred for help and after about six months of therapy felt less depressed.

Her mother died, leaving her a modest inheritance which she is using to complete her education. She has friends, dates casually, and enjoys a variety of outdoor hobbies. Lately she has felt mildly despondent and has experienced fairly serious concentration difficulties. She wants help in becoming more comfortable and functional.

PSYCHIATRIC EVALUATION

Ms. Doe is a thin, tall, blonde, attractive white female who seems a bit serious and flat. She is frankly seeking help with her concentration problems. She is intelligent and forthright. There is no evidence of serious psychiatric disorder. She is appropriately communicative and responsive. She reports no disturbance of sleeping, appetite, or bodily functions. Although she is mildly depressed there are no indications that a depression of any seriousness exists at this time.

PSYCHOLOGICAL EVALUATION

Ms. Doe, a sophomore student, was interviewed and given an MMPI. She was pleasant, communicated very well, and was cooperative. She has been making "Bs" and an occasional "C" in the computer science curriculum.

The results of the MMPI suggest that Ms. Doe is a serious, somewhat obsessional and compulsive person whose usual style of hard work and self-application at present is not operating as well as usual because of mild, intermittent depression. Although not suffering true anhedonia, she does have little fun in her life. She is prone to experience a variety of physical discomforts as a result of stress. Mild depression is the most notable symptom. There is no evidence of psychosis or other severe pathology.

PSYCHODYNAMIC FORMULATION

Ms. Doe is a young woman who has always felt somewhat left out or even deserted as a result of her parents' marital problems, as well as her role as the only girl child in the family. Her mother's death has increased her feelings of desertion, guilt, and depression. As the only sibling who has pursued a college education, she has anxiety about taking this step beyond her more favored siblings. As she proceeds to be successful in college, her ambivalence increases. She is beginning to convert her stress into physiologic discomfort as both a self-punishment and an appeal for help.

RECOMMENDATIONS

Ms. Doe should be referred to the health center for consultation and treatment recommendations regarding her somatic complaints. Individual psychotherapeutic counseling at the student counseling center is also recommended.

Jana M. Green, M.D.
Director, Mental Health Center

Ms. Doe was seen by a physician and treated conservatively for her gastric distress. She began seeing a graduate student psychotherapist weekly at the Student Counseling Center. She soon reported that she was feeling better. At the end of the semester, after approximately 18 sessions of psychotherapy, Ms. Doe decided to drop out of school for a while. She took a job in a midwestern city close to her original family home. Approximately a year later she consulted with a clinical social worker about reentering individual psychotherapy. The psychotherapist felt that a more complete psychological evaluation would be helpful. The following assessment was done:

PSYCHOLOGICAL REPORT
September 17, 1985

NAME: Doe, Ms. Jane   DATE OF INTAKE: 8/26/85
ADDRESS: 2137 Elm Street   TELEPHONE: 697-2483
BIRTHDATE: 1/14/60   EDUCATION: 14
AGE: 25-8   OCCUPATION: Computer
Programmer

REFERRAL

Ms. Doe is referred by G.L. Starke, clinical social worker. Ms. Doe has consulted Ms. Starke for help. She wishes to reenter psychotherapy. She has had two previous psychotherapeutic experiences. Ms. Starke requests a full psychological evaluation to answer the following questions:

1. What are the psychological factors underlying Ms. Doe's recurrent depression, somatization, and inability to be comfortable in her work?
2. What are Ms. Doe's vocational interests and capabilities?
3. Should Ms. Doe return to college?
4. If Ms. Doe enters psychotherapy, where might the focus of attention be best directed?

BACKGROUND

A good deal of background history was included in the report received from the Melville State University Mental Health Center.

Ms. Doe states that following her dropout from school she moved to this city, taking a job with the telephone company as a computer programmer. She dislikes her work.

She is able to visit her father regularly. She finds him as insensitive and unsupportive as ever, but feels compelled to see him once or twice a month.

She is again depressed, sleeping badly and losing weight. Medication and diet control most of her gastric symptoms but she has begun to suffer headaches and general tension. Complete physical examination by Gail Brown, M.D., reveals no physiological basis for her symptoms.

She says she still thinks about her mother even though "we talked about that" in her second sequence of psychotherapy sessions. She is discouraged but hopes that "another round" of psychotherapy might help her. This is why she sought help from Ms. Starke.

It is clear that Ms. Doe is quite distressed. It is also clear that she views her previous experiences in psychotherapy as "counseling." She told her story, discussed her symptoms, frequently asked for and received advice, and felt temporary relief.

When asked what she does for fun or pleasure, Ms. Doe seemed confused and asked "What do you mean?" When it was explained that we would like to know what she enjoys doing for recreation, she responded, "Nothing, I guess."

EXAMINATION PROCEDURES

Wechsler Adult Intelligence Scale-revised, Wonderlic-Fm V, Indiana-Reitan Neuropsychological Screening (Cards 1,2,3 & 27-Aphasia Screening), Nelson-Denny Reading Tests, Strong Vocational Interest-SC II, Vocational Interest Interview, Edwards Personal Preference Schedule, FIRO-B, Minnesota Multiphasic Personality Inventory, Thematic Apperception Test, Sentence-Completion Test, Draw-A-Person Test, House-Tree Test, Interview, Observation and History (11 hours of testing and interviews).

RESPONSE TO EVALUATION

Ms. Doe is about 5 feet and 9 inches tall. She is quite thin, weighing about 110 pounds. She is blond and blue-eyed, and is patently depressed. She volunteers little but she is generally cooperative. When asked her hopes for the future, she said, at first, "Who knows?" She then indicated she would like to work at something she might enjoy. If she "got straightened out" she might want to marry and have children. She worked quickly and effectively throughout the three evaluation sessions.

RESULTS OF EXAMINATION

A. *Intellectual Factors*

Objective results of the Wechsler Adult Intelligence Scale-Revised were as follows:

Factor	Deviation IQ	Percentile
Verbal Scale	119	90th
Performance Scale	117	88th
Full Scale	119	90th

The above results place Ms. Doe in the Superior range of intellectual capacity. She was able to perform at the Average level on subtests measuring general information, ability to pick out key ideas, and small motor control. Variation was not significant.

On the Wonderlic she was able to perform at the 92.4 percentile in comparison with females at all educational levels. In spite of her depression, Ms. Doe performs well intellectually.

B. *Neuropsychological Screening*

Ms. Doe performs all tasks on the Indiana-Reitan within normal limits. No behavioral indications of central nervous system dysfunction.

C. *Reading Skills*

The Nelson-Denny results were as follows:

Factor	Grade Equivalent	Percentile (College Sophomore)
Vocabulary	15.8	70th
Comprehension	16.1	81st
Speed (375 wpm)	15.7	65th

The above results indicate that Ms. Doe has excellent reading skills, quite sufficient for continued university education.

D. *Interest Factors*

Ms. Doe's performance on the SC II indicates strong interests in the Realistic Theme and relatively low scores in the other five vocational themes. This suggests she would be happiest studying and working in areas involving science and practical problems, and in situations where she would have to use words and numbers. She would enjoy a job where the results of her efforts could be viewed in fairly measurable terms.

Her highest scores in Basic Interest Scales included Mechanical Activities and Military Activites. Science and mathematics were also high.

Among specific occupational categories, Ms. Doe was found to be very similar to engineers, physicists, computer programmers and military officers.

Clearly, Ms. Doe is not in the "wrong" vocational field as a computer programmer. Her interests are broader than that and she might be happier pursuing a broader application of her intellect and interests.

She might explore the possibility of continuing school in an engineering college, possibly one with ROTC training at a senior level which would offer options for a military experience after graduation or a military career.

E. *Personality Factors*

(1) *Interpersonal activity.* Ms. Doe demonstrated a number of strong and weak scores on the Edwards Personal Preference Schedule as follows:

Need Drives	Need Avoidances
(Above 75th Percentile —College Women)	(Below 25th Percentile)
Autonomy	
Exhibition	Intraception
Affiliation	Nurturance
Orderliness	Abasement

These results suggest that Ms. Doe is most comfortable interpersonally when she can come and go without restriction, say what she thinks openly and can be independent of others when making decisions. She enjoys saying witty and clever things. She likes to be the center of attention, and to talk about personal achievements. She enjoys also being loyal to friends, joining, making new friendships, doing things with others rather than alone, and forming strong attachments. In her work as well as her personal life, she tends to be neat and organized. She prefers to make plans in advance. In general, she is more comfortable when she can avoid analyzing her motives and feelings, attempting to put herself in another's place, and analyzing the behavior of others. It is very difficult for Ms. Doe to assist those less fortunate than herself, be sympathetic, or to forgive those who hurt her. Ms. Doe had a lot of difficulty accepting blame when things go wrong. She would rather fight than give in. She is depressed by any inability to handle situations.

The FIRO-B indicates that Ms. Doe expresses a limited amount of her real feelings to those with whom she is close, yet she expects persons close to her to tell her everything about themselves, their thoughts, wishes and expectancies. In the area of control, Ms. Doe avoids dominating or controlling those close to her and in turn will tolerate little or no domination or control. In spontaneous affection, Ms. Doe both expresses and expects a lot of warmth.

At a deeper interpersonal level, the personality tests suggest that others see Ms. Doe as being unable to express angry feelings effectively. She is often seen as unsure and "immature." Outwardly she appears to conform, in her passivity. She tends to be rigid and intolerant of playful or childlike behavior of others. She frequently appears to be restless and unhappy.

(2) *Early identification and psychosexual development.* Ms. Doe suffers a significant amount of psychosexual confusion. The projective tests suggest that primary identification is with the father. The picture of the father as seen in the projective material is that of a man who is very stubborn, angry, and suspicious. A rigid person, he is held-in and unhappy. Basically dependent, he denies this. He would appear to be self-centered, interested in his children, but unable to interact with them effectively. He relates by creating fear. He displaces much of his anxiety into hard work. One can see evidence of the strong identification in the many traits noted which characterize Ms. Doe's personality.

The mother appears to be Ms. Doe's primary love object in the projective tests. She was apparently a traditional, available person with limited capacity to accomplish her personal goals. An emotionally sensitive person, she suffered periodic depression. She apparently had great difficulty communicating with her daughter and was more comfortable in child-rearing with male children.

(3) *Sources of anxiety.* The personality tests suggest Ms. Doe suffers a great many specific and diffuse anxieties. Some are experienced directly while some are repressed and are manifested without Ms. Doe's awareness of their origins.

A severe dependence/independence conflict exists. Although Ms. Doe says she seeks success, she is fearful of acquiring power, distrusting her ability to control this energy she sees as dangerous.

She has never felt her parents accepted her. She is sad about the distance between her and the mother. There is grieving and unfinished business regarding the dead mother. Toward the father she is both furious and fearful. She would like the father's support to substitute for the modeling she missed from her mother, but she fears his anger and rejection should she seek this support.

Ms. Doe blames herself for the rejection she has felt from both the mother and the father. She has always felt her brothers were favored. She has felt she is not good enough, since childhood.

Any sort of criticism is devastating to her. She would like to rebel, state her opinion, be critical, but the risk is too great. All males are seen as angry, disapproving fathers and all females are regarded emotionally as likely to withhold approval and acceptance as did the mother. Thus, she has considerable difficulty in forming close relationships with either men or women.

(4) *Outlets and defenses.* The personality tests suggest that Ms. Doe's usual defenses are intellectual. She disposes of her anxieties using such mechanisms as suppression, repression, suspiciousness, obsessional worrying, and focusing on external foci (finances, cleanliness, work schedules, health). Anger is turned inward and she frequently experiences depression, a pattern where she identifies somewhat with her mother.

Less intellectual defenses are characterized by passive-aggressive responses, phobias, and a tendency to be drawn to punishing work and social interactions.

RECOMMENDATIONS

This bright young woman is fixated at an almost adolescent stage of development. She is working at a job that gives her minimal stimulation and satisfaction. The following recommendations should be explored in depth:

A. *Vocational/Educational status.* Ms. Doe is ready for further education. Success is frightening and it is unlikely she will do well until she completes unfinished business in her personality development. Vocational counseling and exploration of a return to college are recommended when Ms. Doe is ready.

B. *Psychotherapy.* By all criteria, Ms. Doe is ready for a serious venture into psychotherapy. She is young, articulate, intelligent, dissatisfied with her current life-style, anxious to be relieved of her symptoms, and somewhat positive toward the therapeutic process.

In some ways, Ms. Doe's previous psychotherapeutic experience may prove to be a barrier. She has had two counseling experiences in which her passivity has fit well with the limited therapeutic ventures she experienced. She is now ready to search deeper in a more active way. Resistance is likely to appear early and with strength as she proceeds in her psychodynamic therapy with Ms. Starke.

It is probably a fortuitous choice that Ms. Doe has made in consulting an experienced female psychotherapist. Her previous psychotherapeutic experiences were apparently helpful to her for a limited period of time. To move on to a more adult, self-satisfying level of adjustment, it will be necessary for Ms. Doe to explore and resolve conflicts in a number of important areas of her life. These areas for therapeutic concentration include:

1. Unfinished business regarding the mother. This includes Ms. Doe's grief not only for the loss of the mother, but for the absence of closeness and role-modeling she has so desperately needed.
2. Her confused relationship and identification with her father.
3. Her confused and frightening views of her psychosexual status and expectancies.
4. The panic regarding "letting go" of any emotion, but especially rage.
5. Her ambivalent feelings about the independence and success she seeks but fears.
6. Ms. Doe's propensity to be drawn to situations in which she is dominated or hurt.

In order to help Ms. Doe to understand the extent and importance of her next psychotherapeutic venture, it is recommended that an interpretation of these results be given to Ms. Doe. This interpretation, in great detail, should be given by the examiner. The session should be taped and the tape should be given to Ms. Doe to listen to, share with her therapist, and review during difficult times, in her personal life or during her psychotherapy.

John H. White, Ph.D.

Ms. Doe began twice weekly psychotherapy sessions with Ms. Starke shortly after she received the results of her evaluation. After six months of psychotherapy, Ms. Doe entered a local university and shortly thereafter was accepted in a naval reserve officer training program. Her grades in her engineering curriculum were very good. She reported strong positive attitudes about her current adjustment and future prospects.

More and more it becomes apparent that the information yielded by a complete psychological evaluation can help the patient to conceptualize the depth and extent of the task they are likely to find in psychotherapy. Mortimer and Smith (1983) have written about the psychological test report as "setting the focus" of psychotherapy. They point out that without such an assessment, the therapist and the patient may fail to explore crucial aspects of the patient's personality which could result in a poor outcome.

The use of a complete psychological evaluation before starting psychotherapy engages the patient in a brief, intense self-search, which results in fairly clear-cut descriptions of the sources of difficulty, present psychological status, and the work to be accomplished in psychotherapy. Psychotherapists report that the assessment represents a commitment to and an involvement with the psychotherapy process, allowing patients to move forward in therapy with greater awareness and impetus than without an assessment experience.

STRUCTURING FOR THE PATIENT
UNDECIDED ABOUT PSYCHOTHERAPY

Many patients who feel a need to change their personal lives are unsure about starting psychotherapy. This ambivalence may be based on fear, unsureness about the process, or other hesitancies.

A conference preliminary to beginning psychotherapy is always an acceptable procedure. Most psychotherapists grant such initial sessions. It is suggested that, although such a conference is quasi-therapeutic, the psychotherapist restrict such a session to a discussion of the general structure of psychotherapy, answering the prospective patient's questions as directly as possible and then perhaps referring the patient to some brief reading material. Extended discussions of the worth and value of therapy as well as demands for guarantees or reassurance should not be encouraged.

A particularly good pamphlet concerning psychotherapy is published by Public Affairs Pamphlets, Inc. In their *The Psychotherapies Today, descriptions of various styles and approaches are presented simply and effectively (Ogg, 1981).*

The American Psychological Association publishes *Women and Psychotherapy*, a thoughtful discussion of the special issues women should consider in choosing a psychotherapist (APA Division of the Psychology of Women, 1982).

STANDARDS AND ETHICS

Every psychotherapist, regardless of professional affiliation, is honorbound to ascribe to basic rules of proper professional conduct. Confidentiality and privilege, critical aspects of the ethics of psychotherapy, were covered in detail earlier in this chapter.

The essence of standards and ethics is *the best interests of the patient.* Although there may be considerable variability in the way psychotherapists interpret specific issues (fee structure, length of the therapeutic session, frequency of sessions, degree of detail in progress notes, etc.), certain general standards are legally or institutionally mandated.

Service Within Competence

Ethical psychotherapists offer and conduct professional psychotherapeutic services only within the scope of their competence. Where a patient's needs require therapeutic skill or knowledge beyond the psychotherapist's education, training, or experience, the therapist must transfer the patient to someone of appropriate competence or arrange consultation and supervision to ensure the patient's best interests.

Avoidance of Personal Involvement

Psychotherapists should avoid nonprofessional contact with their patients or the patient's family. Personal or business involvements with patients are likely to delay or even destroy the effectiveness of psychotherapy. Social contacts with the patient or the patient's relatives must be avoided or kept to the most minimal levels possible.

Physical contact of an affectionate or sexual nature with patients is unacceptable, ethically and legally.

Conflict of Interest

No special favors, services, or involvements of a business nature should take place between the psychotherapist and the patient. Close contacts or business dealings with relatives of the patient in long-term dynamic psychotherapy should also be avoided. It is also probably wise to avoid providing professional services to relatives or close friends of patients in psychotherapy.

Medical Monitoring

The patient's physical health and its effect on the psychotherapeutic process can be an issue of considerable importance. Psychotherapists should require all of their patients to have a recent, complete physical examination prior to beginning psychotherapy. Psychotherapists should further require that their patients receive a physical examination at regular intervals during the course of long-term psychotherapy.

Duty to Warn

Since the Tarasoff decision in California,* psychotherapists have had a legal duty to warn anyone who may be a potential victim of a patient's dangerous behavior. If a psychotherapist makes a determination that a patient is a danger to himself or herself, family members or others, appropriate authorities must be notified. Requirements and procedures vary from state to state. Psychotherapists should become familiar with the duty to warn requirements in the state where they practice.

Practicing psychotherapy in an ethical manner requires good sense, stable moral values and a consistent awareness of the respect to which all psychotherapy patients are entitled.

Tarasoff v. Regents of the Univ. of Cal., 13 Cal. 3d 177, 529 p. 2d, 118 Cal. Rptr. 129.

PART II

Bringing Psychotherapy About

CHAPTER 5

The First Session

The content and outcome of the first psychotherapeutic session can influence the quality of the remainder of the therapeutic contacts. The degree to which the patient feels positive about the therapist is frequently a gauge of therapeutic prospects. Research and clinical experience suggest that when patients develop feeling of friendly cooperation with the therapist and sense a cooperative working toward common goals, psychotherapy is more likely to proceed efficiently.

During the first session it is important to create the beginnings of a working alliance between psychotherapist and patient. This alliance is to some extent based on a belief on the part of the patient that the psychotherapist is prepared to be helpful, understanding, and skillful in the therapeutic setting. The alliance is made firmer if the patient believes that common understandings and expectations are shared with the therapist.

There is no "one way" to begin psychotherapy. Student psychotherapists tend to imitate their supervisors while experienced therapists develop styles of initiating therapy suited to their personality and experience. Some schools of psychotherapy recommend no structuring at the beginning of psychotherapy. The following portion of a first session conducted by a Rogerian psychotherapist illustrates an unstructured approach:

Therapist: Won't you please come in and sit down?
Patient: Thank you (*long pause*) . . . I feel kind of funny.

71

Therapist: The first session can be uncomfortable, at first.

Patient: Well, I've never done anything like this before and I'm not sure what to say or how to begin.

Therapist: Anything you'd like to start with is fine.

Patient: Well . . . , should I tell you what I'm worried about?

Therapist: Whatever you'd like.

Patient: Well, I don't want to waste your time and just ramble on.

Therapist: You're worried about "Doing it right?"

Patient: Yeah . . . well, I don't know. I want to get rid of these tense feelings I always have.

Therapist: Uh-huh . . .

Patient: I mean . . . even early in the morning, while having breakfast, I begin to feel like my wires are being pulled tight.

Therapist: Must be pretty uncomfortable.

Patient: Well, no, not right then . . . I'm so used to it that I hardly notice it anymore. It's there but it's so usual it's like normal for me . . . but I know it's starting.

Therapist: So even though you're used to it, you feel it beginning to build early in the day.

Patient: Yeah . . . even on the weekends it starts in the morning.

Therapist: It never lets up on you.

Patient: I guess not . . . (*long pause*) . . . can't think of what I ought to say next.

Therapist: So you're a little uncomfortable about "How to do it?"

Patient: Yeah . . . I've never done anything like this. I usually talk very little about myself—even to my wife.

Therapist: So talking about yourself is never easy.

Patient: Not nowadays. When I was a kid—a teenager—I could talk the socks off anyone. It seems like during the past eight or ten years I've gotten more and more inside myself.

Therapist: You feel different about yourself than you did ten years ago.

Patient: Yes . . . in a lot of ways. I'm not only a lot quieter but I worry about every little thing. I can't get to sleep sometimes—I worry about this and that—not only what's happened, but what might happen. I'm worried about telling you all this piddling stuff, but it's important to me.

Therapist: At first, most people feel embarrassed or uncomfortable talking about themselves.

Patient: Not my wife! She can tell anybody anything! Last week we were at the beach and she got to talking with a woman working at the re-freshment stand on the pavilion. Before you know it she was telling her about her bowel complaints, her operations, her fights with my mother—everything!

Therapist: You couldn't do that.

Patient: You bet I couldn't. Of course, I don't know why anybody wants to talk about that stuff. I don't believe complaining does a bit of good.

Therapist: It's not your style.

Patient: No—it's hard for me to talk about myself.

Therapist: You're talking about yourself pretty well now.

Patient: Oh? . . . Well . . . I never know . . . you know, how well I do. I mean, I can't tell.

Therapist: It may surprise you to find out you're doing OK?

Patient: Yeah . . . it is a surprise when it happens.

The beginnings of an alliance between a skillful psychotherapist and a fearful patient can come about during a first session, with no formal structuring about psychotherapy.

STRUCTURING

Recent studies suggest that structuring of the process during the first psychotherapeutic session can enhance the process of creating the alliance between therapist and patient (Levine, Stolz, & Lacks, 1983; Bottari & Rappaport, 1983). It was found that the more the patient knew of the therapeutic process and the therapist's role and function during the first session of psychotherapy, the greater the symptom relief and the shorter the therapeutic course. For those psychotherapists who prefer to spend 10 to 20 minutes of the first session in structuring the process for the patient, the following elements are generally of importance:

- The psychotherapist's responsibilities
- The patient's responsibilities
- Time arrangements
- Fee arrangements
- Steps likely to lead to progress
- Evaluation of progress
- Record keeping
- Questions from the patient

The following segment of a first session between a neoanalytically trained psychotherapist and his 45-year-old female patient illustrates a structured approach to beginning therapy:

Therapist: Won't you please come in and sit down?

Patient: Thank you Doctor . . . May I smoke?

Therapist: If you care to—of course.

Patient: I've smoked so long to decrease tension that it's automatic.

Therapist: Being tense at one's first session of psychotherapy is very understandable.

Patient: I suppose . . . What should I do now?

Therapist: I'd like to tell you, briefly, about psychotherapy and how we can work together in your best interests.

Patient: It's sort of funny to hear a doctor say he's going to work with you.

Therapist: It is a lot different from medical treatment. In point of fact, this isn't really a "treatment" procedure. Psychotherapy is more of a learning experience. During our sessions, and in the time in between sessions, you will have a chance to learn about yourself as a person, those things that you do which enhance your life, and the things you do which lower or interfere with your quality of life.

Patient: I think I do a lot of that.

Therapist: Probably so . . . and it will be important to explore that . . . I'd like to tell you something about my responsibilities as your psychotherapist. My first task is to create a sanctuary during our sessions, so that you come to see your appointments as your time in a safe place. We are in a sound-conditioned room. No one but you and I can know what is said here. You have both confidentiality and privilege. What you say is confidential between us. The notes I take can only be read by you and me. Your records or my knowledge of you cannot be subpoenaed to a court of law unless you enter a legal action where you yourself claim your mental or psychological state is part of the proceedings. I'll tell you a bit more of that later.

I have a responsibility to give you my best skills and experience. Should I find at any time during your therapy that I am unfamiliar with what you are exploring, I will tell you so and make efforts to get the knowledge needed to work with you. I will never make believe that I understand when in fact I do not. I must do everything possible to encourage you to talk freely since psychotherapy proceeds best when you are talking and experiencing.

It is my responsibility to avoid giving sympathy. This surprises many patients. Sympathy is a response of helplessness. "I'm sorry you're in such a dreadful state and so helpless." I certainly do not see you in that way. On the other hand, I will always seek to be empathetic to you—to try and sense the kind of feelings you have and the depth of those feelings.

I will rarely give direction or advice. Advice can be as destructive as sympathy. It suggests you are incapable of understanding, deciding, or doing. I will first and foremost be interested in what you feel, what you want, and how you make or avoid decisions. For that reason, I will not "cut you off" by giving advice or telling you what to do.

Of great importance is my responsibility to make no moral judgments about what you tell me. Whether something is "good" or "bad" must be decided by you, and this exploration usually constitutes one of the keys to success in psychotherapy.

As your psychotherapist, knowing that progress depends on your being able to express yourself during these sessions, I must do everything I can to encourage you to take leadership in choosing topics and exploring your feelings.

Patient: Goodness! That's a lot! What am *I* supposed to do?

Therapist: You are not supposed to do anything except pay your fee on a regular basis. That's your only responsibility to me. You may come to sessions or not, you can be late, you can sit silently—if you choose. Psychotherapy works best when I as your psychotherapist have most of the structural responsibilities and you as the patient make more of the choices.

Patient: Well, certainly there must be some things that I can do to make the therapy go better, aren't there?

Therapist: Very much so. We know that psychotherapy will proceed best when you talk about things which give you strong feelings. Your emotions and how you experience these emotions are the stuff that psychotherapy is made of. Any session in which you talk of something that stirs strong feelings right there and then is very powerful for moving psychotherapy forward. Also, when you find yourself talking about things you had no plan to talk about—things which just "pop out"—therapy will proceed best. If you are willing to let your emotions come out as you experience them here, you will be helping advance the therapy. If you can talk about your most uncomfortable, embarrassing, or frightening experiences, thoughts, ideas, and dreams, you will be moving forward in discovering yourself and gaining a greater control of your life.

Patient: How will I know if I'm doing well. Will you tell me?

Therapist: It's sometimes hard to evaluate the effect of psychotherapy. In general, I'll ask you to look for indicators of how you are doing. The first signs of progress may not be in the relief of old symptoms. You may notice changes in the attitudes of your children or your mate.

Patient: That would be a welcome change. My kids have no compassion or understanding . . .

Therapist: That seems troublesome to you.

Patient: Always. It's like a continual battle . . . I am always fearful of what will go wrong next and how I should deal with it. It drives me crazy . . . , I'm sorry—I interrupted you.

Therapist: I'm glad you did. The more you talk, the more we can accomplish.

Patient: I'm not sure I really believe that, but I am here and I'm going to try . . . What if I don't feel like coming to a session? When we decided I would try twice a week, I didn't know it would be—like regular . . . or forever. *(laugh)*

Therapist: It often seems that way at the beginning.

Patient: It's funny. Part of me is scared to death and the other part is looking forward to this. It's like going off to college the first time . . . I don't know . . .

In addition to the structuring covered in the above example, some therapists present details of their fee structure, the ways in which telephone calls and family contacts will be handled, or other logistical aspects of the process.

Of recent significance and concern to psychotherapists is the issue of the psychotherapist's "duty to warn." Most jurisdictions have held that a psychotherapist is limited in the degree of confidentiality which can be promised to a patient. In the original decision laid down in *Tarasoff v. The Regents of the University of California* (cited previously in Chapter 4), the following limits were placed on absolute confidentiality:

> The public policy favoring the protection of the confidential character of patient-psychotherapist communications must yield in instances in which disclosure is essential to avert danger to others. The protective privilege ends where public peril begins.

This ruling places in jeopardy one of the traditional and generally considered essential foundations for the proper conduct of psychotherapy. Experienced psychotherapists believe that patients will be reluctant and withholding of important details of their past lives and their current introspections if confidentiality is in doubt, rendering the psychotherapeutic process fruitless.

This concern is not universally supported. Muehleman and his co-authors (1985) studied the effects of promised confidentiality versus limited confidentiality. Results suggested that notification of limited confidentiality did not significantly limit self-disclosure during the psychotherapy session. This study and similar efforts (Everstine, et al., 1980; Kobocow, McGuire, & Blau, 1983) suggest that patients can tolerate a limited guarantee of confidentiality.

A structured presentation of the limits of confidentiality from a first psychotherapeutic session follows:

Therapist: There is an important exception to the confidentiality rule that I'd like to discuss before we get started. It's called "duty to warn." Because of a number of legal decisions made during the past decade, psychotherapists are required by law to warn any person whom a patient declares serious intent to harm. For instance, should a patient come to a session with a loaded gun and insist he or she is going to leave the session, return to work, and shoot the boss, the psychotherapist would be legally bound to call the boss or the authorities and warn of the impending attack. This happens in only the rarest instances. It's never happened to me, but I am required to tell you this.

Patient: (laugh) Well . . . there are a lot of people I've said I'd like to do in.

Therapist: Certainly . . . and in psychotherapy, the discussion of anger and even murderous rage is not only common and acceptable but an important part of the therapeutic process. It is important to talk about your strong feelings whether they represent behavior acceptable or not acceptable to society. Nothing is too bad or wrong to talk about in psychotherapy. My discussing duty to warn during our first session, even though it is an issue unlikely to be of any importance in our work together, is part of the open interchange between us which will be critical to ensure progress in the psychotherapy. Psychotherapists are also required by law to report incidents of child abuse to certain agencies.

Patient: I don't think I could be harmful to anyone. I'm even uncomfortable when my kids watch violent movies. I don't know how people can be violent . . .

Patients do not seem to question what appears to be a usual and customary procedure during the early phases of psychotherapy.

Some psychotherapists prefer that patients sign a *Duty to Warn* form. Figure 1 presents a commonly used *Duty to Warn* form.

In recent years some psychotherapists have developed a procedure whereby they enter into a *contract* with the patient as part of the therapeutic process. Some suggest that such a contract solidifies the

FIGURE 1.
A Duty to Warn Form

DUTY TO WARN

Although confidentiality and privileged communication remain rights of all clients of psychotherapists according to state law, some courts have held that if an individual intends to take harmful or dangerous action against another human being, or against himself, it is the psychotherapist's duty to warn the person or the family of the person who is likely to suffer the results of harmful behavior, or the family of the client who intends to harm himself.

State laws require that all mental health professionals report incidents of any type of child abuse to appropriate agencies.

The psychotherapist will under no circumstances inform such individuals without first sharing that intention with the client. Every effort will be made to resolve the issue before such a breach of confidentiality takes place.

_____
Psychotherapist

I have read the above and understand the therapist's legal and social responsibility to make such decisions where necessary.

Date _____ By _____

---

patient's commitment to psychotherapy. Some insurance companies have required that such a *contract,* or *therapeutic plan* be submitted prior to reimbursement. Figure 2 presents a therapeutic plan form which may be used, where appropriate, before beginning psychotherapy.

Some additional areas that can be covered in the structuring of the first session include:

- The fact that friends and relatives may become distressed by the patient's involvement in psychotherapy.
- Should the patient ever become uncomfortable about progress in psychotherapy, external consultation or evaluation will be encouraged if the discomfort persists.
- No significant therapy can take place while the patient is under the influence of drugs or alcohol.
- The limits on personal telephone calls to the therapist.

FIGURE 2.
A Psychotherapy Contract

INTERVENTION PLAN

NAME: JONES, Ada   DATE OF PLAN: 7/25/85

REFERRAL SOURCE: Dr. Cramer

ASSESSMENT: 6/15/85 by Dr. Smith. Report and tape to Ms. Jones

ORIGINAL RECOMMENDATIONS:
1. Individual, eclectic-dynamic psychotherapy.
2. Group psychotherapy when appropriate.

CURRENT PLAN:
1. One session of individual therapy per week.
2. Possibly adding an additional session per week during stressful periods.
3. Consider adding/substituting Group when Ms. Jones is ready.

REVIEW OR EVALUATION PLAN:
1. Quality of Life Scale every eight sessions.

FEES:
Individual–$95.00
Group   –$35.00

ADDITIONAL:

AGREEMENT: _____ Therapist
_____ Client

- The options for increasing or decreasing the number of regularly scheduled sessions.
- Vacations and other times when the therapist is likely to cancel sessions.
- Fees and payment schedules.

Structuring Psychotherapy for Adolescents

Children and adolescents usually become psychotherapy patients at the request or insistence of third parties. More are brought against their will than come voluntarily. Reluctance to participate in psychotherapy occurs at one time or another during the therapeutic course with all patients, as a wide variety of defenses or resistances emerge. Most adolescents resist psychotherapy from the first session as part of their relatively normal struggle to free themselves from adult control and authoritarian influence (in spite of their ambivalence about independence). As many as 80 percent of adolescents express quite openly and directly their reluctance to engage in psychotherapy. They refuse to attend sessions or participate only under coercion. Those who continue to attend their sessions frequently justify their reluctance by finding fault with the psychotherapist, the session, the staff, or those responsible for the referral (Taylor, Adelman & Kaser-Boyd, 1985).

It is unrealistic to expect patients to engage actively, with commitment, in a dynamic psychotherapeutic process if they feel they are in a threatening environment. This is especially so if the situation is not of their own choosing. Adolescents represent a special case of the reluctant patient; they resent being "sent" for psychotherapy, but they are at a stage in development where they are desperate for allies, hungry for understanding, power and status, and terribly anxious to discover what is going to happen next in their lives. Psychotherapy is a boon for those troubled adolescents who are able to resolve initial fear and rage to find the sanctuary that psychotherapy can offer.

To help adolescents move through the rocky early sessions of therapy, a pre-psychotherapy psychological assessment can be very helpful. The procedure introduces the adolescent patient to the concept of self-search and the interpretation allows the young patient to grasp a realistic inventory of assets, liabilities, and—most of all—opportunities.

Structuring young, reluctant patients during the first session is of the utmost importance. Expecting the adolescent to simply "come to therapy," session after session, because the parents, guardians, court, or school mandate attendance is unrealistic and incompetent on the part of the psychotherapist. Waiting for the adolescent patient to ease his or her initial resistance rarely works. It goes against all we know about this complex and volatile stage of human development. If introduction into the psychotherapeutic process is to be successful, certain conditions are mandatory because of the sensitivity and fragility of the adolescent personality.

- The patient must see the process as operating primarily in his or her best interests.
- The patient must perceive early on that the psychotherapist is on his or her side, committed to the process of working in the patient's best interest.
- The patient must sense that the psychotherapist is willing to listen to, to understand, and to respect adolescent ideas and values.

Unless the young patient is able to perceive these things during the first three to five sessions one can expect a therapeutic failure regardless of how long the patient is "forced" to attend.

The first session can be difficult. Silence, hostile compliance, or outright rage can be expected. Because of these initial, very trying behaviors, the burden clearly falls on the psychotherapist to decide whether adolescents will be accepted for treatment. Once psychotherapists make a decision to treat these patients, they should be willing to conduct an active first session.

There are many ways in which this can be done. Each psychotherapist must develop an individual structuring style with adolescents. In doing so, the following things about the young patient, at the time of the first session, should be considered.

- The young patient is frightened. He or she may believe that the referral for psychotherapy means that the secret fears of insanity, long a source of private terror, are now confirmed.
- The adolescent patient would be mortified if peers discovered that he or she was seeing a "shrink." Initially, coming to psychotherapy is an embarrassment.
- The adolescent, through experience or peer pressure, usually regards adults as manipulative, untrustworthy, insensitive, and sometimes dangerous.
- No trust will grow between the adolescent and the psychotherapist until limits are tested by the young patient.

The following excerpt is taken from the first session with a 15-year-old boy who had been having problems in school and had run away from home several times. He had long been a victim of his parent's neurotic battling before and after their divorce, which took place when the boy was 11. Professional help was sought after John threw a bicycle lock through a school window at the instigation of peers. A psychological evaluation revealed that John was of High Average intelligence but deficient in reading skills. He was experiencing the many usual conflicts of adolescence, but with unusual intensity. John was suffering a significant degree of depression. The parents agreed to participate in therapy with a family therapy specialist and John was referred for individual psychotherapy.

Therapist: I'm Doctor Harkey, John. Won't you come in?
Patient: (No comment. Takes chair)
Therapist: Is that chair comfortable for you?
Patient: (*Shrugs*)
Therapist: Would you like a coke or root beer?

Patient: (*Shakes head "No"*)

Therapist: We're going to be meeting together once a week for a while to talk. How do you feel about that?

Patient: (*Shrugs*)

Therapist: It was your mother and dad's idea for you to see me, wasn't it?

Patient: Yeah ... (*long pause*) ... (*patient fidgets*) ...

Therapist: I guess if you had your way you'd be somewhere else today.

Patient: Uh-huh ... (*nodding vigorously*)

Therapist: How tall are you John?

Patient: I don't know ...

Therapist: You look to be about five feet five. Come over here—let's mark you on the door sill. (*Therapist takes patient to a door and marks sill at top of patient's head with a pencil*) Let's see. (*taking measuring tape out*) John, hold this end on the mark and I'll run the tape to the floor. (*therapist measures*) That's five feet four and a half inches!

Patient: (*Shrugs*)

Therapist: I'm going to leave that pencil mark up. I've got a feeling you've been growing lately and we can measure you again later to see. How tall would you like to be?

Patient: (*Shrugs*)

Therapist: Are you interested in things like that—height, weight, build?

Patient: Not really ... (*long pause*)

Therapist: I was at your age. I think all people think about this when they are growing ... Where are you at school, John?

Patient: What do you mean?

Therapist: I mean what grade you're in and how you're doing.

Patient: I'm in the 9th. I should be in 10th.

Therapist: Do you feel bad about that?

Patient: Not really ...

Therapist: Tell me about some things you enjoy, John.

Patient: What do you mean?

Therapist: What you like to do.

Patient: I don't know ...

Therapist: Do you enjoy TV?

Patient: Sometimes ...

Therapist: These are a lot of questions, aren't they?

Patient: Yeah ...

Therapist: I'd like to tell you a little about who I am and what we will be doing here. I'm a psychotherapist, which means I talk to people who want to find out more about themselves. The more we know about ourselves, the more we can get what we want from life and the more comfortable we feel with people. Are you ever uncomfortable with people?

Patient: Sometimes . . .

Therapist: Everyone is at times. When it happens too often, we feel bad or mad or depressed or embarrassed. Are you ever depressed, John?

Patient: What do you mean?

Therapist: Like feeling low, hopeless, nobody cares?

Patient: Yeah . . . sometimes.

Therapist: I'd like to help you to understand your feelings. I know that most of your friends call people like me "shrinks," but in truth we are really "expanders."

We don't "shrink" anyone. My job is to provide you with a private, safe time every week where we can talk and you can learn some very good things about yourself and how to use these things you learn. Did you hear the results of your psychological tests?

Patient: Yeah . . . My mother got a tape from the other doctor.

Therapist: Then you know that you're pretty bright?

Patient: (*Shrugs*)

Therapist: At first it's very hard to feel comfortable in psychotherapy and to talk. It's especially hard when being here is somebody else's idea, isn't it?

Patient: Yeah . . . (*long pause*)

Therapist: I want you to try to believe that I'm on your side and I want to help you. That will be hard, but try. What we talk about will be between you and me. I'll answer your questions honestly, and I'll tell you that I don't know when I don't know. You can talk about anything you want and it will be OK.

Patient: I don't want to come here. It wasn't my idea.

Therapist: I know that, John, and that's not fair, but your parents are trying to help with problems they have and you have, and this is part of it.

Patient: They don't care . . .

Therapist: I'm sure it seems that way, and I'm sure they've hurt your feelings in the past.

Patient: They always do!

Therapist: It's been hard on you, hasn't it?

Patient: (*Shrugs*) . . . (*long pause*)

Therapist: I'd like you to come three times, John, and then we'll decide together if we should continue to work with each other—whether you

    like me, feel I understand things that are important to you . . .
Would you try that?

Patient: Then what?

Therapist: Then if you decide it's not as I tell it, or you don't want me to
    help you, we'll stop.

Patient: Yeah?

Therapist: True . . . We'll decide together after three sessions.

Patient: Hmpf . . . (*long pause*)

Therapist: What do you say?

Patient: I don't care . . .

    The remainder of the session continued in this way. At the end of the
first session, John accepted a soft drink and took it with him when he
left.

    The second session began in a way similar to the first. The passive-
aggressiveness, reluctance and suspicion had diminished only slightly. At
the end of the second session the following interchange took place:

Therapist: Do you have a best friend, John?

Patient: Not really . . .

Therapist: Did you ever?

Patient: . . . (*hesitant*) Last year, Ricky . . .

Therapist: Was Ricky in your grade?

Patient: Yeah . . . but he moved away.

Therapist: And you felt bad.

Patient: Yeah . . . I guess . . .

Therapist: It's hard to lose people.

Patient: What do you mean?

Therapist: Like you lost Ricky, and a couple of years ago you lost your
    family.

Patient: I didn't lose my family!

Therapist: Well—they split up.

Patient: Yeah . . .

Therapist: That left you without a family—just a mother and a
    father.

Patient: I guess (*slumps in chair*) . . . (*long pause*)

Therapist: That was hard on you, wasn't it?

Patient: They didn't care . . . They were too busy arguing about the
    money and the cars and the lake place.

Therapist: Parents sometimes pay attention to the wrong things.

Patient: Isn't it time to go?

Therapist: Just about . . . Anything you want to ask me?

Patient: Can I take a coke with me?
Therapist: Sure.

The young patient maintained the adolescent defenses in the second session, responded in a minimal but experiential way to several emotional topics, and ended the session with an interesting piece of ritualistic behavior—refusing a soft drink offered at the beginning of the session, but asking for it as he left. The patient was experiencing the intense dependence/independence conflict so often found among adolescents. John allowed the therapist to give him a soft drink, but would not drink it during the session.

At the end of the third session, the therapist brought up the verbal contract he had offered John in the first session. John hedged and evaded, but said that he'd try "maybe three more sessions." Things went well after that.

As can be seen from this illustration, initiating psychotherapy with an adolescent patient requires far more structure than would be necessary or advisable with an adult patient.

PROGRESS NOTES

Progress notes serve as a journal of the psychotherapeutic process. Such notes need not be detailed. Psychotherapists find progress notes helpful for review purposes. Reviews are particularly helpful during unproductive plateaus and periods of resistance. (These issues will be presented in Chapters 7 and 8.)

Few psychotherapists keep verbatim notes. There is no one standard for progress records. Some therapists take notes during the session, while others summarize following each session. Some therapists record only conflict areas or mechanisms of defense which appear during the session.

Snyder (1947) has proposed a relatively simple scheme for classifying patient and therapist responses. Originally part of a research effort to evaluate the content of the psychotherapeutic interchange, this system can serve as a progress note shorthand.

In this system, all things said by the psychotherapist are labeled "X" categories. Patient responses are "Y" statements. Table 1 illustrates a variation of the Snyder system.

To illustrate the use of this system a segment of the 35th therapeutic session with an accountant, depressed over lack of progress in his profession, will be presented verbatim, following by the progress note based on the interchange.

TABLE 1
A System of Abbreviations for Writing Progress Notes
During Psychotherapy

Category	Abbreviation	Content
Psychotherapist (X)	XST	Structuring comments or miscellany
	XSA	Simple Acceptance
	XRC	Restatement of content
	XDQ	Direct question
	XCF	Clarification of feeling
	XIT	Interpretation to patient
Patient (Y)	YFA	Free association
	YDQ	Direct question
	YSA	Simple acceptance
	YAC	Acceptance of therapist's statement
	YREJ	Rejection of therapist's comment or interpretation
	YDEN	Denial of therapist's comment or interpretation and offers alternative
	YEM	Emotional response
	YLP	Long pause
	YNR	No response
	YPA	Positive attitudes
	YNA	Negative attitudes
	YAMB	Ambivalence

The patient came to the session 10 minutes late and was quite agitated.

Therapist: Won't you sit down?
Patient: Oh God! What a week! I'm in real trouble!
Therapist: A pretty bad time?
Patient: That's putting it mildly. After I left last week, I got to thinking about how I put things off all the time. I was mad about it because for the first time I realized that the putting off was not really a convenience or a choice for me. I wasn't helping myself or getting relief, I was just making future trouble.
Therapist: You were very surprised at this realization.
Patient: Shocked is more like it. I had the idea that putting things off was some sort of cautious or conservative way of handling things. Now I suddenly realize it's just heel dragging—a way of saying, "the hell with it," or something.

Therapist: A form of anger.

Patient: No, not exactly anger—maybe disinterest . . . (*long pause*) . . .

Therapist: You were pleased with your discovery.

Patient: Yeah . . . at least at the time. Then I went into a frenzy of activity. I was working 14 hours a day last week. I was on to everybody—"We're going to change things around here and get more efficient"—I got after everybody.

Therapist: Didn't that help?

Patient: Help? It nearly ruined me! This morning my secretary and a typist gave two weeks notice. They quit. They said I expected too much. I just can't win!

Therapist: What started out well took a bad turn for you.

Patient: Yeah . . . now I'm really upset. (*mops brow*)

Figure 3 presents the progress note written for this segment of the session.

Some psychotherapists prefer to tape record some or all of their sessions. This should be done only with the patient's permission. Reviewing tapes of therapy sessions is a cumbersome, time-consuming procedure, probably best suited for training or supervision.

Progress notes or tapes should be available to the patient. Requests by patients to review records are rare, but the psychotherapist should be prepared to honor such requests.

Good beginnings augur well for an effective, successful psychotherapeutic course (Blau, 1950). If the patient can leave the first ses-

FIGURE 3

Illustrating the Use of a Psychotherapist/Patient Response
Coding System for Progress Notes

PROGRESS NOTES

NAME _____

Date	NOTES
7/31/85	(35)[Pt. 10'late] YEM - insight re: evasion. - Spoiled by over-reaction. YFA, XSA. YEM, XCF, YAC . XIT Anger. YDEN, makes milder. YPA→self. XCF, YAC .. them. YNA→self for spoiling. YEM, XCF, YAC, YEM (still not able to accept own capacity for anger).

sion with some sense of the safety and tranquility of the setting, the sensitivity and skill of the psychotherapist, and his or her own potential to find self-worth, the framework of the psychotherapeutic alliance will have been forged.

CHAPTER 6

Establishing and Maintaining the Psychotherapeutic Process

The psychotherapist's task is three-fold. First and foremost is *the establishment of a therapeutic setting which is a sanctuary*—secure, constant, and as comfortable as possible for the patient. The second, *maintaining the therapeutic alliance through sensitive awareness*, springs from the first. Everything the psychotherapist says or does should support these two essential tasks to ensure a successful therapeutic effort. The third task, *enhancing the therapeutic process*, will be considered in Chapter 7.

The psychotherapist must avoid weighing and judging patients' responses or behavior in personally or stereotypically judgmental ways. At all times the psychotherapist should be aware that those who seek psychotherapy suffer neurotic conflicts and life-styles. The word *neurotic* is simply a way of describing personal conflicts and painful or unproductive styles of coping. People whose conflicts or coping styles are *neurotic* tend to be unable to work consistently in their own best interests. Neurotic behavior requires a considerable expenditure of intellectual and/or emotional energy with relatively little direct return for the investment. Neurotic behavior is "fuel inefficient."

People may seek psychotherapy when this state of inefficiency becomes intolerable. Therapy is an opportunity for a neurotic person to come to understand the imbalance of energies and the source of the inequity. Once the patient is able to discover the patterns which perpetuate the imbalance, a choice becomes possible. The patient may continue the neurotic style or choose to take some emotional risks to modify the old patterns. The goal is to increase personal attainment and fulfillment in relation to energies expended.

People maintain a neurotic balance to satisfy complex needs to continue earlier life patterns, to balance guilt, to reduce intolerable stress, and for other reasons. Beginning psychotherapy is rarely a total commitment on the part of the patient to shed all neurotic encumbrances. There is much fear of change and, as a result, the old ways tend to remain and psychotherapy generally proceeds slowly.

Guilt is frequently a key aspect of the patient's neurosis. Guilt emerges as a topic for therapeutic exploration early in psychotherapy only when an acute episode occurs. It is usually later in the psychotherapeutic course that patients become aware that this pervasive and insidious influence is always there. The following occurred during the 35th session of psychotherapy with a patient who had first mentioned guilt some 10 sessions previously in respect to forgetting his mother's birthday:

Patient: I never realized that I feel somewhat guilty *all* the time. I told you about how I forgot my mom's birthday a couple of months ago, and how guilty I felt. When we talked about it I realized that the guilt was based on anger I didn't even know about! I felt better, but as I've been looking at my feelings more lately, I realize that guilt is there *all* the time, sort of waiting to come out.

Therapist: How does it feel to you?

Patient: It's funny—like a fluorescent light fixture at the office that isn't working right—there's a buzzing, but soon you accept it and don't pay attention. It becomes background. Now that I'm looking more closely at my feelings, I realize that there is a low level of guilt, a feeling of being or doing wrong that's there *all* the time.

Therapist: Uh huh . . .

Patient: That must mean that I feel wrong or bad about things I haven't thought about consciously . . . that I have a lot more to find out than I thought I did.

RESPONSIBILITY FOR PROGRESS

Although psychotherapists identify their responsibilities to create a setting which is a sanctuary and to further the therapeutic alliance in every way reasonable and possible, the therapeutic engagement must be initiated and carried forth by the patient. In the segment of psychotherapy seen above, a patient in his 35th session takes most of the responsibility for initiating topics and carrying forth the exploration. This does not always happen during the early sessions of psychotherapy.

Patients are still unsure of their role. Limits must be tested. Patients frequently show resistance to free expression of feeling. In the early stages of psychotherapy, the patient is less likely to talk openly and at length. The content is less likely to be as emotional or self-oriented as later in the therapeutic course.

In studying therapist and patient responses, Schmitt (1985) found data to suggest that the process of psychotherapy involves patients learning to differentiate between *self* and *behavior,* and becoming aware that inner self and feelings are more closely tied to their own action and beliefs than to that of others. From this, patients become aware of the importance and worth of increased responsibility. The psychotherapist's enhancement task is to respond in such ways as to help the patient increase frequency and intensity of self-exploration.

Constancy of the therapeutic setting and of the psychotherapist's style helps to maintain the sanctuary of the session and encourages the patient to risk exploration and revelation.

LOGISTICAL ELEMENTS

Starting the Session

Each therapist will develop a personal style for beginning the psychotherapeutic session. Establishing a standard, straightforward greeting will increase the probability that the patient will use the time from the beginning of the session to focus on self. The psychotherapeutic session is not a social event and little time, if any, should be wasted on creative amenities. As patients become accustomed to familiar surroundings and familiar responses on the part of the psychotherapist, they are more likely to respond in terms of inner needs and pressures than if the structure of the session is varied.

Smoking

Many psychotherapists, in an effort to focus on *wellness,* forbid smoking during the therapy session. It is sometimes suggested that depriving smokers of the opportunity to smoke during the therapy session increases tension and aids in the expression of emotion. Other therapists feel that allowing their patients to smoke provides an in-process measure of stress, demonstrated by the intensity and frequency of smoking. There are no data to support either view and the issue must be decided arbitrarily.

Feeding Patients

Offering coffee, tea, cold drinks, or water to patients at the beginning of a session is customary for many psychotherapists. Some objection to this practice is found among more traditional psychotherapists. Offering ingestibles is considered by some to be an unnecessary encouragement of dependence and transference. Offering oral rewards to adolescents in psychotherapy helps relieve their inordinate fear of loss of dependence which tends to occur in a successful psychotherapeutic process. This is a condition of the psychotherapeutic milieu to be decided by the psychotherapist.

Initiation

There is no one way for the psychotherapist to begin a session. Some therapists routinely begin with such phrases as "How has your week been?" or "How goes the battle?" Some therapists ask directly, "Where would you like to begin today?" Many patients begin their sessions spontaneously and no initiation by the therapist is necessary. At times patients may be unresponsive at the beginning of the session. When the patient maintains a long silence at the beginning of a session, the psychotherapist may say, "Sometimes it's difficult to get started" or "You seem pensive today." If the patient does not respond, something important may be introduced by silence. This situation will be examined in some detail in Chapter 8.

Proceeding Through the Session

It is the psychotherapist's responsibility to ensure that each session offers the patient as great an opportunity as possible to identify, place in perspective, experience, and resolve conflicts which increase distress and/or decrease quality of life. This cannot be done *to* a patient, but must be done *with* that patient's expressions.

Most experienced psychotherapists recognize the patient who hopes or expects to improve in psychotherapy by *absorption*—assimilating wisdom or relief by listening. This is unlikely to happen. The raw material of psychotherapy lies in the patient's revelations, recollections, responses, explorations, and experiencing. The psychotherapist who panders to this "listening" need on the part of the patient has become a counselor—advising and directing. Little or no psychotherapy is likely to take place when the therapist's responses are more frequent than those of the patient. The psychotherapist must do everything possible to create a setting where the patient may explore and the psychotherapist can act as a *catalyst,* ensuring that the exploration is rewardingly experiential and likely to lead to further exploration.

In an effort to measure the impact of psychotherapy sessions, Stiles (1980) studied the responses of both patients and therapists. He found that two factors were associated with psychotherapeutic progress and benefit. The first was called *smoothness/ease.* This represented feelings of ease and pleasantness during the session as opposed to perceptions of unpleasantness and danger. The second factor was labeled *depth/value,* representing feelings by the patient that ideas brought out or experienced were good, valuable, deep, and rich as opposed to bad, worthless, shallow, or empty.

The sequence and style of a psychotherapist's responses, clarifications, questions, interpretations, etc., determine to a large extent the quality and thus the likely success of the psychotherapeutic venture. These matters will be considered in detail.

THE PSYCHOTHERAPIST'S FIRST TASK—MAINTENANCE

The psychotherapist's primary task is to maintain the therapeutic setting as a sanctuary. All that was promised to the patient during the initial structuring session must be constantly and consistently provided: tolerance, acceptance, awareness, sensitivity, and skill. The therapist must not conduct sessions when ill, overburdened, distracted, or annoyed. Unless the appropriate quality and ambience of psychotherapy are maintained, all that is likely to occur is a facade of psychotherapy, leading nowhere.

This cannot happen for all psychotherapists at all times. Part of the psychotherapist's value is in his or her humanness, which means there will be bad days, poorly conducted sessions, and therapeutic errors. The ideal, however, must be recognized, known, and constantly sought by the competent psychotherapist.

THE PSYCHOTHERAPIST'S SECOND TASK—SENSITIVE AWARENESS

Once the proper setting is established, the psychotherapist must be prepared to constantly monitor the expressions of the patient. These expressions may be verbal or nonverbal. The way a patient communicates in psychotherapy tends to replicate the patient's usual and customary presentation of self in everyday life. Long periods of silence, as noted previously, may be a powerful message from a patient. What the patient says, does, or implies is of importance in every psychotherapeutic session. The psychotherapist must be guided, even directed, by the patient's communications.

Patient responses during the psychotherapy session fall into three broad categories: *Intellectual Exploration, Experiencing,* and *Integration.* Each of these will be analyzed in detail, since appropriate therapist activity should follow an evaluation of the quality and depth of the patient communication.

Table 2 presents these broad categories and a representative group of patient responses within each category. The importance of these patient responses in moving the psychotherapeutic process forward is in ascending order, with Intellectual Exploration being the least helpful patient activity. Experiencing and finally Integration are ordinarily the most therapeutically productive patient responses.

PATIENT RESPONSES—INTELLECTUAL EXPLORATION

Except for deeply disturbed patients, hysterics and character disorders, intellectual exploration is likely to be the communication style of choice by most patients during the early and middle phases of psychotherapy. Intellectual focus represents an outcome of society's expectation for adults. It is usually the acceptable, controlled, safe, approved way of looking at or experiencing life.

Intellectual exploration reveals the patient's outward self. This is the person, the values, the capacity that the patient is willing or able to reveal with relatively little anxiety. This is the "outside" story. It may include confidential material, embarrassing thoughts, frightening experiences, or intellectual expression of emotional burdens. Deeply uncomfortable topics are usually avoided or disguised.

Intellectual exploration may be fraught with petty details, evaluative commentary on the therapeutic process, history-giving, or self-justification. The focus of attention may be on others in the patient's life. The patient at times may deliver a philosophical dissertation on some topic more or less connected with the patient's life. When patients explore intellectually, the psychotherapist should be cautious and conservative. Challenges, interpretations, and detailed analyses of symbolic meanings should ordinarily be avoided. Rejection of the psychotherapist's response is a signal that the therapist has gone too far. Some examples may be helpful to illustrate this category of patient response:

Patient: It's very difficult for me to leave the house, even to go shopping . . . I plan my day and when it comes time to go out, I find

TABLE 2
Categorization of Patient Responses During Psychotherapy Sessions: Ascending Order of Value for Therapeutic Progress

Intellectual Exploration

Avoiding uncomfortable topics	Obsessional focus
Discussion of therapy issues with friends and family	Petty details
Dissertations	Phone calls to the therapist
Evaluative commentary	Projection, and other-blaming
Expecting counseling and direction	Rationalization
Focus on others	Silence
History details	Statements and descriptions of problems
Justification and displacement	Psychobabble Questions Reading psychology texts Withholding and censoring strong feelings

Experiencing

Discussing and analyzing dreams	Negative attitudes toward the therapist (transference)
Emotional reactions	Positive attitudes toward the therapist (transference)
Fantasies	Parapraxes
Flight into health	Recapitulation identified (family patterns being repeated by the patient)
Discussion of risky, embarrassing, or frightening subjects	Silence
Free association	Nonverbal experiencing
Insight	

Integration

Confrontations	Reality testing
Future talking	Recapitulation patterns predicted
Leaving therapy	Recapitulation patterns prevented
Independent decisions and action	Unfinished business
Acting in own best interests	

all sorts of reasons to avoid going. I telephone . . . I clean . . . I watch TV and pretty soon I find it's time to start supper.

Therapist: So one way or another you avoid going out.

Patient: Yes. I've done this for years. When absolutely necessary, I will go shopping with my husband or my mother, but recently I've been avoiding even that. That's why they decided I should see you.

Therapist: So it wasn't really your idea to consult me.

Patient: No . . . but I realize something ought to be done. I mean . . . I realize it's not normal to be afraid of going out of your own house . . . but I am —so there you are.

Therapist: What would you like to happen?

Patient: I suppose I'd like to be rid of this thing and to be able to go out whenever I want—alone, even.

Therapist: You say "suppose." Are you sometimes unsure?

Patient: What do you mean?

Therapist: Often when people say, "I suppose," they really haven't made up their mind . . .

Patient No . . . that's just a figure of speech.

This excerpt, from the first psychotherapeutic session of a 32-year-old housewife referred by her mother, her husband and her gynecologist, illustrates *intellectual exploration* and rejection of the psychotherapist's too early efforts to explore dynamics. Some of the more common intellectual presentations by patients found in psychotherapy follow:

Statement of the Problem

This form of intellectual exploration is common early in psychotherapy, but may appear at any time. It often represents patients' efforts to master or intellectually control their involvement in psychotherapy and to avoid the revelation of deeper, more disturbing ideas. The following is from the seventh session with a 50-year-old executive who was deserted by her husband of 25 years and whose subsequent suicidal venture resulted in her referral for psychotherapy:

Patient: Everything was going so well. We enjoyed the same things—oh—we had our little problems but who doesn't. It upset everything when he left. I must have been hard to live with as he said. If he would come back, I'd feel better immediately.

Therapist: So his leaving has upset you considerably.

Patient: Well, it's upset everything—our home, our children, our

finances. He even wants to file separate tax returns. That's foolish—
the accountant says that will cost us a bundle.
Therapist: You're worried about your finances?
Patient: Not really. We've planned carefully but it's just set things out of
line and made a lot of trouble.

Intellectual responses are ways of revealing and concealing at the
same time. Efforts by the psychotherapist to probe more deeply or to explore motivation are usually too threatening to be accepted.

Rational Explanations

Although most commonly found in the earlier sessions of psychotherapy, rational explanations as an intellectual exploration may
occur anywhere in psychotherapy as it can in everyday life. This effort to
explain one's behavior in a reasonable manner, avoiding deeper searching
and more threatening possibilities, can represent the patient's efforts to
justify self and relieve underlying guilt. The following example is taken
from the 20th session of a 31-year-old securities salesman discussing his
relations with his current girlfriend:

Patient: I'm just going to have to see less of Jane. I can see that she is
starting to get too serious. She is beginning to ask too many questions. Pretty soon I'll have no privacy at all. I have no intention of
marrying her and I don't want to mislead her.
Therapist: She might get the wrong idea about your interest.
Patient: Yeah . . . I mean she's a nice girl and all but I'm in no position
to offer her what she probably wants and it would be unfair to let this
go further. It's time to cool the relationship. I don't want to hurt her
or disappoint her.

Although the real issue is the patient's intense fear of close relationships, he is not ready to face this. In his psychotherapy as in everyday
life, there is an avoidance of self-focusing by attending to the "needs" or
values of others in a perfectly rational matter. The response of the patient
makes sense, but represents an avoidance of inner conflicts.

Questions

When the patient seeks counseling or asks questions in the psychotherapeutic setting, the purpose is to keep the patient's involvement

at a minimal emotional level and avoid inner exploration. This method of intellectual exploration can also express dependence. The following excerpt from the second session of a 45-year-old female obstetrician illustrates this level of response:

Therapist: Then you're not always happy in your work.
Patient: It's not that. It's simply a matter of logistics. There are only so many hours in a day. How many hours a day do you see patients?
Therapist: Well, that varies . . .
Patient: Even so, don't you find there are so many things to do for the time available?

The effort to seek and avoid help at the same time may take the form of telephone calls to ask questions which the patient believes to be too important to await the regularly scheduled psychotherapy session. The following call was made by the same patient as above:

Patient: Doctor?
Therapist: Yes . . .
Patient: I had to call you. I'm feeling terrible about fighting with my husband.
Therapist: I understand . . . and we will explore that . . .
Patient: You don't understand—I just am so depressed—I'm not sure I can work. Is there anything I should do now?
Therapist: This is a difficult time for you and we'll talk about this . . .
Patient: Are you sure this is going to work out? Should I apologize to him?
Therapist: Well . . . we will certainly . . .
Patient: (*interrupting*) I really hate to call you this way but I'm so unsure that anything good is going to come of this. Do you have any suggestions as to what I should do?
Therapist: We have an appointment tomorrow and we'll go into this at that time.

During the next session it was revealed that the patient had a circle of friends she called whenever things weren't proceeding well. Her therapist had simply been added to the list. It is unlikely that psychotherapy can move forward via telephone consultation. There are emergencies which may require special decisions in respect to patients' needs and behavior (see Chapter 9), but telephone consultations generally do not serve any productive psychotherapeutic purpose.

Obsessional Focus

In the therapy session, as in everyday life, obsessional fears and attention to trivial detail use energy, decrease tension, and ensure limited emotional exploration or focus on the inner self. They represent, as do other intellectual explorations, a heartfelt but over-controlled effort to find or explain sources of distress. The following is from the 65th session of a 32-year-old management supervisor and shows clearly that intellectual exploration can appear later as well as earlier in the psychotherapeutic process:

Patient: I've been thinking about my mother again. You remember I've told you before that she was always too busy with my stepfather to really take care of us.
Therapist: Yes, I remember.
Patient: He demanded too much of her—all the time. She didn't even worry about whether we were dressed right or whether we had enough lunch money. I guess I told you how I was embarrassed by having to wear my brother's clothes.
Therapist: Yes . . . you . . .
Patient: (*interrupting*) These pants had a hole in the back. I asked her to fix it. She put a patch on that was of a different color. I was pretty embarrassed.
Therapist: Yes . . . you told me that. How do you feel about that now?
Patient: She could have found a piece of material that matched the pants. It was like she didn't care.
Therapist: It was disturbing.
Patient: It's not *that* hard to match a piece of material for a kid's jeans. They even make these patches that you can iron on.

Nothing the therapist can say seems to deter the patient from a repetitious cataloging of complaints with little or no focus on his feelings regarding the mother's behavior.

Projections

Most patients at one time or another will focus their attention on the behavior or motives of others. This intellectual exercise again helps to avoid self-exploration. The following example is taken from the 85th ses-

sion of a deeply depressed 57-year-old executive who had stopped going to
work a year previously and had become completely dependent on his wife.
He is discussing his 24-year-old son:

Patient: I absolutely cannot tolerate John. He is a complete idiot!
Therapist: You're pretty annoyed.
Patient: He absolutely refuses to get out of the house! He gets up late,
    fiddles around, cadges money from his mother, and then spends the
    day at the beach!
Therapist: You resent that.
Patient: It's not normal. He's a complete sponge—sleeping until
    noon—hmpf!
Therapist: Do you see some of your own situation there?
Patient: Me? I get up at 5 or 5:30 every morning. I *can't* sleep late.

Silence

Some patients express their difficulty in experiencing emotion or committing themselves to the psychotherapy with silence. The silent patient
may be fearful, angry, suspicious, confused, or manipulative. Most inexperienced therapists are uncomfortable when the patient is silent. With
experience, psychotherapists generally learn that patient silence is a
means of slowing psychotherapeutic progress. It is a way of avoiding or
postponing *experiencing,* which the patient fears.

Some patients who seek to improve their lives in psychotherapy hope
that this can be done through absorption. They suggest that simply being
in the setting, listening to the therapist, or in group situations listening to
others will lead to insight and/or conflict resolution. This is a sophisticated and fairly manipulative form of silence. It is sometimes quite bla-
tant ("I'm paying the money—you should do the advising") and sometimes it is presented with an aura of charm ("I really get a lot out of it
when you talk about the mechanisms and how things work").

There are many styles and forms of intellectual exploration. They represent a fairly neutral approach to psychotherapy. This form of patient response may appear whenever the patient is threatened about searching
deeper. Although a common and probably necessary mode of patient response, intellectual exploration can become a barrier to psychotherapeutic progress. This will be further explored in Chapter 8.

PATIENT RESPONSES—EXPERIENCING

The real work of psychotherapy takes place when the patient is sufficiently comfortable to explore and experience feelings. The psychotherapist can expect strong affective responses at any time during psychotherapy. Sometimes these occur early in the process and frighten the patient into a retreat to intellectual exploration. In some instances, strong early experiencing can stir the patient to leave psychotherapy.

Only by venturing into the experiencing mode can patients discover their own repeated patterns of arranging neurotic behaviors which are punishing, failure-seeking, and unenhancing. Explaining why a patient behaves neurotically is unlikely to lead to anything but increased resistance and intellectual exploration. This is why the reading of self-help books produces little or no change in neurotic patterns of living.

The patient begins to venture toward experiencing in psychotherapy from the beginning. The tension reported by most patients when they begin psychotherapy often represents fear of exploration and revelation. Although patients speak of a wish to change, there is an underlying, often unconcious *need* to maintain the neurotic balance. The patient wishes to learn and move ahead, but fears change.

Many experiential responses by patients are accompanied by emotion. These emotional responses are sometimes very strong. Inexperienced psychotherapists are sometimes distressed by such patient experiencing. Rarely, if ever, is this concern justified except in the unusual situations which will be considered in Chapter 9. Spontaneous emotional experiences during the psychotherapeutic session are extremely important in the process of forwarding the therapeutic process. The major forms of the experiencing response will be considered in some detail.

Free Association

When the patient talks openly and without interrupting the flow of spontaneous thoughts during psychotherapy, experiencing is very likely to occur. Most psychotherapists suggest during the initial session that the patient speak as freely as possible. This kind of structuring may sometimes be helpful in encouraging free association during later sessions. The following illustrates free association by a 42-year-old high school teacher which took place during his third session of psychotherapy:

Patient: I don't seem to have to have much to say today... (*long pause*).

Therapist: Sometimes it's hard to get started.

Patient: Yeah... I have all kinds of thoughts, but nothing very—you know—pertinent.

Therapist: When you talk about everything that crosses your mind, you can sometimes come across important ideas and feelings.

Patient: You mean just *everything*?

Therapist: Yes... that's often helpful.

Patient: Well... I guess I can try... Gee! That's hard.

Therapist: Yes... it takes a while to get the hang of it.

Patient: I'm thinking of my trip to San Francisco last summer... I was excited... Also I guess scared. I'd never been there. I wasn't sure I wanted to go. I heard all about it but it was scary. I wasn't sure about what to wear. All the others in our group who were going to the meeting seemed so... so *sure* of what they would do and where they would go. I had all these fears about how to do things. I was raised in a pretty sheltered home. My father was a small town minister, you know. I wasn't allowed to... well... I wasn't allowed to do and learn much of anything. I think that I never married because of that. I broke away, got a football scholarship for college... but I never *fit*. I just didn't know what to say or what to wear or anything. I still feel that way sometimes.

In this session, the therapist responded to the patient's hesitancy by first encouraging, then structuring for free association. Although the patient's associations are anecdotal and narrative, some emotional content begins to emerge. This movement from intellectual exploration to experiencing is an essential step for therapeutic progress.

As the patient gains experience and comfort in psychotherapy, free association is more likely to become a stream of consciousness with ideas and feelings emerging rapidly. Sometimes the free association lacks contextual structure. Exploration and emotional experiencing are primary, as in the following excerpt from the 34th session of the school teacher:

Patient: What to do oh what to do? I don't want to stay where I am now—there's no real future for me. There never was—it's like it's been all my life—I get into something, realize it's not for me but I'm stuck—or I *make* myself stick—playing the piano, the college I went to, my marriage, my job—it's all the same pattern—Stick to it whether you like it or not. As a kid my friends thought I was a "simp." I was, I am! I'm sick of it... but I'm scared to change...

My father was like that. He could never make a decision . . . I had an uncle who kidded the old man "You couldn't find your ass with both hands behind you"—and I'm following in my father's footsteps . . . I really admired Uncle George. He said what he wanted to say and did what he wanted. I wish I could . . . .

The flow of ideas is much freer than in session three. The patient *experiences* what he is talking about and remembering. There is *congruence* between the inner thoughts and feelings and the free external communication. Therapy is moving forward.

Catharsis

When the patient experiences emotion which expresses inner stress, a lessening of anxiety and a sense of positiveness usually follow. Although the free expression of emotion may occur at any phase of psychotherapy, a sudden release of long-withheld feeling can take place early in the psychotherapeutic course. As the patient becomes aware of the safe aspect of the psychotherapeutic setting, the burden of "holding in" is sometimes suddenly released. The following occurred during the fourth session of psychotherapy. The patient, a 32-year-old advertising executive, started therapy in order to deal with depressive symptoms:

Patient: All my life I've believed that if you work hard and do the right things, you'll succeed and be happy. Now I'm not at all sure it works that way.

Therapist: It's discouraging to find one's style or principles not working.

Patient: Yes . . . I've invested so much in . . . in . . . (*weeps silently*) I'm sorry . . . I'm sorry.

Therapist: It's important for your therapy to feel free enough to feel.

Patient: Oh . . . (*weeps*) I've never been . . . I just can't hold it any more . . . I feel so *awful* . . . (*continues weeping*) . . . I've never done this . . . in front of anyone. I feel *so* bad.

Therapist: It's all right to feel bad openly here.

Patient: I know . . . I mean . . . I didn't . . . I was afraid this might happen. I've heard that people break down in therapy. I never have . . . I mean . . . I always felt I (*sob*) shouldn't . . . (*weeps quietly*) . . . .

Therapist: You've held in a long time.

Patient: Oh yes! (*sobs loudly*) For *so* long.

It is clear that the patient is draining out a lot of emotion—with no particular focus or direction.

Later in psychotherapy, catharsis is likely to be connected with fairly specific areas of conflict or even conflict resolution as the neurotic patterns the patient has been sustaining or creating are discovered. The following strong emotional experiencing or catharsis occurred with the account executive during her 42nd session:

Therapist: What would you like to talk about today?
Patient: Well . . . I don't know . . . I've been thinking about my sister. I talked to her last week. She never comes to visit me. I've always wanted to be close . . . I asked her to come down for the Labor Day weekend. She said she'd like to but will be too busy . . . I usually say, "That's OK," but this time I got mad. I told her that I'm the only sister she'll ever have and it's time to stop acting like I'm imposing on her when I want to see her. I actually got mad! She tried to joke and turn it back but I said, "Goddamn it—one day you'll wake up and you'll be old or sick or scared or alone and you'll wonder why you didn't love me and realize I love you. We're *sisters* not just a couple of ex-college roommates! That means something!" Damn it. (*crying loudly*) I didn't realize I felt so strongly . . . I guess I've felt that way for a long time but never realized it . . . She was shocked . . . *I* was shocked . . . I don't know, but . . . it had to be said and I feel better now that it's in the open. *She* has to face this now—I have! From now on we'll be open—or we can't communicate. This will be good for both of us, I think . . . .

One can see elements of catharsis as well as other experiencing phenomena in this response.

Recapitulation

Neurotic patterns or their underpinnings usually form relatively early in the child's developmental cycle. As these patterns stabilize in early and middle maturity, parental behavior models, environmental expectancies, and early response patterns occur and reoccur. The neurotic personality becomes a victim of long-established arrangements. Rarely does that patient understand, acknowledge, or experience his or her active involvement in arranging the old patterns to reappear with new people and new circumstances. *Recapitulation*—reexperiencing old patterns of unhelpful behavior—keeps the neurosis alive.

The psychotherapist must be continually aware of, and sensitive to the patient's propensity to recapitulate earlier patterns. Whenever patients report a situation in which they work against their own best interests and are puzzled as to why they did this to themselves, it is important for the psychotherapist to speculate, "Who in the patient's life might have done this to the patient or to themselves?" or "Who might have expected the patient to act in this manner?" Frequently, as the psychotherapy proceeds, the therapist will find that the patient's repetitive behavior is an imitation of an important figure in the early life of the patient. The following exchange occurred during the 20th session with a 27-year-old guidance counselor:

Patient: I simply can't make an application for a new job. Every time I try I get flustered and I simply can't proceed. I can't . . . It's as though I don't expect myself to be worthy or competent.

Therapist: This sounds like what you described as your father's attitude about your entire academic and professional life.

Patient: That's right. He always said, "I don't understand how any of you people can make a living with what you do."

Therapist: Does this mean that you're carrying through the identification with your father, and simply criticizing or shaking your finger at yourself?

Patient: I don't know—it seems like it. It's funny, though, several weeks ago I found myself having a tantrum in almost exactly the same way that my mother did at one time. And that surprised me. I have never acted like that before. My way is to hold in . . . (*long pause*) That's really funny! The evening after I had that tantrum, I was able to sit down and make out an application for a job I was thinking of getting.

Transference

The transference phenomenon was originally described by the psychoanalysts (Freud, 1912). Considered an essential element in the psychotherapeutic process, it represents the patient's unconscious identification of the therapist and the therapeutic process with pleasant and unpleasant aspects of the patient's family and early development. The patient *transfers* early feelings, experiences and conflicts to the psychotherapist, the therapy setting, and the therapy process.

Transference is a recapitulation phenomenon which occurs within the structure of the psychotherapeutic setting.

Positive transference may represent the affections, warmth and sensuality that the patient had or missed having during the developmental years. *Negative transference* can represent the fears, doubts, and rages suppressed or repressed during the growing years. When the patient expresses strong, spontaneous affect toward the psychotherapist, it may be the first conscious experiencing of previously repressed earlier feelings. In other instances, the patient may be presenting, in therapy, an example of transferences which characterize his or her own life-style. This is the case in the following segment of the 52nd session of psychotherapy with a 29-year-old securities salesman:

Patient: Life is *really* much better. I can *see* what I've been doing to myself. I like myself more . . . and I owe it all to you. You've given me something I've never had before. . . . I think about that a lot. I think about you a lot. When I face a decision that's tough, I imagine how you would go about handling it.

The patient all but aggrandizes the psychotherapist. He imparts to his therapist complete wisdom and perfect modelship—as a child might to a trusted and idolized parent.

In contrast, the 58th session with the same patient included the following:

Therapist: You seem troubled.
Patient: Well . . . I'm disappointed . . . in you . . . I used to think you were pretty helpful . . . and caring. Now I realize that you really don't give a damn! It's just one patient after another for you . . . My being so anxious and miserable doesn't mean a thing to you . . . you don't *really* help . . . I could be talking to a computer!

Later in the psychotherapeutic process, the patient related both these positive and negative transference feelings to incidents with his parents during his developmental years. This will be presented in the section of this chapter devoted to patients' *integration* responses.

Resistance

Silence, obsessional questioning or focus, criticism, and other negative responses to psychotherapy may be either intellectual or experiencing ventures. Resistance represents an effort on the part of the patient to stall or prevent progress in psychotherapy which might lead to frightening discoveries or affect. When resistance occurs in an emotional context, the response usually represents the anxiety of being close to the painful issue or a recapitulation of an early developmental experience.

The following excerpt is from the 25th session of a second effort at psychotherapy by a 28-year-old female graduate student. She had started psychotherapy at age 23 but stopped after 10 sessions because she "felt much better." During her initial psychotherapeutic effort, she had frequent silences with no visible emotion.

She returned to continue psychotherapy after five years. She had recently married and found her happiness marred by uncomfortable obsessions and morbid thoughts. Emotional resistance occurred as follows:

Patient: ... (*long period of silence*) ... (*sigh*) ...
Therapist: You seem troubled.
Patient: (*no response*) ... (*long period of silence*) ... (*patient begins to weep silently ... weeping becomes open sobbing*) ... I guess I'm pretty angry. You don't help very much.

Although the silence was similar to earlier silences, in the current instance the resistance was accompanied by spontaneous, deep emotion. The appropriate responses to resistance will be considered in Chapter 7.

A special form of resistance to continuing in the psychotherapeutic process has been called the *flight into health*. In this situation, the patient denies fear of progress and revelation by insisting the psychotherapy has been successfully concluded. Ordinarily a phenomenon of earlier sessions in psychotherapy, like other patient responses it represents some aspect of the patient's neurotic life-style—in this case, unrealistic optimism. The following took place during the sixth session of psychotherapy with a 26-year-old medical technician:

Therapist: You seem very animated and pleased today.
Patient: Oh, yes! I feel marvelous! I can't understand it but somehow I'm cured! I'm sleeping well ... I'm OK at work and I see everything as bright. I think that I'm over the hump and everything will be right ....
Therapist: Uh hu ... well ....
Patient: (*interruption*) And it's you and this treatment I have to thank for this. I could never have done this without you.
Therapist: Well ...
Patient: (*again interrupting*) I just feel like calling all my friends and telling them they should see you ... I feel better than I have in years. It seems like a miracle.
Therapist: Yes, so it seems.

Clearly the patient was *experiencing* a *flight into health*. All problems were solved. The psychotherapist had worked a miracle. Most importantly, the patient was relieved of the burden of returning to therapy and searching through painful experiences and emotions. The resistance expressed in the *flight into health* served as a barrier, a protection against further exploration.

Unconscious or conscious efforts to delay or halt psychotherapy, such as being regularly late for sessions, cancelling appointments, shifting appointments, forgetting sessions, not paying for sessions, etc., may or may not include *experiencing*. Efforts to explore these behaviors may produce intellectual efforts or can result in fruitful experiencing.

Although patients express the need to resolve conflicts quickly, rapid conflict resolution is very frightening to most people who seek psychotherapy. It is as though their defenses are islands of safety and removal of these will result in drowning. The psychotherapist may find that following a very intense and emotional session of discovery, appointments are cancelled. Some tenacious obsessional patients do not cancel, but simply do not respond during the next session, resulting in an "emotionally cancelled" session.

As many as 30 percent of psychotherapy patients terminate early. Early or premature termination may represent a resistance to proceeding with psychotherapy. Those entering psychotherapy for the first time, those patients with serious thought disturbances, and those with very painful and compelling problems are more likely to terminate prematurely (Hoffman, 1985). A detailed exploration of this phenomenon will be presented in Chapters 8 and 10.

Fantasies

Fantasy represents a uniquely human capacity to utilize experience in creative, personalistic ways. The ability to create whimsical, capricious, quaint, bizarre, frightening, quixotic, grandiose, or resolution ideas and daydreams is probably essential if a person is to be a complete human. Fantasies are very useful in the psychotherapeutic process. They represent an expression of the extremes of our fears, our hopes, our abilities.

It is almost impossible for patients to fully discuss their fantasies in psychotherapy without *experiencing*. The essence of fantasy is the involvement of self.

Freud suggested that unsatisfied, neurotic people fantasized. He specifically related active fantasy to frustrated sexual drive (Freud, 1906). Later research failed to confirm his observations, suggesting that fantasy, particularly sexual fantasy, is consistently experienced by active, adjusted, intelligent persons (Epstein & Smith, 1957; Hariton &

Singer, 1974; Brown & Hart, 1977; Moreault & Follingstad, 1978). Although most studies have emphasized sexual fantasies (Arndt, Foehl & Good, 1985), the research suggests that fantasies in general are important experiences for well-functioning persons.

The introduction of fantasies into the psychotherapeutic setting can reflect patients' comfort in the setting as well as the psychotherapist's ability and interest in dealing with these rich expressions of the patient's unique self. Psychotherapists vary considerably in the degree of interest and tolerance they are able to devote to patients' fantasies.

Since active fantasy involves a great deal of experiencing, patients frightened of revelation will tend to avoid discussing their fantasies or will discuss fantasies in very general terms. An example of this occurred in the initial psychotherapeutic effort of the female graduate student cited in the section on *resistance*. During her fifth session, the following occurred:

Therapist: During the periods of silence while you are here, do you have fantasies or daydreams?

Patient: What do you mean?

Therapist: Most people have an active "inner life"—like thoughts or daydreams about themselves. Situations—sometimes pleasant—sometimes fearful.

Patient: Just some thoughts maybe, nothing important.

Therapist: Such as?

Patient: I don't know—like making a marvelous discovery here and getting all better. (*laughs*)

Therapist: What is it like to you?

Patient: I just told you . . . (*long pause*).

Although admitting to the experience of fantasy, the patient is too defensive to be explicit or free about her fantasies.

During her second effort at psychotherapy, fantasy became an important explorative tool. As the patient became more secure in the psychotherapeutic setting and less afraid of exploration and revelation, she was able to respond as follows during the 40th session (after one of her long silences):

Patient: You once asked about my daydreams . . . when I was so quiet during my first therapy . . . I didn't want to tell you. I'm not sure I want to now . . . but I notice that when I'm scared or angry, I stop talking in here . . . I often get a picture of taking off my clothes and getting into a warm bubble bath. I think about drifting off—warm and secure. I block out everything and drift off. Sometimes I

think about producing something *great*—like a book or a sculpture
... or better yet a great idea which influences everyone.
Therapist: You feel good when this happens?
Patient: Yeah ... but I wouldn't tell you before. I was afraid ... I
  don't know ... maybe of being silly ... or not facing reality ...
  Oh! ... (*long pause*) ... When I was a kid, I used to lock myself in
  the bathroom if my mother or father was mad or critical. I'd make
  believe I was only visiting and that soon I'd go back ... to a different
  set of parents maybe ... (*laughs*) It's about the same. I guess I felt
  as bad about talking then as I do now. (*smiles*)
Therapist: Perhaps it's a bit easier now.
Patient: (*laughs*) Perhaps.

The patient is able to experience some emotion as she discovers a
relationship between her current methods of coping and her efforts to deal
with stress in the childhood years. In reaching the point where she can describe and experience fantasy, she has moved ahead in the psychotherapeutic process.

Dreams

The nature and meaning of dreams have long interested scholars,
scientists, artists, and religionists. The scientific investigation of dreams
began in the mid-19th century, focusing on the external and internal
stimuli which could account for dream content. The French philosopher,
Henri Bergson, in 1901, predicted that the exploration of "the most secret
depths of the unconscious ... will be the principal task of psychology in
the century which is opening" (Hall, 1984).

Bergson's prophecy was validated by the growth and influence of the
psychoanalytic movement. A significant element of the psychoanalytic
psychotherapies is the analysis of dreams to uncover the origin and purpose of neurotic symptoms.

Research from mid-twentieth century to the present has suggested
that dreaming occurs four or five times per night. Dreaming is associated
with deeper levels of sleep during the rapid eye-movement phase (REM).
Later explorations showed that all phases of sleep produce dreams
(Aserinski & Kleitman, 1953; Dement & Kleitman, 1957).

It is believed by many psychotherapists and dream researchers that
dreams contain a *manifest*, or obvious content which symbolizes or dis-
guises *latent* content—the description or expression of repressed, hidden
feelings (Hall & Van de Castle, 1966).

When the patient describes a dream, little or no emotion may be experienced. If the description of a dream is followed by very little free

association, it likely represents an intellectual exploration. The following dream was reported at the beginning of his 30th session by a 58-year-old business executive who entered psychotherapy because he had become paralyzed by depression and was unable to work. He also suffered a superabundance of functional aches and pains.

Patient: Well, I finally remembered a dream. I honestly believed I didn't dream. I don't remember all of it . . . I was there and . . . well, this person I worked for before I came down here. He was just like my last boss—started fine and ended up to be a sneaky, unscrupulous son-of-a-bitch!—was there haranguing me about something that wasn't done. I was telling him I couldn't do it—my leg was broken and that was that . . . .

Therapist: That is all you remember?

Patient: Yeah . . . There was some other vague stuff.

Therapist: As you think of the dream, what feelings do you have?

Patient: Like what?

Therapist: Anything.

Patient: Just like I told you—that's all I remember. (*defensively*)

Somewhat reluctantly the patient admits that he dreams. A figure of conflict appears in the dream. After a very brief flurry of strong negative feeling, the patient retreats from the dream, fearful of going further.

Later in the session, after the patient recited a seemingly endless list of complaints about his aches and pains, the incompetence of his children, and his wife's limited ability, the therapist approached the dream again:

Therapist: In the dream you reported that your leg was hurt.

Patient: What? . . . Yeah, in a hospital . . . but my legs never bother me. It's my back and these bouts of flu and the headaches.

Therapist: Have you any other thoughts as you think of your dream?

Patient: Only what I told you already.

Therapist: Which leg was hurt?

Patient: Which? Oh! The left leg—I don't know why.

Therapist: Have you ever hurt your leg?

Patient: No . . . I don't think so . . . .

Therapist: Do you know of anyone close to you who . . .

Patient: (*interrupting*) Oh! My father got some kind of bone infection from a lawn mower accident. I was only six or seven . . . it got worse and worse. He had a couple of operations. He was laid up for years— in fact, that's when he lost his business. Later he worked for the

> post office, but he wasn't much good . . . I'd forgotten about that for years.
> *Therapist:* Which leg did your father hurt?
> *Patient:* The left leg. Why?
> *Therapist:* In the dream your left leg was hurt . . . and you couldn't do what your terrible boss wanted you to do.
> *Patient:* Yeah . . . that's an interesting coincidence.

The patient reluctantly examines the manifest content of the dream but is unable to associate freely to the content. The psychotherapist earnestly pursues a content analysis, trying to help the patient to gain some experiential benefit from the first dream reported in 30 sessions. In spite of the patient's reluctance, the therapist plows ahead, "forcing" an association from the patient. No real experiencing takes place. Rather than producing progress, the therapist has pressured the patient and perhaps has threatened the sanctuary aspect of the psychotherapeutic setting.

Most experienced psychotherapists who use dream interpretation as part of the therapeutic method agree that the patient must lead in the association to manifest content. Some suggest that the first dream never be interpreted in order to avoid threatening the security of the patient in the therapeutic setting. Some procedures for dream interpretation will be presented in Chapter 7.

Parapraxes

"Slips of the tongue," or "Freudian Slips," are forms of *parapraxes* or speech intentions which are not carried out or are distorted in some way. Such expressions can be useful during psychotherapy. Slips and distortions may reveal an unconscious need or wish which represents an area of conflict. Examination of the meaning of such slips can be a helpful exercise in discovery and experiencing in the psychotherapeutic setting.

Not all psychotherapists accept the identification and examination of parapraxes as an important part of the therapy process. While Freudian and other dynamic psychotherapists believe that most parapraxes express conflicts, hidden wishes, or ulterior motives, others believe that such common behavior as slips of the tongue is devoid of hidden meaning.

Psycholinguistic research has explored the occurrence of parapraxes. Results suggest that errors in language are not random. Some errors seem to originate from transposition of discrete elements of sound (phonemes). Thus, a person may say, "I have a *thor* thumb" instead of "I have a *sore* thumb." Other slips involve meaning as well as sound: "I think we had an *interior* motive," the slip substituting *interior* for the intended *ulterior*. Some errors are sequential disordering such as *"burly erd"* for *"early bird."* Linguistic explanations focus on the nature of memory elements and predictable, orderly substitutions and distortions (Fromkin, 1973). No research has identified a predictable formula for parapraxes. Many experienced psychotherapists, however, believe that parapraxes can be used as a helpful part of the experiencing process.

The propensity to "slip" varies widely among people. People with obsessive personalities have been found to exhibit parapraxes only rarely. People who are prone to frequent slips of the tongue are found to be equally prone to substituting and forgetting names.

Sufficient interest and support for the psychoanalytic view on parapraxes exists to justify exploring the identification and analysis of these occurrences in psychotherapy.

A 29-year-old male patient, a college graduate student, during his 45th session of individual psychotherapy was talking about his extremely positive feelings toward the therapist, and at the same time about his deep anxieties that something might happen to the therapist. He described a fantasy of the therapist dying of a heart attack and the patient attending the funeral and bringing flowers. During the course of the discussion, the therapist indicated that sometimes transference which seems extremely or unusually positive can be a denial or a reaction formation to some strong negative feelings. The patient became very agitated, sat upright, and said, "for the like of me I don't see what's bad about you." When asked if he could see the difference between what he said and what he intended to say, he began to smile and said, "I said 'like' instead of 'life'." After several moments of silence, the patient (who had analyzed other parapraxes in previous sessions) said, "I guess it's not so much that I like you, as it is terribly important to feel that you like me."

Parapraxes should be treated as another opportunity for patients to experience deeper elements of their personalities by exploring more than the manifest meaning of what they say or do, as is the case with dreams and fantasies.

Insight

The highest or most complex, or perhaps the most important, experiential phenomenon in psychotherapy occurs when the patient achieves insight. Long before psychotherapy became a formalized treatment process, the concept of insight was regarded as a crucial aspect of self-awareness. The ability to see oneself was viewed as the antithesis of foolishness or madness. In the fifteenth century, an obscure German poet wrote:

> For fools a mirror shall it be
> Where each his counterfeit may see
> His proper value each would know
> The glass of fools the truth may show

Traditional psychoanalytic theory proposes that the analysis approaches conclusion when the patient brings unconscious ideas into conscious awareness. *Insight* is seen as self-visualization (Finkle, 1984). At the beginning of psychotherapy, most patients are to a larger or lesser degree unaware of their private logic and the underlying motives for feelings, thoughts, or actions (Mahl, 1971). Insight is the experiential awareness by the patient of self-defeating behavior, compulsions to recapitulate unhappy early experiences, and unrealistic assumptions (Schulman, 1984).

During his 81st session of psychotherapy, the previously mentioned 29-year-old graduate student experienced insight concerning one aspect of his irrational behavior as follows:

Patient: I do it . . . *I*, nobody else . . . stupid *me!* . . . I can't believe it but it's so . . . wow!

Therapist: How does that work?

Patient: It's so stupid . . . and simple . . . so as soon as someone confronts me and looks me in the eye, I back down. I'm scared . . . angry . . . but most of all I feel *wrong.* I can't look them in the eye. Any dummy can look *me* in the eye and act . . . well . . . tough, or strong, or sure . . . even, maybe, uncaring . . . and I will back down. I don't want to but I *have* to . . . and all because I can *not* stand for anybody to say no, to *think* anything bad about me . . . *I* make this all up. I don't know what they're really thinking. (*weeps softly*) All these years . . . I've given everybody . . . anybody . . . all the power over me they want—probably more than they want. What for? For safety . . . safety first . . . be safe, no matter what . . . even if there's nothing to be safe about . . . I can be afraid of *nothing.* All somebody has to do is act like they are insisting. No, it isn't that they act that way . . . No, I *see* people as acting that way. If they don't, I will arrange it! I'll imagine it . . . (*long pause*) Oh what a fool . . . all these years . . . I'm *not* wrong . . . I've just insisted that I am.

Therapist: So . . . when others have power over you in most cases . . .

Patient: (interrupting excitedly) I've *given* it to them. I've always automatically believed that *ought* to be . . . a foolish imitation of what I believed was "reasonable" or "sensible" . . . or just "safe." Shakespeare was right.

Therapist: How is that?

Patient: "What fools these mortals be." Certainly, what a fool *this* mortal has been! *(laughs)*

The patient's insight into his own behavior is clear, painfully clear, yet at the same time revealing, clarifying, reassuring. There now remains but one step to the consolidation of gains and completion of psychotherapy—integration.

PATIENT RESPONSES—INTEGRATION

Although some psychotherapists perceive the insight phenomenon as the end of formal psychotherapeutic activity, most experienced therapists have found that the patient must experiment with the newfound self-awareness which has arisen from experiencing. Experiments by patients in their real world integrate and reinforce the self-awareness. These experiments by the patient can create anxiety and sometimes lead to *regression*. The patient may be as fearful of success as of failure. Both can exist simultaneously (Gelbort & Winer, 1985) and a regressive withdrawal to earlier neurotic coping styles is not an uncommon event as patients try themselves in the real world. The reality testing begun during *experiencing* continues with increasing frequency and practical application during *integration*.

Some of the integrative steps which suggest that the patient is moving toward success in psychotherapy follow:

Future Talking

During the greater part of the psychotherapeutic process, patients talk about the past and to some extent about the present. Self-initiated discussion of the future is rare. As patients reach the integrative stage of therapy, they are more likely to feel safe than during earlier stages of psychotherapy. At that point patients begin to think about tomorrow. They make efforts to anticipate and exert some control over their own future.

A 36-year-old financial executive of alternate sexual life-style reflected as follows during his 136th session of psychotherapy:

Patient: I don't *really* know how it's going to be but I'm going to
    start looking for a new job. I've been here too long. I know that, but
    now I'm not as frightened of moving on . . . and moving up. I'm too
    good for the kind of stuff I've been doing. I am good and I should ex-
    pect others to know this. In my next job I want to be appreciated, but
    I will have to expect it . . . I'm going to apply for an accounting
    management slot. I've really been doing that level of work for years
    but I've been treated—I've *arranged* to be treated—like a clerk . . .
    No more. Never again.
Therapist: Do you look forward to this?
Patient: Yes . . . and no. It's strange but not really. I know I've been
    scared of success and power. I don't *have* to be any more. The same
    socially . . . I *can* meet people outside of gay bars. I am going to lead
    a more normal, a less frenetic social life. The gay community isn't
    enough. It's like my work, it's limited . . . I can do better . . . .

Recapitulation Predicted

Having identified and experienced the compulsion to repeat earlier
unhappy patterns of behavior, the patient's next step in therapeutic progress is to integrate self-awareness by predicting situations likely to encourage or support recapitulation.

A 32-year-old computer specialist who had been in and out of mental
hospitals for years, as well as having attempted outpatient psychotherapy
with almost a dozen psychotherapists, spoke as follows during his
212th session:

Patient: When I was really crazy, I just didn't know what was
    going on. I was terrified of everything, but now I can see that I would
    find things to scare me . . . and my family was no help. They still
    aren't. My mother, always the martyr, enjoyed the tragedy of a
    nutsy son, so she treated me like a sick child and loved it . . . She
    still does. If I go to visit her on the weekend she'll start with, "Did
    you work too hard this week?" and before I can answer, she'll turn to
    my aunt and say something like, "He works too hard, you know. He
    doesn't know when to stop," talking away like I'm a retard and don't
    know that she's talking about me. I'll be furious, but that scares me,
    so I'll shut up. If I say anything, I'm afraid I'll be playing her game
    and I'll lose . . . and that has made me crazy for years . . . so now I

don't want to go home. I go as seldom as possible. I know the game now.

Clearly this patient has more to learn and more things to try, but he has come a long way from his schizophrenic life-style. He has learned about his own compulsions to enter into a recapitulation of earlier mother-son interaction, to his detriment.

Recapitulation Patterns Prevented

Once the recapitulation pattern is identified, the patient may avoid involvement, as noted above. A more integrative way of dealing with such situations may require the exercise of a certain degree of power and mastery by the patient. This can be frightening and push the patient toward "safer" but less integrative responses. If the patient can become sufficiently self-aware and comfortable, and willing to take the risk of trusting the self, destructive recapitulation can be prevented.

In his 225th session, the same patient described above reported the following incident wherein he prevented recapitulation:

Patient: Well . . . I changed the game. I went home but I didn't let my mother treat me like a cretin. (*laughs*)
Therapist: You're pleased?
Patient: Yeah . . . yeah . . . I guess so . . . (*long pause*) I'm reluctant . . . I want to tell you but I'm afraid you will expect too much . . . no . . . you won't . . .
Therapist: It's scary to have power.
Patient: Yeah . . . yeah but maybe more scary not to . . . Well . . . I got the power. I went home to visit but what I did . . . I invited my mother and my aunt to meet me at a restaurant. I got there early and got a table. When they came, I sort of took charge. I said "hello" and told them I was hungry and hoped they were. We talked about the menu. My mother asked me how work was, and before she could start in, I asked her what she wanted to eat . . . and she got into that instead of doing that "poor sonny" business . . . and we ate and talked about the food . . . Then afterwards I wouldn't let her pay. I paid, then told them I was late for a meeting at the Unity Church where I was going to meet a girl. We were going to plan a program . . . so before anything could happen I was gone! I think that was pretty good.

This patient has surely come a long way.

Confrontation

As patients move into later phases of the psychotherapeutic process, as experiencing becomes more comfortable and more frequent, self-defeating patterns of behavior tend to be identified and avoided in both the therapeutic sessions and in patients' everyday lives. It is rare that psychotherapy can be completed by the patient learning to "avoid trouble"—real or imaginary. Some issues are too compelling to head off or to work around. Some important issues must be *confronted*.

Confrontations are feared and avoided by most patients during the early phases of psychotherapy. The very term *confrontation* is seen by many as a battle with no winners.

The following excerpt is from the 25th session of psychotherapy where the financial executive introduced several pages ago spoke of his difficulty being straightforward with supervisors:

Therapist: You seem to feel unsettled today . . . .

Patient: Yes . . . I'm pretty unhappy . . . (*long pause*) . . . My work isn't going well . . . no . . . not the work but my boss. I told you before . . . he doesn't like me and that makes things hard.

Therapist: The last time we discussed this, you said he was unfair.

Patient: Very unfair would be more accurate. He called me into his office Monday—that's his worst time. He complained that last week's totals were late . . . . They were in his "in box" and he didn't even see them. He just kept complaining to me.

Therapist: What did you say?

Patient: I almost cried . . . it was so unfair. I kept control of myself. I quietly told him the sheets were in his "in box." He was surprised . . . but he didn't even act embarrassed. He said, "Why didn't you tell me in the first place?" . . . I was so mortified I didn't know what to say . . . I just left . . . It's so unfair.

At this point in his psychotherapy, the patient can only describe and to some extent experience his fear and inability to act in his own behalf. Although he knows what is fair and what is right, he is not able to *confront* the issues in his own best interests.

This man completed psychotherapy after 142 sessions. He took an executive position with a company several hundred miles away. About six months after he left psychotherapy, he wrote the following letter to his former therapist:

Dear Dr. Blau:

I left psychotherapy feeling very good and only a little bad. I knew it was time to leave and this job was an important opportunity for me to move forward.

Within a month or two, I began to feel uncomfortable with my boss, the Vice-President for financial affairs. He is a short-tempered former military officer. At first I acted fairly passive in response to his challenges, but a month ago he accused me of delaying some reports. Without realizing what I was doing, I quietly closed the door of his office and walked up to his desk, leaned over, looked him in the eye and told him that the delay was *his* fault for taking three of my staff the previous week and using them for a pet project of his own. I told him I had sent him a memo warning him that he was undercutting our effective functioning and that the delay was his fault.

He was shocked. He admitted he hadn't read my memo. He apologized. I was scared, but I had confronted him (as I've talked about so many times but never did!). I was not sure of how this would work out.

Yesterday I received a call from the Executive Vice-President. I'm being promoted to head a new department—the VP had recommended me as "Competent and straight shooting!"

I can now really see how therapy works.

With sincere thanks,
Jim Brown

Although the patient's *confrontation* of an old and painful interaction occurred after he had terminated psychotherapeutic contacts, it was clear that this integrative response was the result of his hard work and accomplishments in psychotherapy. He was able to integrate what was learned and experienced in psychotherapy by facing the previously overwhelming issue of dealing with authority realistically, appropriately, and in his own best interests. Confrontations are often opportunities for patients to test reality, and to identify and utilize significant opportunities—in the psychotherapeutic setting and in real life.

Unfinished Business

This special form of recapitulation resolution coupled with integrative confrontation arises with some frequency during the late stages of a successful psychotherapeutic course. *Unfinished Business* refers to important personal exchanges with significant figures from patients' developmental experience which never took place. These figures are usually family members or family surrogates who in some way impeded the patient's personal growth by things they did or things they should have done. The harsh, unloving, manipulative, brutal, insensitive, withdrawn, selfish, seductive, deserting, or ignoring parent is a frequently found figure of conflict in the early lives of patients. In addition to parents, such figures may be other relatives, siblings, or teachers.

The patient may remain loyal, attached, fearful, or anxious in relation to such figures through a major portion of the therapeutic process. Most patients are terrified of confronting these significant figures directly. In many instances, the significant figure with whom the patient has unfinished business has died. The unfinished business may be angry feelings, recrimination, termination of the attachment, or open expressions of long-hidden warmth and love. The following occurred during the 12th session with a severely obsessive/compulsive accountant who began psychotherapy in order to deal with chronic headaches and stomachaches which had no apparent physical basis:

Patient: When I think about my mother I'm furious. I *know* she is a bright and capable person. She does such *stupid* things though—in her work, in her contact with us, with her husband. I don't think she has ever done anything right with me . . . or my brother and sister!

Therapist: Have you ever told her?

Patient: Oh no! I couldn't do that . . . She's old and frail now. She's almost 70 . . . well . . . 65.

Therapist: You don't want to hurt her?

Patient: Well, no! Well . . . , yes . . . , maybe I do . . . but I can't. It would do no good.

During this patient's 75th session, he presented the following report of an unfinished business confrontation:

Patient: I drove down to my mother's home for her birthday. That's the first birthday I've been with her for 10 years. This year I suddenly decided I had to see her and get some things out in the open.

Therapist: You planned?

Patient: Yes . . . and no. I planned to go but I didn't really know what I would say. We've talked a lot about unfinished business here and I knew I had a lot of that. I guess I decided I better do it before she died . . . I guess we talked about that, too . . . See—I'm still obsessing to avoid issues. What I did—I drove down by myself. I didn't take my wife and son. I brought her some flowers and candy for her birthday. I've never done that. When I came in, she opened the door and before I could say anything she said, "I'm baking" and she started to go back. I got really mad. I followed her to the kitchen . . . she was going back to her cooking . . . I took her arm and turned her around and said, "Sit down, you've been running away all your life but today I'm going to tell you some things I should have said a long time ago." Then I told her what a rotten mother she'd been and how hard it had been on us . . . on *me*! I wouldn't let her interrupt. When I was through, she started to whine and tell me how hard things were and how bad my father had been to her—and I suddenly realized that after my father left *I* took on the burden of what he did. *I* felt guilty . . . and she helped by blaming me . . . and my brother and sister . . . for her being left as *her* burden. I looked her square in the face and said, "*I* didn't leave you. I was never to blame . . . but you let me be part of the blame." She started to get mad . . . She said some things and then she just started sobbing. I put my arms around her and said that this should have all come out a long time ago. She just nodded . . . (*long pause*).

Therapist: And then . . .

Patient: Then for some reason I told her to stop cooking and I made her come out with me . . . I took her to lunch. I felt good . . . we talked . . . she was puzzled or uncomfortable but I felt good. Afterwards I took her home, gave her the candy and flowers. I wished her a happy birthday and kissed her goodbye . . . I haven't kissed her in 10 years. I guess I've forgiven her . . . You once said I wouldn't forgive anybody until I could forgive myself . . . I didn't believe it or maybe I didn't understand it . . . It's true though . . . I had to face her with all that and forgive myself for all that guilt . . . It was easier then to understand . . . or maybe accept her as she was . . . and is.

There are many ways in which patients integrate the self-awareness they have learned in psychotherapy which will not be taken up explicitly at this time.

Not all of the risks, ventures, and successes by the patient will be reported to the psychotherapist. Toward the end of psychotherapy, patients who have come to understand and resolve their dependency on the therapist begin to enjoy, even treasure, their independence as they move toward completion of the therapy.

Leaving psychotherapy is a part of the integration process. This will be explored in a later chapter.

The degree of skill with which psychotherapists can create and maintain the therapeutic setting will be dependent on their emotional stability, training, supervision, and experience. All of these are dynamic and changing. In later chapters, the issue of maintaining and improving therapeutic skill will be examined.

CHAPTER 7

Enhancing the Psychotherapeutic Process

Once the psychotherapist creates the therapeutic sanctuary and joins with the patient in the psychotherapeutic alliance, primary effort should be directed toward maintaining the *sanctuary* and the *alliance*. This is done through a sensitive awareness of what is being expressed by the patient. While always attending to these two tasks, the therapist must, whenever possible, *enhance* the process within which the patient moves from *intellectualization,* through *experiencing,* to *integration.* Errors of commission are more likely to adversely affect the process than errors of omission. Inexperienced psychotherapists report feeling a need to "do more." This anxiety-based response may result in the psychotherapist pressing the patient by word or attitude to "move faster." Such impatience can delay or even destroy the psychotherapeutic process.

WHAT DOES THE PSYCHOTHERAPIST DO?

There are many things that a psychotherapist may do or say during a session. Wogan and Norcross (1983) studied the dimensions of therapeutic skill and technique. They found 14 categories of things which psychotherapists "do" during a therapeutic session. Table 3 presents these activities.

There is probably no reason why a therapist shouldn't use most of the techniques or responses identified in Table 3 (other than *physical contact* which is unethical and potentially destructive). The issue in competent psychotherapy is clearly to enhance the patient's progress through the therapeutic course without damaging or destroying the conditions essen-

TABLE 3
A Factor Analytic Description of What Psychotherapists Do
(After Wogan & Norcross)

Component	Activities
Psychodynamic Techniques	Analysis of transference Analysis of resistance Interpretation of the patient's past
Fantasy and Imagery	Use of active imagination Fantasy techniques Use of imagery
Rogerian Skills	Striving for accurate empathy Expressing warmth Trying to understand the patient's reality
Education	Providing information about other services or agencies Assertiveness training Educating the patient to improve deficient abilities
Authenticity	Making patients take responsibility for their actions Total honesty in expression Attempting to be genuine
Planning and Structuring	Planning the course and content of the session Structuring content and direction Specifying the length of a session or therapeutic course
Self-disclosure	Talking about the psychotherapist's personal feelings Revealing facts and experiences of the therapist Exchanging self-disclosure with the patient
Physical Contact	Touching, holding or embracing the patient Sensual contact with the patient
Direct Guidance	Giving specific advice Giving guidance
Psychometric Testing	Giving projective tests Giving intelligence tests
Frustration	Making the patient angry Creating frustration for the patient
Nonverbal Evaluation	Interpreting body movements or postures Interpreting gestures and facial expressions
Flooding	Flooding (exposure to feared stimuli) Implosion therapy (provoking intense anxiety)

tial to the establishment and maintenance of the setting. Anything the therapist does which enhances the patient's movement through therapy, when done correctly and at the right time, is likely to be done without significant disruption of the sanctuary of the psychotherapeutic setting and the alliance established between patient and therapist.

The process of preparing to respond to the patient in psychotherapy is fairly complex. Psychotherapists of different "schools" are in strong disagreement as to how therapists should act. At a recent meeting where the most noted psychotherapists in the world were gathered at an *Evolution of Psychotherapy Conference* (Zeig, 1987), little agreement as to the nature of psychotherapy was reached. Fifteen major schools of thought represented by such luminaries as Thomas Szasz, R.D. Laing, Virginia Satir, Bruno Bettelheim, Joseph Wolpe, Rollo May, Albert Ellis, Jay Haley, Carl Rogers, Judd Marmor, Lewis Wolberg, Carl Whitaker, and others presented their views and critiques. The closest thing to a central idea which emerged was that the patient already has the answer to the problem deep within and the psychotherapist simply helps bring it out. That is certainly a premise for the method of psychotherapeutic intervention proposed in this volume.

PSYCHOTHERAPEUTIC RESPONSES

What the psychotherapist may do or say during a session constitutes the most complex aspect of psychotherapy tradecraft. It is not only what is said, but the timing, the manner, and the style of response that determine whether the process will be enhanced.

The therapist's responses can be soothing. They can be threatening or intimidating. Although the "correctness" of the therapist's response is of great importance, even very accurate labeling or interpretation too early can seem too threatening to the patient and can delay the therapeutic process.

When patients feel intimidated during a psychotherapeutic session, they are more likely than not to *regress*. This means that they will feel less trustful of the therapist and of psychotherapy as a sanctuary. The psychotherapist must be prepared to accept and work with these regressions, which are a natural and frequent occurrence in the therapeutic course. On the other hand, regressions which are caused by inexperience or poor judgment on the part of the therapist must be rehabilitated and recurrence must be prevented. To enhance the psychotherapeutic process, therapists must understand the degree to which their responses will enlighten, clarify, and encourage as opposed to responses which are too intense, intrusive, and threatening.

Making painful discoveries often places the patient in conflict. Although the patient comes for help, he or she has lived a lifetime of hiding from painful realities. Facing and modifying old beliefs and behaviors broadly describes the therapy process. Some common painful discoveries which patients tend to avoid early in the therapeutic course include:

- Facing one's own compulsion to spoil one's own success.
- Discovering how others, including family, have used them.
- Discovering promises that were made by parents that will never be fulfilled.
- Understanding that the rules used since childhood don't work or no longer apply.
- Finding out that one is not as bad as one has been given to understand, and that much of life to date has been wasted trying to live up to a negative image.
- Understanding that injustice is commonly tolerated, even promulgated in society.
- *Accepting* that Godot will never come.
- Realizing that love does not conquer all and, in fact, can be very destructive.
- Learning that loneliness is a fairly useless childhood behavior and should not be aggrandized and supported.
- Being able to tolerate that nothing is forever.
- Discovering that one can contribute to or arrange one's own failure.
- Becoming aware that self-destructive patterns can be repeated for years, while the individual believes, each time they recur, that they are new and unexpected.

The kinds of responses psychotherapists make can be viewed in terms of the degree of intensity and probing inherent in the response. There are no sharp dividing lines, but, in general, the intensity of therapists' responses can be described as *least intrusive, moderately intrusive* and *intense and probative*. Table 4 presents various therapist activities or responses and the degree of threat and probative effect likely to be felt by the patient.

The directness with which a psychotherapist helps patients to prove or test their ideas, values, or fears is a matter of the most delicate judgment. Too little encourages a slow or evasive therapeutic course. Too much may deter or abort the process.

There is probably more choice-making toward or away from progress by patients than by therapists. Once the patient "commits" to the therapeutic process, the psychotherapist's primary and oft-repeated question should become, "What interferences or barriers am I likely to raise that can be avoided?"

TABLE 4
Degree of Intensity and Probative Effect of Various
Psychotherapist Responses

Level of Intensity and Probative Effect	Therapist Response or Activity	
A. LEAST INTRUSIVE	Simple acceptance Empathy Encouragement	Information Guidance and advice Restatement of content Similes and analogies
B. MODERATELY INTRUSIVE	Structuring Direct questions Reflecting patient's questions or statements	Clarification of feeling Structuring and limit setting Guidance and advice
C. INTENSE AND PROBATIVE	Analysis of resistance Analysis of transference Focused questions Guided fantasy Interpretation Confrontations 　• *Paradoxical intention* 　• *Posed hypothetical choices* 　• *Flooding*	Dream analysis Analysis of parapraxes Analysis of gestures or expression

The therapist must demonstrate patience, tolerance, and a degree of courage in stepping in at the right time while avoiding challenging interventions which are inappropriate.

To proceed in therapy, the patient must learn that the process involves certain acceptable losses. This can be a crucial barrier. The losses are diffuse and symbolic. They include such powerful defenses as controls against anger, loss of childhood dependency, giving up illness as an excuse and weapon, and giving up the control of or by parental figures. Most people in psychotherapy, at one point or another, develop paralyzing fears of loss of control. For the psychotherapist to insist or press for the patient to accept a very threatening interpretation directed toward closely-held beliefs before the patient is ready may cause the patient to shut down therapeutic operations.

LEAST INTRUSIVE THERAPIST RESPONSES

Statements and expressions by psychotherapists which support the patient's responses with little or no pressure to intensify or enhance the patient's self-exploration are ordinarily best used under the following circumstances:

- During the beginning sessions of psychotherapy.
- After the patient has missed several sessions.
- When the patient is actively and experientially engaged in self-exploration.
- When the patient seems fearful or defensive.

Examples of the more common *Least Intrusive* therapist responses follow:

Simple Acceptance (Empathy)

This therapist response was originally described by Snyder (1947). It is a statement that should indicate to the patient that the therapist understands what the patient has said. The response implies neither agreement nor disagreement.

Patient: I'm not sure I can continue in school—it's just too hard.
Therapist: Uh huh . . .

The patient is reassured that the therapist is listening. There is an implied encouragement to go further.

The psychotherapist may choose to use a simple acceptance *with empathy*. In this response the therapist attempts to convey to the patient that the situation is not only understood but that the therapist can sense how the patient feels about the issue:

Patient: I could take more time with my studies, but then I'd probably have to give up my job in the evening.
Therapist: Yes . . . I can see that . . . .

The words alone cannot convey *empathy*. The tone, articulation, and pace of the therapist's response transmit the therapist's interest and sensitive awareness. For this to happen, the therapist must genuinely concentrate on the patient's communications and make every effort to sense the patient's feeling tone.

This is the least intrusive response which can be made by a therapist. It is valuable early in the psychotherapeutic course when patients tend to be defensive and easily threatened. It can be a useful enhancing response when the patient is moving along well, serving as a subtle marker of the therapist's attention and continuing support:

Patient: We've been talking for only 10 minutes but I realized that this man was attractive *because* he was planning to use me. I was feeling a compulsion to go along with his manipulations . . .
Therapist: Uh huh . . . .
Patient: But for the first time that I can remember, I *knew* it was happening . . . and I could . . . sort of step back and say, "You don't have to do this any more." I was *so* pleased and excited!
Therapist: Mm . . . Yes!
Patient: I felt a sense of strength . . . and comfort.

Restatement of Content

This therapist response is an extended form of *simple acceptance*. It has additional value as a least intrusive therapist interaction of signaling patients that the content of their statement has been received and understood. It is somewhat easier to convey empathy with *restatement of content* than with *simple acceptance*. The psychotherapist chooses those elements of what has been said by the patient that most clearly express the essence of what the patient has said:

Patient: My wife won't do a thing at home . . . She comes in, puts her things down by the door, and flops down to watch TV. All she wants to do is watch those damned soaps!
Therapist: Getting to the TV is the first priority when she gets home.
Patient: Every day! Nothing else seems to matter! She doesn't consider me or the kids or anything like getting supper started or talking. No—right to the boob tube!
Therapist: She doesn't seem to worry about your needs.
Patient: Right! I come home all keyed up. I want to talk, wind down, but I can't. She's glued to the TV.

Restatement of content is a response which offers an opportunity for the psychotherapist to reassure the patient that the therapeutic alliance is in operation. This response further implies that the therapist is interested, alert, processing the things being said by the patient, and ready for more—when the patient is ready to provide more.

Similes and Analogies

These are the most complex forms of least obtrusive therapist responses. They require a good bit of intelligence and creativity on the part of the psychotherapist. These responses are best used where the patient has expressed loosely some ideas which have a central theme:

Patient: I don't really want to make a lot of trouble, but what am I gonna do? If I don't tell people what I want, they won't know. So I'm "aggressive"—so what? That's the way life is . . . I don't understand some people. If something goes wrong, they complain, "Why didn't you say something?" So—I say something whenever I've got something to say. You don't get anywhere by hoping people will read your mind.
Therapist: So . . . the squeaky wheel gets the grease?
Patient: Exactly.

Similes and analogies (including literary references) should be selected to fit, as much as possible, the cultural and educational background of the patient. In an exchange similar to the example above with a professor of education, the following occurred:

Patient: I don't understand why my colleagues are so distressed when I put myself forth aggressively at the Senate meetings. After all, we're elected to review and revise the University's procedures. If I sat there like some of them, dozing and listening, nothing would ever change.
Therapist: Nothing ventured, nothing gained.
Patient: Exactly so!

A simulated exchange between a police sergeant and his psychotherapist further illustrates adaptation of similes and analogies to the patient's culture and environment:

Patient: It's true that I'm tough on new recruits. If I wasn't, they wouldn't survive. The Captain says I've got to realize that we have a "new breed" of police. Bullshit! Explain that to the bad guys out there! If I'm not hard on a new guy, he's gonna run into a tough deal and not know what's coming down. Then he's really in trouble. When that happens, he'll be glad I was tough on him during his training.
Therapist: No pain, no gain?

Patient: That's it—no pain, no gain.

In the hierarchy of psychotherapist responses, the use of similes and analogies borders on and sometimes becomes moderately intrusive when the therapist's response is a *clarification of feeling* rather than a summary of the content of what the patient has said. Such a response in relation to the police officer's complaints that he is criticized for doing what he believes is a critical part of proper training might be:

Therapist: It's like the comedian says, "I don't get no respect?"

Here the psychotherapist goes beyond *restatement of content* and *similes* and *analogies*. The patient's subtle anxiety is brought out. If this occurs too early in therapy, the psychotherapist's efforts to enhance the patient's progress may fail. The following is what actually happened in the second session with the police sergeant:

Patient: It's true that I'm tough on new recruits. If I wasn't they wouldn't survive. The Captain says I've got to realize that we have a "new breed" of police. Bullshit! Explain that to the bad guys out there! If I'm not hard on a new guy, he's gonna run into a tough deal and not know what's coming down. Then he's really in trouble. When that happens, he'll be glad I was tough on him during his training.
Therapist: It's like the comedian says, "I don't get no respect?"
Patient: (*pause*) Well . . . no . . . I mean . . . It's not me . . . That's just the way the world is. Too many people think that a few nice words or a college education is all they need. Well, I'll tell you—it's tough out there and anybody that wants to get into this work better believe it!

The psychotherapist went too far, too soon. Clearly the sergeant was not ready to face his own anxiety concomitant with the fear that younger, better educated police recruits were a threat to his role and status. The patient ceases to relate freely and responds with a subtle attack on the psychotherapist ("a few nice words and a college education"). This patient was not ready for moderately intrusive responses from his psychotherapist.

Encouragement

Some psychotherapists believe that when the patient is encouraged during psychotherapy, disruptive dependency interactions develop.

Other therapists see encouragement as an enhancing response. Although each psychotherapist is likely to choose differently, encouragement responses should probably be used earlier in the therapeutic course than later. The following excerpt from a first session illustrates encouragement:

Patient: I don't know . . . It was a very hard decision to start therapy . . . but it's hard to continue. I really don't know. I really try . . . .

Therapist: Many who start therapy feel this. The beginning is often the hardest part of the therapy.

Patient: I *do* want to change.

Therapist: That is important. It's the best starting point.

When used in response to a patient's ambivalence regarding significant life choices, encouragement can be a therapeutic error:

Patient: It's hopeless. Lord knows, I've tried, but I just can't stand that woman . . . . She drives me nuts. I'm going to consult a lawyer.

Therapist: Perhaps it's time to do that.

The danger which is bound to arise if encouragement is used regularly lies in the implication that the psychotherapist is a judge, weighing the patient's decisions and then awarding approval or disapproval. Patients may seek this kind of interaction, but it is counterproductive when therapists become the givers of rewards or blessings.

Information

Most requests for information during psychotherapy are diversions or dependency-seeking responses. There are occasions when psychotherapists can provide information in keeping with their role of enhancing the process:

Patient: My sister called me. She has finally admitted that she is unhappy and must do something about it. She's frightened though . . . She has just moved to St. Louis and doesn't know who she should see.

Therapist: I'll give you the names of three qualified therapists after our session. There are many good people in St. Louis.

The therapist should carefully evaluate requests for information before responding, since such requests rarely advance psychotherapy:

Patient: I'm really confused about whether to go home to see my folks or not this year . . . and it's so expensive.
Therapist: The airlines are cutting fares for the holidays and the fares are extremely reasonable.

The foolishness of that therapist response speaks for itself.

Guidance and Advice

Most patients approach the psychotherapeutic experience with the literal expectancy of "getting help." Although initial structuring may help patients to begin to understand that the efficiency and effectiveness of the psychotherapy process require their active exploration and participation, early expectancies for advice and direction can be persistent. The value of guidance and advice during psychotherapy remains an issue of considerable debate (Leo, 1985a). The position taken in the context of *Psychotherapy Tradecraft* is that such responses are usually of little value in furthering the process of psychotherapy.

When a patient requests advice or guidance, the psychotherapist should help the patient explore dependency needs and attitudes. An authoritarian solution to the immediate problem is ordinarily of less importance therapeutically than the opportunity available for the psychotherapist to help the patient explore within. The following interchange is constructed from a session of psychotherapy with the patient "Jim Brown" who wrote the letter in the last chapter.

Patient: I *know* I ought to have a raise. I've been with the company almost two years. My boss is that way—if I don't push for the raise, I'm sure I won't get it. I *hate* to push or demand. (*weeps*)
Therapist: Perhaps you could write him a memo outlining what you've done since you started and pointing out that you should be rewarded for the value you've brought to the company.

The therapist's suggestion is reasonable. It is perhaps clever. It may be good counseling practice. It does not enhance the process of psychotherapy. The patient's emotional expressions are ignored. The immediate problem might be solved but the patient's anxiety and suffering related to fear of his own worthlessness would probably remain. The following is what really happened in that session:

Patient: I *know* I ought to have a raise. I've been with the company almost two years. My boss is that way—if I don't push for the raise, I'm sure I won't get it. I *hate* to push or demand. (*weeps*)

Therapist: ... (*pause while patient continues to weep*) ... Perhaps it's even frightening.

Patient: Oh God! You don't know ... My father would terrify me by acting cold and distant ... and he'd stare at me. I never knew what I'd done wrong. I felt it must be *something*. (*weeps*) I've never been able to stand up for myself ... even when it has nothing to do with me or what I've done.

Therapist: Uh huh ...

Patient: Maybe my father even *wanted* us to be terrified ... I never thought of that.

The therapist first *clarified the patient's feelings* (a *moderately intrusive* response) and then provided *simple acceptance,* allowing and encouraging the patient to continue experiencing emotion associated with important ideas and memories, without pressure or threat.

There are, of course, instances where guidance and advice are not only helpful but perhaps mandatory, as in the following example:

Patient: This stomach pain is still bothering me ... but I suppose it's only stress ... or guilt.

Therapist: These pains are pretty recent.

Patient: Yeah ... the last month or so.

Therapist: Perhaps it would be a good idea to see your physician and check it out.

Patient: Don't you think it's stress?

Therapist: I don't know, but you should check this out with your doctor.

Information, guidance, advice, and encouragement should be used very sparingly, especially when the patient is in an experiencing phase of therapy.

Being able to give up encouragement, information-giving, and advice as frequently-used responses is a sign that the psychotherapist is becoming comfortable with the concept that the patient will proceed through the therapeutic process most efficiently with the least steering, manipulation and moral judgment by the therapist.

MODERATELY INTRUSIVE THERAPIST RESPONSES

The concept of *intrusive* as used in the context of psychotherapy refers to those things which the psychotherapist does or says which intimidate or menace the patient. The perception of peril or jeopardy is the patient's interpretation. Objective evaluations of what is threatening or intrusive do not apply in psychotherapy. This constitutes a paradox of psychotherapy: The experiences and insights which the patient seeks are frequently blocked by feelings of danger raised by any approach to these experiences and insights. Much of what is described or labeled as therapeutic skill is the ability of the psychotherapist to sense that the patient has developed sufficient security within the psychotherapeutic sanctuary to risk exploration.

If the psychotherapeutic venture is to be successful, the patient must eventually confront emotional perils—real or fancied. If the psychotherapist confronts the patient with painful issues too early in the process, the patient will withdraw. Moderately intrusive therapist responses offer a way of bridging the gap between least intrusive and confrontation responses. Moderately intrusive therapist statements offer the patient opportunities to take modest risks in self-exploration.

Structuring

A therapist response which describes the psychotherapeutic process is a moderately intrusive response. In all structuring there is a tone of expectancy. The structuring suggests or implies that there are things the patient should or could be doing to further the process. Structuring responses are more likely to occur early in psychotherapy than later. Structuring is often a psychotherapist's response to a patient's question. The following example is from the 10th session with the police officer alluded to earlier:

Patient: (*long pause*) . . . I guess I don't have much to say . . .
Therapist: Nothing comes to mind.
Patient: (*long pause*) . . . What do I do when I have nothing to say when I'm here?
Therapist: This happens at times to almost everyone during therapy.

The psychotherapist assures the patient that the uncomfortable pause is a "part of the game." At the same time, there is an implication, without pressure, that this will pass as the patient presses on.

Limit Setting

When the psychotherapist is required to set limits, it should be done in the least intrusive way possible. Limit setting is a form of structuring meant to emphasize and preserve the sanctuary of psychotherapy. Sometimes the limit setting is a response to reasonable requests or questions, as in the following:

Patient: I'm somewhat uncomfortable about taking this particular hour for my therapy. It's such a . . . *pattern.* I would really like to make an appointment each week for the time that's most convenient. Can I do that?

Therapist: Sometimes the regularity of the therapy appointment is inconvenient, but this *pattern* or consistency is very helpful in encouraging you to explore your life in the most efficient psychotherapeutic way. Scattered appointments could interfere with progress. If a different time on a regular basis would be helpful, we can try that.

In some instances, limits must be set more stringently, as when testing of limits by the patient threatens the psychotherapeutic process. The following occurred with the police sergeant during his 15th session of psychotherapy:

Patient: I find that I'm attracted to your secretary . . .

Therapist: Uh huh . . .

Patient: I've been thinking of calling her up and . . . you know . . . getting together or something. Then I thought I'd better bring this up, but I figured you wouldn't care what she does on her own time.

Therapist: That's certainly understandable—your being attracted to her—but you have some "doubts" about whether it's OK?

Patient: Yeah . . . but what the hell? Do you mind?

Therapist: I don't mind, but I have to tell you that the staff are instructed not to socialize with patients. This is to protect you and your work in psychotherapy. Once you develop a friendly or social relationship with the psychotherapist or anyone closely connected with your therapist, safety is lessened. You would find yourself less able to speak freely about your ideas, your thoughts, and especially your feelings. As I've told you before, success in psychotherapy depends a lot on our being able to create a comfortable, safe place for you where you can look at anything. Social contact with me or my staff would interfere with that. Your *wanting* to date my secretary, however, is an important thing for us to talk about.

Patient: Well . . . I'm not sure that this is reasonable . . . I find myself annoyed and I really don't know why.

Therapist: Your feelings and finding out the "whys" are the most important things. Can you talk a bit about how your interest in Ms. Smith began?

Clearly the issues are important and go much deeper than a superficial interest in the psychotherapist's secretary. In this exchange, the therapist set the limits firmly but not threateningly. This was followed by another moderately intrusive therapeutic response—the *direct question.*

Direct Questions

As demonstrated above, a direct question by the psychotherapist is a request for the patient to *focus* on an issue perceived by the therapist to be important for psychotherapeutic progress. The purpose of a direct question is to help the patient to move from *intellectualization* to *experiencing.* The question should help the patient move from a general involvement in an experiential issue to a more focused interaction. The following example is from a session with the patient who objected to his wife's attachment to television above all else:

Therapist: She doesn't seem to worry about your needs.
Patient: Right! I come home keyed up—I want to talk—wind down—but I can't. She's glued to the T.V.
Therapist: Have you told her, as you've told me so clearly, how much you would like her to be concerned with some of the pressures you face?
Patient: No . . . I guess . . . well . . . she wouldn't . . . no . . . (*long pause*) . . . (*weeps softly*) . . . I'm sorry . . . (*long pause*) . . . I guess I can't— I can't ask for anything I want . . . even when I *know* I deserve it, I feel that I don't . . . I hope she'll understand but I can't ask. Then I get mad at her and don't tell her why I'm mad. (*weeps*)

The answer to the psychotherapist's question is unimportant. The result of the direct question—the patient's focusing on a painful and longstanding emotional barrier—is critical to therapeutic progress.

Guidance and Advice

Although guidance and advice by the psychotherapist are ordinarily least intrusive responses, they can be moderately intrusive. In the following interaction, the psychotherapist uses this technique to encourage a patient to focus on a significant aspect of her life:

Patient: I don't really understand why I have such ups and downs with my mother.

Therapist: It's pretty distressing.

Patient: Yes . . . but it's a blank for me.

Therapist: Have you read the book "My Mother—Myself" or the one called "Best of Friends—Worst of Enemies"?

Patient: No, should I?

Therapist: Both of these books explore the complex and often painful relations between grown daughters and their mothers.

Patient: Oh . . . well . . . maybe I'll do that.

In this example, the therapist used guidance and advice to direct the patient to some reading material which described issues and conflicts with which the patient was struggling.

As a moderately intrusive therapist response, guidance and advice can threaten patients and impede progress, as in the following:

Patient: The whole business of what to do, when to do it . . . it's just hard . . . I just can't meet people . . . be comfortable . . . (*long pause*)

Therapist: You might try one of the singles clubs.

Patient: Are you serious? Have you ever been to one of those?

Therapist: No . . . but . . .

Patient: They are a zoo! You can't believe what kind of misfits and weirdos go to those clubs. Is that how you characterize me?

A therapeutic error has clearly been made. The patient has been unproductively threatened. Guidance and advice should rarely, if ever, be given in psychotherapy. When they are used, they should be specific, limited, and well within the psychotherapist's knowledge and experience. There should be a clear-cut highly predictable goal for the guidance and advice.

Reflection of Questions

Questions by patients can reflect confusion, information-seeking, manipulation, dependency-seeking, or other traits and state of the patient. As psychotherapy proceeds, questions seem to occur less frequently. Questions should never be treated lightly. They represent a subtle effort to interact directly with the psychotherapist. Issues of transference and resistance frequently make their first appearance in the form of questions to the therapist.

Rarely, if ever, should the psychotherapist answer questions directly. There are occasional instances, usually early in the psychotherapy, where encouragement, information, or guidance and advice may be appropriate. If the psychotherapist is to encourage movement by the patient toward experiencing and integration, confidence in the patient's potential must be expressed by reflecting rather than answering questions. The following demonstrates a direct answer:

Patient: I notice that you always wear a blue suit. Do you ever dress
     casually at the office?
Therapist: Yes, sometimes.
Patient: Oh ...

An appropriate response to the patient's question would be as follows:

Patient: I notice that you always wear a blue suit. Do you ever dress
     casually at the office?
Therapist: You've been wondering about whether I ever dress
     differently.
Patient: Yes ... I guess everybody wonders about their therapist—what
     they are *really* like. Sometimes I have fantasies that you were once
     the President's analyst or something like that ... I guess it's sort of
     adolescent but ... I guess ... I ... er ... I'm sort of embarrassed
     ... I admire you but I feel ... uncomfortable about it.
Therapist: Perhaps you find that even pleasant feelings and thoughts
     can be uncomfortable.
Patient: Yes ... yes ... I have a lot of anxiety about that.

In this example, the psychotherapist properly reflected the patient's question. This led to an experiential revelation by the patient. The therapist then responded with a moderately intrusive psychotherapist response—reflection of feeling.

Reflection of Feeling

When the psychotherapist responds with reflection of feeling, it provides the patient with an opportunity to identify and explore the emotional aspect of what has been said. It is an opportunity for focusing, provided by the psychotherapist. To be done properly, it requires that the therapist identify the emotional essence of what the patient said. The therapist must then present this essence without interpretation or elaboration. This minimizes threat and allows the patient to explore or evade without undue defensiveness. In the following example, the patient indicates that she is not ready to carry the exploration further:

Patient: Of course, when he starts criticizing me, I just leave. I'm past the point where I will allow people to abuse me.
Therapist: At the first sign of criticism you react.
Patient: Well . . . yes. (*long pause*)

In a similar vein, a patient responds to reflection of feeling with further exploration:

Patient: I could tell that nothing I could do would please him, so when he blamed me for misplacing the key, I just left.
Therapist: So when you see he is in a critical mode, you react.
Patient: Well . . . yes . . . I can see he is going to blame me for everything that's gone wrong for him. I don't need that. I've had enough of that kind of unfairness in my life! I don't *have* to take it!

In both cases, the patient has the choice of whether to go further or not.

Clarification of Feeling

This therapist response attempts not only to identify the focus of feeling in what the patient says but to clarify the essence of that feeling, encouraging the patient to experience that essence. Never as obtrusive as interpretation, which goes beyond what the patient has said, clarification of feeling goes beyond reflection of the feeling stated by the patient by simplifying, relabeling, or putting the patient's emotional expression into a different context. Using the last example of reflection of feeling presented above, the psychotherapist's response is given as a clarification of feeling:

Patient: I could tell that nothing I could do would please him, so when he blamed me for misplacing the key, I just left.
Therapist: You felt not only angry about being accused, but decided that you couldn't correct the situation.

Rather than simply reflecting the patient's feeling, the therapist simplified the patient's emotional response, clarifying the presence of frustration and hopelessness.

If the patient accepts the clarification and pursues the focus on emotion, experiencing is likely to follow, as in the following exchange during a 43-year-old executive's 102nd session:

Patient: I'm not foolish about it—simply realistic. Being a 43-year-old divorced woman earning more money and having more status than the available men I meet, for all practical purposes takes me out of the mating market.
Therapist: Most men seem too fragile to relate to and enjoy a powerful woman.
Patient: You're damned right! They may admire me at work, but won't risk sharing themselves on an equitable basis. They are *afraid* to laugh, to play . . . and I *won't* give up the status and respect I've earned by changing to a simpering, fatuous female partner in the personal setting.
Therapist: So being yourself, your honest self, can be emotionally costly at times.
Patient: It's true . . . (*pause*) . . . (*weeps gently*) . . . but I won't play that game.
Therapist: Doing the right thing is not always easy.
Patient: Yes . . . but in the end . . . it's best.

The clarifications of feeling helped the patient focus on the core of emotion and experience without going beyond into more threatening interpretative or confrontational responses.

Patients can be threatened by clarifications of feeling which touch on emotional structures the patient is not yet ready to experience, as in the following:

Patient: I know it's wrong, but I was so distressed by my wife's behavior . . . actually her *lack* of behavior. Well, so I called a woman I went with before I married Jane . . . I know it was wrong but I wanted someone to really *talk* with.
Therapist: You felt really fed up with your wife . . .
Patient: No . . . that's not it. She is just not sensitive to my needs.

The psychotherapist clarifies the patient's rage toward his wife, but the patient is not ready to experience this. The clarification is rejected and the patient intellectualizes. The psychotherapist might have enhanced the patient's efforts by a reflection of feeling as follows:

Patient: I know it's wrong, but I was so distressed by my wife's behavior . . . actually her *lack* of behavior. Well, so I called a woman I went with before I married Jane . . . I know it was wrong but I wanted someone to really *talk* with.

Therapist: There are times when a person not only *wants* but really *needs* someone to be interested and to listen.

Patient: It's really not too much to ask . . . after all . . . I'm human too!

The subtle differences between reflection of feeling and clarification of feeling lie in the degree to which the patient's defenses against anxiety are threatened by the psychotherapist's response. Making the choice between reflection and clarification is determined by the psychotherapist's sensitive awareness of how safe the patient seems to feel. This is a reliable predictor of the risks in emotional exploration the patient is able to take.

INTENSE AND PROBATIVE THERAPIST ACTIVITY

This group of responses includes the most powerful efforts the psychotherapist can make in attempting to enhance the patient's movement from *intellectualization* through *experiencing* and finally to *integration*.

These therapist responses must be based on clear indications from the patient's dialogue that the probative response is warranted and appropriate to the patient's life and times. The psychotherapist should be reasonably certain that the patient feels enough comfort, safety, and trust in the therapeutic setting to risk experiencing as a result of probing by the therapist. The further a patient proceeds in the psychotherapy, the more frequent will be the opportunity for the therapist to use probative responses, since maintenance of the sanctuary of the setting creates a backlog of trust. This, in turn, encourages or allows the patient to tolerate and use probative information from the therapist.

The success or failure of the psychotherapist's probative efforts can be evaluated. If the patient responds to the therapist's statement and proceeds to experiencing, the therapist's venture was appropriate. When the patient responds with defensiveness, puzzlement, evasiveness, or withdrawal, the psychotherapist's response has been too intense or premature.

Focused Questions

The psychotherapist may choose this probative response when the patient has revealed a series of episodes where a strikingly similar series of events have been described. In the following passages, a 26-year-old computer supervisor reports a recent incident during the 36th session of psychotherapy. In previous sessions, the patient described feelings of physical illness and nausea whenever his father returned on weekends from his job as an itinerant accountant. At these times, the father reviewed the children's school work, performance on household tasks, and behavior in general. Although the father was never brutal, the approach of Friday evening each week resulted in anxiety and fear for the patient. In later sessions, the patient described similar physical symptoms associated with examinations at school. A similar response at work was reported as follows:

Patient: I like my new job although I'm not always sure of exactly what they expect of me. What bothers me is that the old symptoms of stomachache and nausea seem to be back. I haven't had those for a while.

Therapist: So the new job has been stressful enough to bring back some of your old symptoms?

Patient: I guess . . . it's disappointing. I thought I had that whipped.

Therapist: When has this happened?

Patient: Well . . . I told you I like my boss a lot. He's helpful and he encourages me. He *really* wants me to do well, but when I report to him at the end of the week—during our "closeout" session for the week—I get tense and then nauseous. It's worse when we do the monthly "closeout" . . . (*long pause*)

Therapist: You had similar symptoms in high school and college at exam time didn't you?

Patient: Yes, the same thing.

Therapist: And I think you told me that you would feel nauseous or get stomachaches when your dad came home for the weekends when you were a kid?

Patient: Yeah . . . that's right.

Therapist: Could all of these be associated? Fear of your father's judgments, fear of test performance, and fears about your job performance?

Patient: Gee! I don't know . . . You're right, the feelings were the same . . . As I think about it, I feel a little . . . queasy in the stomach!

Therapist: So, you react the same way to all of these?

Patient: I guess so . . . but at work . . . my boss is nothing like my father . . . Some of my teachers were . . . gosh . . . that's weird! Just thinking about it gives me stomach twinges! I guess I'm expecting my boss to act like my father!

The psychotherapist asks the patient to relate three events which seem to trigger similar symptoms. The therapist does not interpret the meaning of the events. The patient's attention and thoughts are focused by several questions. The patient accepts the focus, perceives a pattern, and experiences the symptoms being explored. The therapist's focused question has enhanced the patient's progress in psychotherapy.

Although the focused question is usually the least threatening of the intrusive therapist responses, threat and rejection can occur if the psychotherapist is not constantly mindful of the patient's degree of confidence in the sanctuary of the setting. In the following example, the psychotherapist used focused questions too early in the therapeutic process. During the fourth session of psychotherapy, a 36-year-old dental assistant discussed feelings of discouragement and depression:

Patient: It just comes on me. Sometimes just a day or two and sometimes it lasts longer. I feel rotten . . . and hopeless.

Therapist: Is it more at work or at home?

Patient: Gee . . . I don't know . . . (*long pause*)

Therapist: Does it happen at any particular time? Like when someone criticizes you?

Patient: Gee . . . maybe . . . I don't . . . I guess I ought to think more about those things.

The psychotherapist is too eager. The questions may be appropriate, but clearly the patient is not sufficiently secure to accept this intrusive therapist response. The patient becomes bewildered and self-blaming, and withdraws from the topic. It should be noted that an interpretation posed as a question is not a focused question. The focused question does not include a suggested underlying dynamic principle to account for the patient's behavior.

Guided Fantasy

This procedure is most effective with patients who have moved from intellectualization into experiencing with relatively little discomfort. When such patients reach a barrier and seem unable to move beyond description, the psychotherapist must be creative but cautious. The guided fantasy should be based on elements common to the patient's life and experience.

In the following exchange, the 26-year-old computer supervisor, during the 38th session of psychotherapy, struggles to explore his shyness in social settings:

Patient: I've always had trouble starting any kind of social conversation . . . especially with women . . . especially attractive or self-assured women . . . even in work situations . . .

Therapist: It's always difficult.

Patient: Yeah . . . I'd *like* to be able to be smooth, easy—you know.

Therapist: Like?

Patient: I don't know.

Therapist: Try to imagine yourself at work. A fellow executive is visiting from another office. You told me that you are sometimes asked to show these visitors around.

Patient: Yeah . . . sometimes.

Therapist: Imagine that it's 10 in the morning. You are supposed to meet J.A. Jones to play host, as you've done before. You are introduced to J.A. Jones, who is an attractive and articulate 26-year-old woman accountant.

Patient: Gee . . . I don't know.

Therapist: Try to imagine yourself being introduced. Make up a story or a fantasy of what happens.

Patient: Well . . . OK . . . I introduce myself . . . and . . . I feel kind of funny . . . her being a good-looking woman and all . . .

Therapist: Try to experience the feeling.

Patient: Well . . . it's like . . . excited and still a little nervous like . . . like I might say something stupid . . . or I wonder if my clothes are OK.

Therapist: Looking for something wrong.

Patient: Yeah . . . assuming she'll find something wrong.

Therapist: Does it feel bad?

Patient: Yeah . . . sort of . . . but not really bad . . . more like—"Uh oh—be careful."

Therapist: Go on . . .

Patient: I have to be careful that I don't act the fool in some way . . . I'd get pretty stiff and formal. I'd look away from her and talk about the organization. . . . Boy! . . . Am I stiff . . .

Therapist: Not doing well?

Patient: Hell no! . . . the more I try to be cool and avoid embarrassing feelings . . . the stiffer and maybe unfriendlier I act . . . People tell me that.

Therapist: So you're telling this attractive woman about your organization. What are you feeling? Try to imagine it as if it were happening right now.

Patient: Gee? . . . I keep wanting to look at her . . . but I'll blush . . . I am blushing! She'll think I'm a real nerd . . .

Therapist: You fear you're spoiling it?

Patient: Yeah . . . I'm messing it up . . .

Therapist: Messing up what?

Patient: Well . . . you know . . . a pretty girl . . . I'd like . . . well, even if it's business, I'd like her to think well of me.

Therapist: Be attracted to you?

Patient: Yeah.

Therapist: Imagine you've shown her around. You're back in your office. As you talk, she says she's enjoyed the morning. Imagine, then, she asks if the two of you can have lunch.

Patient: Just like that? Gee! That's never happened. No! It has! I forgot . . . that happened about a year ago! . . . God! was I upset . . . I made excuses and said I had other plans.

Therapist: Did you?

Patient: No . . . I was too scared to accept.

Therapist: Imagine yourself saying, "Yes, fine" to your visitor. Make a fantasy of taking her to lunch.

Patient: Well . . . Gee! I'd drive to a pretty nice place I guess. I think to Bogies. I've been there a couple of times. It's kind of an "in" place . . . I'd ask her what she'd like . . . or maybe she'd ask what's good . . . We'd talk about ourselves I guess. I'd ask her about where she went to school . . . and then . . . I guess if it went OK, I'd ask her out to dinner . . . No . . . Maybe that would be too quick . . .

Therapist: Afraid again?

Patient: Yeah . . .

Therapist: It's *your* fantasy . . . You can imagine anything you want.

Patient: Well . . . she'd say she had a good time . . . and I'd say I did too . . . and then I'd ask her if we could get together again.

Therapist: How do you feel?

Patient: Good . . . I guess . . . Yeah, it feels good . . .

The guided fantasy was well within the patient's experience. The patient was comfortable in the psychotherapeutic setting. Although somewhat intrusive, the guided fantasy was accepted by the patient. Areas of conflict were approached and experienced. The patient has moved forward.

Interpretation

Various forms of interpretation constitute the most complex of the intrusive psychotherapist responses. The origins of most of the interpretive techniques are in psychoanalytic theory and practice. Effective and skillful use of these responses requires that the psychotherapist be well-rounded in dynamic theories of personality, as well as in principles of human development. Interpretation goes beyond focusing patients' attention on congruities and incongruities of their behavior and ideas. An appropriate interpretation helps the patient associate feelings and behavior with a general principle or an overarching concept which directs or shapes the patient's thinking and behaving.

In making an interpretation, the psychotherapist presents the patient with an explanation—a cause and effect model of the purpose served by the patient's symptoms or neurotic behavior. Such a presentation threatens the continued, hidden existence of the mechanism. Unless the patient is able to tolerate the anxiety and personal discomfort which usually follow an appropriate interpretation, the patient will be overly fearful or angry. The interpretation will be rejected in some way. If the interpretation touches the patient's neurotic substructure too deeply, therapeutic progress may be disrupted.

Inappropriately presented interpretations can drive a patient out of therapy. Interpretations which are inconsistent with the patient's personality or threatening beyond the patient's readiness or tolerance can increase the patient's discomfort and create unnecessary and possibly damaging reactions. There are some general rules for psychotherapists to follow in selecting and making interpretations:

- The interpretation must be based on material brought up previously by the patient.
- The underlying concept or personality dynamic being proposed in the interpretation should be consistent with the patient's history and neurotic behavior patterns.
- The interpretation being proposed should be appropriate to behavioral patterns demonstrated by the patient in situations or circumstances other than the instant situation to which the psychotherapist directs the interpretation.
- The therapist must be relatively sure that the patient is ready and able to experience a variety of emotions, as evidenced by the patient's previous responses to moderately intrusive therapist activity.
- The psychotherapist should choose to make intepetations at such times when there is reasonable evidence that the patient is relatively secure within the therapy session and seems to be communicating easily and comfortably.
- The interpretation must never be made as an accusation, moral judgment, or expression of the psychotherapist's personal values.

There are ways for the psychotherapist to evaluate whether the interpretation has been made appropriately and effectively. The following tend to occur when the psychotherapist has made an appropriate interpretation for which the patient is ready:

- The patient accepts the interpretation and proceeds to describe *experiencing* strong feelings as the concept presented in the interpretation is explored.
- The patient is stirred emotionally by the interpretation even though unable at the moment to explore the emotions triggered by the interpretation.
- The patient reports an increase of emotional responses, parapraxes, or dreams following the session in which the interpretation was made.
- The interpretation is followed by a flood of free associations or memories. Sometimes this occurs in the sessions subsequent to the session in which the interpretation was made.

When interpretations are made inappropriately with regard to content or timing, there are indications of the psychotherapist's error. These are signs of such an error:

- The interpretation is followed by puzzlement or confusion on the part of the patient.
- The patient flatly rejects the interpretation.
- The interpretation is followed by withdrawal by the patient into long silences.
- The patient retreats to meaningless intellectual responses.
- The patient cancels one or more appointments subsequent to the interpretation.
- The patient breaks off psychotherapy.
- The patient criticizes the psychotherapist or the therapist's staff.
- The patient becomes uncharacteristically passive.

Interpretations should include some element of *recapitulation*. The patient's neurotic style or behavior is likely in some way to reflect a feared or desired element of the patient's developmental experience. It may imitate the behavior of the patient's family members or of early influential others. It may reflect significant incidents, traumas, or missed experiences during the patient's developmental years. The more the psychotherapist knows of the patient's history and life-style, the more effective the interpretations are likely to be. Interpretations early in the psychotherapeutic process are less likely to be effective and useful than those made after the psychotherapist knows more about the patient's life and times.

Analysis of resistance. Resistance tends to occur in psychotherapy when the patient perceives, usually unconsciously, that hidden fears, wishes, motives, or memories are being approached during the psychotherapeutic process. The patient's comfort and security with neurotic ideas or behaviors are threatened by the self-exploration natural to the psychotherapeutic process. Just as naturally, the patient is reluctant to give up or disturb the neurotic balance. Resistance represents the patient's efforts to prevent discovery at the same time discovery is taking place. Resistance is a signal to the therapist that the patient is fearful and wishes the therapeutic process to slow down.

The resistance may be outwardly associated with some element of reality, such as being critical of the psychotherapist's staff, schedule, vacation plans, or behavior. At times it may appear as passivity, withdrawal, silence, or missed appointments. The following exchange occurred during the 7th session of psychotherapy with a 32-year-old attorney whose psychological assessment suggested he had never been able to express warmth and love to an admired but feared father:

Patient: (long pause) Somehow or other I don't feel like telling you what I'm thinking . . .
Therapist: It feels more comfortable to hold back.
Patient: Yeah . . . well no . . . I just don't think you'll be very helpful . . . I know the therapy and all . . . about saying everything that's on your mind, but . . . I'm reluctant to do that. It's probably an exercise in futility. You're not going to help me, or give advice or anything like that.
Therapist: It seems sort of frustrating.
Patient: Yeah . . . and I wonder if it's worth continuing.
Therapist: Uh huh . . .

The patient is exhibiting resistance, but at a stage in psychotherapy much too early for the therapist to make an effective interpretation. *Simple acceptance, reflection of feeling* and *restatement of content* are the therapist's best response choices.

Toward the end of the 38th session, the same patient demonstrated similar resistance. During previous sessions, the patient had expressed much emotion regarding his inability to engage in exchanges of warmth and closeness with his father. He described a number of events during early development where efforts to win the father's attention, approval, or closeness ended in the patient being rebuffed and ridiculed. The psychotherapist is now confident that an interpretation may not be too threatening and there is a fairly clear basis for a probative, enhancing response:

Patient: This is one of "those" sessions. I really don't feel like telling you anything.

Therapist: They seem to come up now and then.

Patient: Yeah ... I know they are not supposed to be helpful ... but I really don't want to say anything. I probably should have cancelled today.

Therapist: So it's like a "resistance" or "braking."

Patient: Yeah ... I'll start to talk and stop myself.

Therapist: As though it might be painful or frightening to go on?

Patient: No ... well, yeah ... maybe ...

Therapist: Can you look at those feelings?

Patient: (*long pause*) ... I talk to myself ... look at what I might say ... then my stomach gets tense. I don't want to look at you. It's like I'm a little mad ... and a little scared ... I don't know.

Therapist: You've described similar feelings when you would try to get your father interested in what you were doing.

Patient: Yeah ... something like that.

Therapist: You've also talked about feeling resistant when you felt a need to talk to one of your seniors at the law firm about litigation on which you were working. You've said you are uncomfortable and reluctant to discuss what you really think.

Patient: Yeah ... I guess the feelings are similar.

Therapist: If you couldn't talk openly with your father ... express yourself freely without bad results, is it possible that now as an adult you are repeating a pattern of self-protection with significant people in your life?

Patient: I don't know. What do you mean? (*tense*)

Therapist: As I've told you, psychotherapy tends to be a miniature representation of your life-style and experience. Learning in your early life to be resistant to being open and direct with your father may have become a style of not being open and direct with any person who might represent your father—such as your senior at the firm ... or me ...

Patient: (*long pause*) I sure feel funny.

Therapist: Tell me.

Patient: Well ... I want to tell you, I want to laugh ... but I'm a little sad ... and even a little weepy ... (*long pause*)

Therapist: If this pattern is true ... you resist being open, creative, or

even loving and love-seeking with important people in your life
because the risk of rejection and ridicule is too painful.

Patient: (*weeps softly*) He was a son-of-a-bitch . . . (*pause*) . . . All I
wanted was for him to *see* me and *know* I'd do almost anything for
him . . . (*weeps*) . . . I'm not sure how this relates to anything.

At this point the session was over. Significant material associated with
emotional pain or anxiety is often brought up at the end of the session to
express another form of resistance to discovery of long-hidden, painful
emotion.

A week later, the patient began his sessions by reporting portions of a
number of dreams. About halfway through the session, the patient
brought up the topic of his resistance during the previous session:

Patient: . . . (*pause*) . . . Last session was pretty confusing . . . I've
thought a lot about it . . .
Therapist: It seemed important to you.
Patient: Yeah . . . but confusing. Everything you said made sense. . . . At
first I was annoyed . . . or maybe suspicious. But . . . as I listened to
you and thought about it, I became more and more emotional.
Therapist: Uh huh . . .
Patient: I never did tell you what I wasn't able to talk about . . . I was
going to tell you about an experience with Mr. Jones, the senior
partner . . .
Therapist: The one who frightens you.
Patient: Yeah . . . that's what is odd. . . . Last week . . . I mean the week
before last, he came to my office to ask about a case I was working
on. I assumed he had something critical to say. I went over the file
and when I was finished I was actually sweating . . . My shirt was
wet. I don't know *what* I expected . . . but . . . he stood up and said
I'd done a great piece of work and that he enjoyed working with
me!
Therapist: A very welcome surprise.
Patient: Yeah . . . but when I came to my session, I did everything *but*
talk about that. . . . I even had some trouble today. . . . So . . . that
idea of resistance makes sense. That's what happened . . . but that's
stupid! To avoid something good like that . . .
Therapist: Perhaps avoiding something good so as to not be reminded of
something bad in the past.
Patient: Yeah . . . I have that funny feeling again. I guess my father is
still in my head.

Although an interpretation can focus on a specific incident in the patient's current life, this probative therapist activity enhances the patient's progress most when the interpretation includes the identification of a recapitulation pattern. The interpretation above includes all the elements of an enhancing venture by the therapist:

- The therapist's interpretation was made when *the patient was ready*.
- The interpretation focused on a *current, emotional experience* reported by the patient.
- The patient's behavior and response were *characteristic of a series of problem behaviors* spanning the patient's adult life.
- An *overarching concept* explained the "sense" of the neurotic behavior.
- The pattern was identified as a *recapitulation* of an important, powerful early experience.

Analysis of transference. Transference and resistance inevitably occur in dynamic psychotherapy. Theoretically or by definition, transference occurs when a patient endows another (the psychotherapist) with qualities, attitudes, expectancies, or debts of a figure (usually parental) from the patient's developmental years. The transference may be *positive* (strong father, warm mother, fair parent, protective older sibling). Transference can also be *negative* (abandoning, ignoring, jealous, seductive parent; jealous, critical, vindictive sibling; cruel parent surrogate). A little-discussed but often-found form of transference is *expectant* (almost unlimited provision of tolerance, support, reassurance, excusal, and downplaying of reality). *Expectant transference* includes all that patients feel is *owed* to them. The patient's unfilled needs and expectancies from childhood are *transferred* to the psychotherapist.

Transference relates to early experiences of great emotional significance which remain unsettled in the individual's personality. As one matures, one develops a great sensitivity to the reoccurrence of similar phenomena, giving the individual a chance to reexperience early emotions and perhaps resolve early conflicts. It is probable that recapitulation, the repetition of neurotic patterns over and over, presents the individual's willingness to sacrifice happiness and tranquility for an opportunity to deal with significant earlier conflicts. The following represents an example of this in therapy. Resistance transference and recapitulation all occur in this session where the patient integrates patterns of his life with what he has learned in psychotherapy:

Patient: I missed my last session on purpose. I really didn't want to come.

Therapist: Sometimes it's pretty frightening to anticipate therapy.

Patient: Yeah. . . . It wasn't as bad as usual, and I think this is the first time I've told you that I did it purposely. Usually I make some kind of an excuse, but I have the feeling you know that I really feel frightened of coming.

Therapist: A lot of people in therapy feel this way.

Patient: Sometimes, when I feel I'm not working very hard, I become uncomfortable and unhappy. . . . It's as though I feel that you have certain expectations for me and I am not meeting them. It's funny, but actually I almost create these things by being silent and missing sessions. . . . Huh! It's like I set up my own feelings of being unfavored.

Therapist: Have you had this feeling of "not doing what is expected" often?

Patient: Yes, I have . . . especially with my father. No matter what I did or, for that matter, what I do now, he always has a comment that leaves me feeling that I didn't quite do well enough.

Therapist: So, in some ways, talking in here about yourself is like talking with your father.

Patient: No, not really. I *know* that you don't make the kinds of judgments he does. . . . Yet, in a way, I'm afraid I'll do something to disappoint you.

Therapist: Although it may be less fearful, it's a similar kind of thing.

Patient: I guess it is. . . . I never thought of it that way, but, yes, I will create situations here where I'll suddenly say to myself, "He won't like this—why am I doing it?" I've never had an answer before, but I think I do now. . . . I'm not sure. In a way, it gives me a safer chance to deal with it than when I do it with my father. . . .

Therapist: So, you couldn't talk this way with your father.

Patient: Oh, my God, no! He would just find fault with that . . . I guess. . . .

Therapist: Why do you say "I guess"? Does this mean you're not sure?

Patient: You know, now that I think about it, it has been literally years since my father has been critical of me. As I think about how I've talked to you about it, I am acting as though it always happens and it really doesn't! It's as though, even though I don't like it to happen, I *need* it to happen.

Therapist: How does this *need* feel?

Patient: Well, it's hard to say, it's like I need to feel that I'm about to be criticized or that someone—like you—is starting to be critical of my not performing, and then I go through a whole series of self-accusations, little fits of anger, fears—a whole routine. Gee! I've been doing this since I was a kid.

Therapist: So, being here is not much difference from the way you were at home many years ago.

Patient: Yes and no. If home had been like this, I guess I wouldn't be doing this now. At home my thoughts and ideas were never very acceptable. At least, I didn't think they were . . . Gee! I didn't realize I'd been doing this in a pattern for so many years.

In this sequence, the psychotherapist helps the patient move toward integration with a combination of nonintrusive and probative responses. Encouragement, restatement of content, direct questions, and interpretations all occur. The patient develops insight as to his repetitious pattern of recreating painful experiences.

Interpretations of dreams. The use of dreams to understand human motivation has a history dating back to biblical times. The interpretation of dreams has been an important element of Freudian psychoanalysis. Psychotherapists of many theoretical persuasions view patients' dreams as behavior worth noting and using during the psychotherapeutic course.

There are many ways in which the psychotherapist may approach the interpretation of dreams. In a nonintrusive way, the therapist may simply await the report of dreams by the patient and encourage the patient to discuss dream content. The following took place during the 16th session of psychotherapy with a 42-year-old elementary school teacher. No structuring concerning dreams had been previously given by the psychotherapist:

Therapist: Well, how was your week?

Patient: You know—rush, rush, rush . . . never enough time.

Therapist: Um huh. . . .

Patient: Something though. . . . I had a dream. . . . Will we talk about dreams?

Therapist: As you wish. . . .

Patient: Well . . . I don't remember all of it. . . . I think it was on Tuesday night, no, Wednesday night . . . after the big storm. I dreamt that I was in my grandmother's old house . . . where I used to visit. . . . I was in her bed . . . very frightened. . . . I used to crawl in with her when I was small. . . . I felt that "something" was coming . . . to get me. . . . That was all. Then I woke up. . . . (*long pause*)

Therapist: How did you feel about the dream?

Patient: Then or now?

Therapist: Either one.
Patient: Well, when I woke up I was still frightened. Now . . . gee . . . it
seems to me that I've had dreams like that before.
Therapist: Frightening.
Patient: Yes . . . usually. (*long pause*)

The therapist chose to allow the patient to set the pace. No interpretation takes place. The patient chooses to pursue or not to pursue the meaning of the dream.

Whether or not a psychotherapist has been trained and supervised in
dream analysis, it is likely that most patients will bring up the question of
dreams and their place in the psychotherapeutic process. Those who practice dynamic psychotherapy of any sort should expect this and be prepared to respond to patients' reports of dreams. Dreams generally involve
strong emotional responses. Hall (1984) has written:

> Whether dreams are analyzed by free association, amplification, ex-
> istential analysis or content analysis, they supply a rich source of
> information about the structure, dynamics, development and ab-
> normalities of human personality. They visualize that which is in-
> visible. Dreams are the kaleidoscope of the mind. (p. 390)

All psychotherapists should be familiar with the concept of dream interpretation. Reading in the basic literature on this subject is important
so that the psychotherapist can make informed choices about dealing
with dream material during psychotherapeutic sessions (Freud, 1960;
Hadfield, 1954; Mahl, 1971; Hall, 1966; Hall & Van de Castle, 1966;
Hall, 1984).

Some psychotherapists prefer to prepare or structure their patients for
dream material, suggesting that dreams and their meaning are important
elements of the therapeutic process. The following illustrates such a
structuring in a first session:

Therapist: As you proceed with psychotherapy, you are probably going
to remember your dreams with greater frequency.
Patient: I don't dream.
Therapist: Many believe this because dreams are often "forgotten."
Dreams frequently represent important areas of conflict in our lives.
Dreaming seems to relieve some of the pressure of these conflicts.
The dream is then "forgotten" so that we can have some relief, yet
not have to face these threatening conflicts.
Patient: I just don't remember dreams . . . at least since I was a kid.

Therapist: Many people feel that way. As you become more comfortable in your therapy, you are likely to remember some of your dreams. When this happens, if you discuss them during your session, we will try to use your dreams to help you understand yourself better.

The above patient, a 48-year-old businesswoman suffering recurrent depression who was in therapy with a 68-year-old female therapist, reported her first dream at the end of the 12th session as follows:

Patient: Oh yes! I had a dream! Finally.

Therapist: You seem pleased.

Patient: Well . . . I really believed I didn't dream. . . . (*long pause*) . . . It wasn't much. . . . I was driving down a dirt road past an old, old house . . . I was apprehensive . . . and I don't remember anything else.

Therapist: In the beginning of therapy, dreams tend to be remembered as fragments. Later you'll probably dream more about what this dream may have meant. . . . Well, our time is up today.

Early in psychotherapy, patients tend to report dreams at the end of the session. This may be an unconscious effort at self-protection by the patient in order to avoid exploration of painful ideas. It may represent a testing of limits to see if the psychotherapist will adhere to "the rules" as to the length of the session. The session should not be extended to explore a dream. Some psychotherapists routinely avoid interpreting the first dream. In the session following, the psychotherapist chooses to bring up and explore the first reported dream:

Therapist: Last week you reported the first dream you've remembered in a long time.

Patient: I did? Oh, yeah! About the old house. . . . I'd forgotten.

Therapist: Did you recognize the house?

Patient: No, not really . . . but something was familiar. . . .

Therapist: The house was the focus of your attention?

Patient: Yes. . . . That was the dream.

Therapist: When did you have the dream?

Patient: The night before my last session, I believe. . . .

Therapist: Dreams the night before a therapy session sometimes represent feelings about the therapy. . . .

Patient: I don't see anything about that dream that has anything to do with you or the therapy.

Therapist: Mm . . . tell me about the house. . . .

Patient: I don't know.... It was pretty elegant, but old.... I was afraid.... I don't know why....

Therapist: Houses in dreams sometimes symbolize people.... The house is seen as representative of "mother" in many cultures.

Patient: I can see that. I always thought of our house and my mother.... Sometimes I still do.... (*begins to weep softly*).... Sorry.... (*long pause*)

Therapist: I believe you told me your mother died two or three years ago.

Patient: Three years next month. (*continues to weep*)

Therapist: You still miss her.

Patient: Oh ... well ... yes.

Therapist: She was ill before she died?

Patient: Yes, it was terrible.... She was such a lovely, elegant person, but she deteriorated from the cancer....

Therapist: Like the elegant house?

Patient: Oh my! ... Is that it?

Therapist: What do you feel?

Patient: Oh ... heavy and light—very funny—oh my! ... So that house could be my mother and I was fearful about her deteriorating?

Therapist: How does that seem?

Patient: OK.... Yeah....

Therapist: Could the dream also be connected with therapy?

Patient: How do you mean?

Therapist: You had the dream the night before your session?

Patient: Yes....

Therapist: Could anything in the dream represent your therapy or therapist?

Patient: I don't know.... (*pause*).... Sometimes you remind me of my mother.... (*pause*).... That's a little embarrassing.

Therapist: Do you worry about me sometimes?

Patient: (*long pause*).... Well ... I had this thought.... I'm embarrassed ... like ... well ... what if you became ill ... or retired.... (*long pause*)

Therapist: And perhaps left you as your mother did?

Patient: (*cries... then begins to laugh*) I know it's not funny but I feel funny about all this. I certainly never talked this way with my mother....

Therapist: Yes.... It is different in therapy.

Few inexperienced psychotherapists would or could present an interpretation of this patient's dream so quickly and effectively. The psychotherapist's gender, age, and experience all supported this aggressive approach.

Dreams (as well as slips of the tongue and most fantasies) involve both *manifest,* or direct, information and *latent,* or symbolic, hidden content. Patients' needs and fears (the essence of maladjustment and the driving energy of psychotherapy) often appear directly or symbolically in dream material. The following dream was reported during her 23rd session by the 48-year-old businesswoman to our experienced psychotherapist:

Patient: I dreamt last night that I was with my daughter. She was much younger than she is now. We came to a long iron staircase. We started down and I became extremely frightened. Suddenly she broke away and seemed to be acting dangerously. The scene shifted, and I saw her running to meet a man and things seemed better. I had my left hand, however, stuck in the iron staircase. I was afraid to pull it out directly, and I'm not sure why. . . . (*long pause*)

Therapist: What sort of thoughts do you have about the dream?

Patient: Well, it felt good and it felt bad. I have no idea what the iron staircase meant. The only person I recognized was my daughter, but she was much younger.

Therapist: The manifest or the direct content told you that this dream involves you and your daughter and a man that you do not recognize. Is that correct?

Patient: That's right.

Therapist: Do you recognize any symbols in the dream?

Patient: The staircase seems important, I mean the iron stairs.

Therapist: You called it a staircase and then iron stairs?

Patient: Well, the iron stairs seemed much colder and more rigid than a stairway.

Therapist: Frequently in dreams, the staircase represents the sexual act. Does this help in understanding the meaning of the dream.

Patient: I don't know. . . . Why would it involve my daughter?

Therapist: Have you ever had a deep concern about your daughter's sexuality during her earlier years, were you ever frightened as you were in the dream?

Patient: . . . . Yes. . . . When she was a teenager, she almost got into trouble sexually. . . . It was just like in the dream. I was frightened . . . terribly frightened, but it worked out.

Therapist: Often in a dream there's something old, something new, and wish fulfillment. Is there anything in the dream that represents a recent event?

Patient: I don't know. . . . Recently my daughter's father has appeared on the scene, and has been showing her some attention. I think this is good for her. . . . Could the man in the dream that I didn't recognize be her father acting in a different way?

Therapist: How does that feel?

Patient: That feels right . . . but why was my hand stuck in the stairway?

Therapist: If a stairway is sexual behavior, could an iron stairway be cold, rigid sexuality?

Patient: That's certainly the way I've always looked at my own sexual response.

Therapist: Which of your hands was caught in the stairway?

Patient: The left hand. . . . Oh yes! Left is feminine and right is masculine! I remember that from another dream interpretation. Am I afraid to let go of my cold sexual response? Is that possible? Feels right. . . .

Although no symbol is absolute, the therapist must use his or her judgment in making these kinds of suggestions.

It is far beyond the scope of this book to teach dream analysis. The references cited previously will help inexperienced psychotherapists to learn more about this interpretive technique. Without formal training in dream interpretation, it would be wise for the inexperienced psychotherapist to explore dream material in the least probative way. A sequence of interpretive ventures can include:

- Simple acceptance.
- Encouragement to explore feelings, to identify places and persons which appear in the dream and questions regarding symbols.
- Relating the dream to the day preceding.

If the patient does not pursue an exploration of the dream spontaneously, yet seems fairly comfortable, the psychotherapist may use moderately intrusive questions to encourage the patient, as follows:

Patient: Last night I dreamt that I was a young child and I was at a zoo with an older person. That's all I remember. . . .

Therapist: Um hum. . . . (*pause*). . . . How did you feel in the dream?

Patient: Oh . . . I don't know . . . more like I was watching myself when I was younger. . . . (*pause*)

Therapist: Was the zoo or anything familiar to you?

Patient: No . . . not exactly. . . . Maybe the weather. It seemed to be cold

and bleak. . . . I grew up in Michigan. It was often like that. . . .
(*pause*)

Therapist: Did you recognize the person you were with?

Patient: Not really—just a vague feeling it was an older
woman . . . maybe like a grandmother. . . . (*pause*)

Therapist: Your grandmother?

Patient: I don't know. . . . Maybe. . . . I don't remember my grand-
mothers. Both died when I was young. One when I was two and the
other I think when I was six. . . . (*pause*)

Therapist: Was there anything that struck you as unusual that appeared
in the dream?

Patient: (*pause*) I was wearing mittens. . . . I guess it was cold. . . . I
don't know (*somewhat tense*). . . . (*long pause*). . . .

Therapist: Do you remember what night you had the dream?

Patient: I guess it was Sunday night. . . . Let's see—yes . . . we had the
birthday dinner for my mother Sunday. I had the dream that night.

Therapist: Tell me all that went on that day. . . .

Patient: Well . . . nothing much. . . . We went to church and then spent
the afternoon getting ready for my mother's birthday dinner. It's a
tradition. I always prepare it and my sisters and brothers come
over. . . .

Therapist: And your mother?

Patient: Oh yes! She'll be 82. I've always made her birthday dinner. She
loves for me to fuss over her. She always has. There were five of us
and I was the oldest. . . . She never had time to do things and I
always helped her. She says she doesn't want a fuss made over
her . . . but she does. . . . (*long pause*)

Therapist: That must be difficult for you at times.

Patient: Well . . . yes and no. . . . She can be demanding but . . . well,
I'm the oldest and she expects it. . . .

Therapist: Did she ever take you to the zoo?

Patient: Oh no! She was too busy to take us anywhere. . . . The only time
I ever went to a zoo was with my best friend and her family. . . . They
once invited me on a trip with them to Chicago. . . . I seem to
remember that one thing we did was to visit the zoo. It wasn't too
much fun. . . . It was cold . . . but the rest was fun. . . . We stayed in
a hotel and my friend and I had a room to ourselves. It was such lux-
ury . . . our own bathroom! At home there were seven of us . . . and
one bathroom! I remember that trip.

Therapist: It was a real contrast to your everyday life.

Patient: Oh my, yes. . . . I guess life on the farm was not all peaches and
cream.

This sequence developed as a result of sequential dream exploration by a relatively inexperienced psychotherapist. He responded to the patient with *simple acceptance,* and after it was clear that the patient would not continue spontaneously, the psychotherapist encouraged the patient to explore feelings and to identify places and symbols in the dream. Finally, the psychotherapist's request that the patient relate the events of the day preceding the dream resulted in a flood of rich memories of a very positive experience which had occurred during the patient's rather stark and demanding childhood. Although no specific interpretations were made which related the dream to significant events or patterns in the patient's life, the dream interpretation efforts by the psychotherapist enhanced the session.

Interpretation of parapraxes. Slips of the tongue often present an opportunity for patients to explore hidden or conflicted aspects of their lives and personality (Freud, 1968/1901). These "slips" are more likely to occur as patients come closer to experiencing inner conflicts. Parapraxes can be interpreted more directly than dreams since they frequently "say what the patient means." They usually appear after the patient has moved beyond the initial phases of therapy, is relatively comfortable in the psychotherapeutic session, and has had some successful incidents of experiencing.

The psychotherapist can enhance the process by asking the patient to first acknowledge the parapraxis. If the patient did not hear his or her slip of the tongue, or rejects the idea, some structuring may be helpful. This usually occurs at the first instance of a parapraxis. Later in the psychotherapeutic process, patients seem to accept their parapraxes as opportunities.

Patient: So I thought that if I just hang around with guys who know what they're doing . . . you know . . . seem to have social skills . . . I'd be more comfortable.

Therapist: You might learn from them. . . .

Patient: Yeah . . . This one guy at work . . . the women are crazy about him. He has more than he can use. I asked him to go fishing with me Saturday. He's never been deep sea fishing . . . so I told him to bring two holes . . . er . . . poles and we'd go. So we're going. . . .

Therapist: You said "two holes."

Patient: Did I? I meant two poles. . . . Everybody sets two or three lines on these trips. . . . I meant *two poles.*

Therapist: Everyone has "slips of the tongue". . . . Sometimes they're of little meaning. In psychotherapy such slips are called "parapraxes." They are symbolic, like dreams, but usually much more direct. It's like a gift from the unconscious. It means that the thing we say instead of what we meant to say is an unconscious intention. You meant to say "bring two poles" but instead—what did you say?

Patient: Uh . . . I forgot! Gee—that's odd!

Therapist: Not really. That often happens. The unconscious intention is often hidden. You said, "Bring two holes."

Patient: Oh yeah—I meant "two poles". . . .

Therapist: If you allowed the sentence to stand as "bring two holes," what might that mean?

Patient: I don't know . . . gee . . . that's sort of silly. . . . I, uh . . . that's embarrassing . . . like . . . I'd want him to bring two women—huh! . . . Yeah. . . . So I was saying what I *really* wanted—for him to help me get a woman. . . . Yeah . . . I guess that's true. . . . That's pretty strange!

Unconscious intentions are expressed in all sorts of slips of the tongue, forgetting, and misplacement of familiar items. Extensive descriptions of these behaviors can be found in the standard editions of basic psychoanalytic literature (Freud, 1962).

Interpretation of gestures. Facial expressions, body posture, and gestures can all be channels for communication of feeling. Such communications are not always clear and the psychotherapist must be cautious in identifying and interpreting muscular messages.

In the following segment, a patient sits with her hands tightly clenched into fists:

Patient: I know he was probably right. I did not treat him as well as I could, so I can't really blame him for leaving me for another woman.

Therapist: You feel no blame or anger.

Patient: Not really. He's always told me that 95% of our conflict was my fault and if I'd do my part, he'd do his. (*fists clenched even more tightly*)

Therapist: So you're not angry or resentful?

Patient: Not really. . . . I could have shaped up and prevented it.

Therapist: Look at your hands.

Patient: . . . . What? (*opens hands and rubs them to restore circulation*)

Therapist: What were you doing with your hands while you were telling
me you are not angry with your husband?
Patient: Well . . . I . . . uh. . . . *(laughs weakly)* I guess I was a little tense
and was clenching my fists.
Therapist: What does it mean when someone clenches a fist?
Patient: Usually, uh . . . I guess they're mad. . . . *(long pause)*

In the following exchange, a gesture commonly observed during psychotherapy is interpreted by imitation. A 41-year-old man suffering depression is discussing his wife:

Patient: Sometimes I wonder why I ever married. I seem to get more
pressure at home than I do at work. . . . I guess it was . . . I don't
know. I *do* love my wife. *(shaking head from side to side as he
says this)*
Therapist: So you love her in spite of the pressures you feel she puts on
you.
Patient: Yeah. . . . *(continuing to shake his head in a negative
gesture).* . . . I guess I still love her. . . .
Therapist: Let me repeat *what* you said, *as* you said it. "I love my wife."
(shaking head from side to side) "I guess I still love her."
Patient: Oh, my! . . . Did I do that? *(smile on face)* I mean. . . . Oh,
my! . . . Does that mean I'm saying "No" while I'm saying
"Yes"?
Therapist: Does it feel that way?
Patient: *(pause)* I guess it's true . . . uh . . . sometimes I *don't* love her.

Such *interpretations* are intrusive responses by the psychotherapist
and should not be used early in the psychotherapeutic course.

Confrontations

The most probative responses which can be made by psychotherapists
directly challenge the patient to judge, experience, and decide. Such responses present opportunities which ordinarily provoke much anxiety in
the patient. Confrontations must not be a routine response choice. They
should occur at opportune moments in psychotherapy where the patient
has already provided all the pieces and it is clearly time to put together a
matrix of ideas and emotion. The psychotherapist must be sure these
segments explain a significant, long-standing conflicted behavior or
reasoning process in the patient's life. Some common and uncommon
confrontation techniques will be considered.

Paradoxical intention. This technique addresses behavior or emotion which patients suggest is involuntary. The technique instructs the patient to *emphasize* or *elaborate* a bothersome idea or symptom. In effect, the patient is asked to practice the neurotic behavior or thought in order to test reality and gain control of the behavior. This procedure raises cognitive dissonance, increasing the patient's opportunity to choose alternate thoughts or behaviors (Kercher & Smith, 1985).

In the following example, a 32-year-old bookkeeper in his 85th session obsessively discusses doubts about his relationship with his mother. This same topic has appeared frequently, in almost the same manner, with little or no experiencing. The psychotherapist chooses to intervene with a paradoxical technique:

Patient: I can't believe my mother cares for me. . . . It's the same. I'll call her and she just rambles on about nothing. I'm late again in sending a birthday present. I know that's a way I have of showing how angry I am. I don't believe she really cares for me at all. . . .

Therapist: You are correct of course. You should listen to yourself and see that she doesn't care. She is not like a mother at all. Instead of getting a present late, she should get no present at all. . . . She doesn't deserve your caring since she doesn't care for you.

Patient: (*long pause*) Hmm . . . I don't know. . . .

Therapist: Of course you do. . . . You've told us time after time. It must be true. She deserves no present at all. . . .

Patient: Well . . . I guess I've never really thought of it that way. I've been mad but I never really *got* mad. I guess I *want* her to deserve a present from me . . . by doing things for me I deserve. I guess I haven't done much to bring this about. I've just been kind of waiting for something good to happen.

The purpose of the technique is to allow the patient to see what he is doing (or not doing) to continue and maintain the neurotic thinking. By clarifying and intensifying the dissonance in the patient's behavior, the opportunities for decision-making become more clearly apparent.

In the following portion of the 50th session with a painfully shy man of 28, the psychotherapist decides to use a paradoxical intention technique to increase the patient's awareness of an insoluble conflict and of the potential for choice-making:

Patient: I just can't play the game right. There are lots of girls I meet at work or at the spa where I work out. . . . I think about ways of being friendly or asking them out. . . . I just can't do it. . . . It's too frightening. . . . (*long pause*)

Therapist: This has been happening for some years. You want to communicate with these girls but you think they will reject or embarrass you. It must be true. . . . They will. . . . They'll ridicule you or laugh at you. . . .

Patient: Well I don't *know* that.

Therapist: You must assume it. You wouldn't have spent years thinking about being rejected if you didn't have good reason.

Patient: Well . . . they haven't.

Therapist: But imagine what one of the girls you've been interested in at work might say. . . .

Patient: Well . . . I don't know. . . . Maybe, "I'm busy."

Therapist: No. . . . Think of it as you've feared it at the worst. She'd laugh at you—ridicule you—say that you're too funny looking, a nerd.

Patient: Hey! It couldn't be that bad!

Therapist: Why not?

Patient: Well . . . that's extreme . . . but I guess I feel "extreme."

Therapist: Say it. . . . "If I ask a girl to have lunch with me, she'll laugh, ridicule, call me stupid."

Patient: . . . . I, uh. . . . If I ask a girl to have lunch with me, she'll laugh, ridicule, call me stupid . . . uh . . .

Therapist: A nerd, ugly. . . .

Patient: A nerd . . . uh, ugly. . . . (*laughs*). . . . *This* is stupid. (*laughs*)

The technique of paradoxical intention can be applied to alleviate pressure, invalidate neurotic premises, or make unacceptable actions conscious (Frankl, 1960).

Posed hypothetical choices. This probative confrontation response can be used by the psychotherapist to help the patient gauge the depth and extent of feelings in conflict situations where the patient uses evasion or denial to avoid focusing on important emotions.

This is illustrated in the case of a young man who has had multiple contacts with various females, never allowing himself to become "emotionally involved." In fact, he had been deeply involved with three females over a period of 12 years. His pattern has been to meet a new female and "fall in love" during a series of brief but intense encounters. During the most current of these, in the third week of their relationship, the woman decided to go on a week's vacation. The patient suspects that she is meeting another man. As she leaves, he says to her, "I will miss you." Reporting this in psychotherapy, he says that this was a "maneuver":

Patient: As she was getting on the plane, I said, "I'll miss you". . . . (*long pause*)

Therapist: I have the feeling that this was not so much a statement as an invitation.

Patient: You're right! I was hoping she would say, "I'm going to miss you, too." That would be important.

About two weeks later, the patient came to his session. He started as follows:

Patient: My first thought was, "I've missed you". . . . (*long pause*)

Therapist: Do you have some feelings about that?

Patient: Just that I "missed you." Nothing really important.

Therapist: Do you recall saying the very same thing in another situation recently?

Patient: No, I don't. . . . (*defensive*)

Therapist: Remember what you said when Jane was leaving?

Patient: Yes, now I remember. I told you that I said, "I'll miss you" at the airport. I was giving her an invitation to say, "I missed you, too." Is that what I want from you?

Therapist: Did you want very much to have Jane say that she missed you?

Patient: Yes, very much.

Therapist: Do you suppose you very much want me to say that I missed you?

Patient: I don't really know . . . maybe.

Therapist: Suppose you are offered a choice. You could say the same thing to Jane and the same thing to me. Which one, if you had only one choice, would you want to say, "I missed you too"?

Patient: You . . . you by a hundred miles!

The posed hypothetical choice used a situation reported by the patient to allow him to experience, judge, weigh, and value a transference experience occurring during the psychotherapeutic session.

In the following situation, our 32-year-old bookkeeper in his 89th session is helped to face the extent of his internalized rage by a posed hypothetical choice:

Patient: Of course it wasn't fair. . . . I'd worked very hard on that report and Mr. Brown just said, "I don't think we'll use this." No explanation or apology.

Therapist: You must have been mad. . . .

Patient: No . . . not really mad . . . disappointed.

Therapist: He asked for the report, set a deadline, made you work overtime, then simply threw your work aside and you're not mad?

Patient: Well . . . I don't see it as mad . . . perhaps unfair.

Therapist: If you could, magically, have two buttons—red and green: If you push the red one, the president of your company would call Mr. Brown tomorrow and tell him he's doing a good job; if you push the green one, the president would call and tell Mr. Brown he is a nit-picking, critical nincompoop and if he doesn't shape up, he's going to have to wear a dunce cap at the office for a week. Which would you pick?

Patient: (*laughing*) Oh my. . . . Wouldn't that be something! (*laughs at length . . . wipes a tear from his eye*) I guess I'd be really tempted to push the green button. (*laughs*) It might do him some good. . . .

Therapist: Would it do *you* some good?

Patient: (*long pause*). . . . Yeah. . . . I guess I'm really mad at him. . . . I've been mad at him a long time.

Flooding. This is a technique used to help delineate and then extinguish maladaptive responses to aversive stimuli. The purpose is to confront the patient with a feared concept. Where the exposure is to stimuli symbolic of unconscious conflicts, the technique may be called *implosive therapy.* In its mildest form, flooding may be instituted with a "Say it again" technique. This is done by the psychotherapist in the following illustration:

Patient: I was so mad I could have said . . . no, I guess I couldn't.

Therapist: You were going to say . . .

Patient: Well . . . I can't tell my mother, "Go to hell."

Therapist: Say it again.

Patient: "Go to hell."

Therapist: Say it some more.

Patient: "Go to hell. . . . Go to hell. . . . *GO TO HELL!*" . . . (*weeps*). . . .

Therapist: You've thought that a lot.

Patient: . . . . Yes. . . . (*continues to cry*)

Therapist: And that is something you've said your father could not do.

Patient: What?

Therapist: Confront your mother honestly. . . .

Patient: Oh yes. . . . (*continues to cry*). . . .

Therapist: So you have been repeating a pattern . . . recapitulating your father's ways.

Patient: . . . . Yes. . . .

In a more implosive style, a 58-year-old depressed patient, having described during many sessions his strong attachment to his married daughter and his inability to show this because of unnamed, unspecified fears, is confronted by the psychotherapist as follows:

Therapist: So you can't hug or kiss your daughter.

Patient: No.

Therapist: You're afraid.

Patient: I guess—but I don't know.

Therapist: In group therapy, some of your fellow group members suggested you might at times have had sexual feelings about your daughter.

Patient: Yes. . . . That was disgusting! I've read about this but I can't believe it!

Therapist: In describing the females you've sexualized during business trips, you've said they are "young, slim, blond, perky, cute."

Patient: Well, yes. . . .

Therapist: Is your daughter "young, slim, blond, perky, cute"?

Patient: Well, yes . . . but sex with my daughter . . . unthinkable!

Therapist: Think of it. . . .

Patient: No! . . . I . . . uh, can't.

Therapist: Think of the time you told me about your business trip to England and the blond daughter of your host came into your room in the middle of the night.

Patient: That was different.

Therapist: She looked like your daughter?

Patient: Yes. . . .

Therapist: Imagine she was.

Patient: Oh, my God! I'm getting nauseated! I can't!

Therapist: Think it again!

Patient: This is painful. . . . (*sobs*) Oh my. . . .

Three sessions later, the patient reported remembering a dream in which he was sexually stirred while tussling with both his daughter and granddaughter.

The variety of confrontative techniques possible in psychotherapy is limited only by the creativity and experience of the psychotherapist. Confrontation is a powerful psychotherapeutic intervention, but it must be used intelligently and with caution. Unless used when the patient has become comfortable and trusting, and with material or ideas previously considered by the patient, serious barriers to continuing psychotherapy can easily occur. Early or frequent use of confrontation is ill-advised.

MAKING THE RIGHT CHOICE

The psychotherapist's third task—enhancing the patient's progress—requires and reflects the sum total of professional education, training, and experience. Whether the patient's progress is enhanced or disrupted depends on the psychotherapist's skill in choosing and providing interventions appropriate to the patient's level of security and readiness for experiencing. To be effective, the psychotherapist must continually ask:

- Is there a covert as well as overt message in what the patient says?
- What theme is being presented or suggested?
- Is the patient ready?
- Is there a therapist response which is most likely to encourage experiencing?
- If the patient is not ready to experience, can a less intrusive response be made that will help the patient become *aware* of some important pattern in his or her life?

Table 5 presents a general sequence of appropriate psychotherapist activity.

In order to monitor patient responses with sensitive awareness, the psychotherapist must constantly listen and observe. The patient's messages may be direct, covert, or symbolic. Before an appropriate response can be made, the psychotherapist must consider:

- *At what level is the manifest response?* Does the patient's message appear to be at the intellectual, experiencing, or integrative level?
- *How vulnerable is the patient?* Does the patient appear to be unusually tense? The psychotherapist must take care not to destroy the sanctuary by making threatening and intrusive responses to the patient's tentative explorations. The therapist must always be concerned as to whether the patient is ready to face covert or symbolic meanings.
- *Does the patient's response recapitulate an early or consistent life*

TABLE 5

Appropriate Therapist Activity at Various Stages of Psychotherapy

Stage of Psychotherapy	Patient's State of Vulnerability	Patient's Primary Focus of Response	Appropriate Therapist Intervention
Beginning	Threatened	Intellectualization	Nonintrusive responses
Early	Some sense of security	Intellectualizaton & some experiencing	Nonintrusive & some moderately intrusive responses
Mid-Stages	A backlog of security & stress tolerance	Experiencing	Moderately intrusive & probative activity
End Stages	Secure and strong positive attitudes toward self	Experiencing & integration	Probative & nonintrusive responses

pattern? From the first session on, the psychotherapist should attempt to identify the patterns of the patient's behavior which repeatedly express and maintain the neurotic balance. In this painful adjustment, the patient is a victim of his or her own arrangements. The psychotherapist must first verbalize such patterns to the patient. Though often rejected at first, these patterns can later in the psychotherapy be associated by the patient with experiences and circumstances remembered from the developmental years.

With training and experience the psychotherapist learns to listen with greater sensitivity to what the patient says, as well as to gauge the emotional state of the sayer. Each patient will choose a unique pathway through the psychotherapeutic process. The experienced and skillful psychotherapist molds the procedures and tradecraft of therapy to the communication mode, interactional style, and emotional state presented by the patient. This not only minimizes threat but ensures that the therapeutic process is truly a product of the patient's own doing.

CHAPTER 8

Identifying, Diverting, and Rehabilitating Psychotherapeutic Errors and Barriers

Psychotherapeutic errors and barriers are those behaviors and occurrences which needlessly delay or interfere with the patient's progress toward self-understanding. All psychotherapists, from beginner to master hand, must accept fallibility as a part of psychotherapeutic practice. This acceptance is a necessary precedent to any kind of prevention, intervention, or postvention. To reject the idea that mistakes occur in all psychotherapeutic ventures is to be insensitive to such occurrences. Under such conditions of unawareness or narcissism, the psychotherapist is more likely to ignore or compound therapeutic errors.

No complete outline of error classes is possible. Each therapist and each patient is capable of creating new styles and classes of behavior which can interfere with the therapeutic process.

Psychotherapeutic errors, or pitfalls, may be characterized as either *avoidable* or *inevitable*. Avoidable errors are those committed by the psychotherapist. These include such behaviors as intimacy with the patient, accepting gifts from the patient without examining the dynamic meaning of the gift, or frequently canceling the patient's regular appointment. These behaviors are therapeutic errors. Some tend to occur in one form or another with every psychotherapist over a long professional career. Repetition of avoidable errors suggests a deficit in the psychotherapist's skill, competence, or personality and should be subject to evaluation and resolution as early as possible.

Some barriers or pitfalls are inevitable in all dynamic psychotherapy. These are often labeled resistance or transference. Patients demonstrate needs, wants, and a neurotic life-style by creating in the therapeutic setting miniatures, or models, of the ways in which they have developed and learned to cope with life. Falling in love with the psychotherapist, nit-picking criticism of the psychotherapist, and forgetting appointment times of sessions are common forms of inevitable pitfalls or barriers to therapeutic progress. They can be opportunities for the psychotherapist to help the patient move forward in self-evaluation and understanding. Inevitable patient barriers which are ignored or improperly perceived or resolved mechanically by the therapist represent therapists' errors indicating deficiencies in training, experience or personality.

Avoiding or ignoring inevitable errors is common among inexperienced or poorly trained psychotherapists. Patients create barriers as hesitancies to begin the exploration of painful areas of their lives or to demonstrate their neurotic style of responding to conflict. These conflicts are as frequently fears of success as of failure. The effective psychotherapist must recognize and accept these as opportunities to help the patient resolve barriers and move forward in the therapeutic process.

A detailed exploration of *patient barriers, psychotherapeutic errors,* and *external barriers* (disruptive events not instigated by the patient or the psychotherapist) follows.

PATIENT BARRIERS

No experienced psychotherapist believes that the process is easy or comfortable for the patient. Giving up (or even revealing) a neurotic life-style is often painful and frequently embarrassing. In this context, the word *barrier* will be used to describe those things done by the patient which impede, delay or abort the process of psychotherapy in order to avoid painful awareness or to maintain tenuous but seemingly safe neurotic adjustments. The concept of *therapeutic error* will be reserved for those acts of omission or commission knowingly or inadvertently done by psychotherapists which interfere with therapeutic progress.

The things which patients do to impede progress in psychotherapy can be described in a variety of terms. The concepts of *resistance* and *transference* have already been considered in Chapter 6 and 7. In order to help the psychotherapist conceptualize things which patients do which will slow or stop progress in psychotherapy, these will be considered under the headings of *mechanical, defensive,* and *confrontational* patient barriers. These categories are not mutually exclusive but are presented in this way for illustrative purposes.

Mechanical Barriers

Those behaviors by patients which at first seem ordinary requests, social interactions or omissions, and which can interfere with the psychotherapist's efforts to create a sanctuary and preserve the patient-psychotherapist alliance are mechanical barriers. Some of the more commonly occurring forms of this will be described in some detail.

Telephone consultations. In its usual form, this barrier is raised when a patient insists on contacting the therapist outside of the scheduled appointment time. The reasons may range from "I just have a question" to "I am so upset I can't wait until our next session." The psychotherapist who responds to these invitations without evaluating the deeper meaning of this subtle barrier to therapeutic progress can expect such calls to continue and begin to substitute for the patient's commitment to therapeutic work during regularly scheduled sessions. This barrier must be dealt with early and directly by the psychotherapist.

Social invitations. The psychotherapist may be invited directly or receive an invitation in the mail to an event important to the patient. The patient may even get someone to invite the psychotherapist to a social gathering the patient plans to attend. Since any interaction between the patient and the psychotherapist outside of regularly scheduled sessions is very likely to interfere with the therapeutic process, the psychotherapist is safe in assuming that such invitations should be avoided, but discussed during a regular therapy session.

Gifts. An extremely bad psychotherapist in a large community is known for his unique approach to the Christmas season. He puts up two large folding tables in his consulting room to hold all the gifts given to him by his patients. Gifts represent strong patient feelings, sometimes affection, sometimes guilt or even fear. Such patient behavior must be handled in a therapeutic manner. The psychotherapist who receives gifts regularly from patients may be encouraging this through one or more therapeutic errors. Even the rare gift must be viewed as a mechanical barrier which should be given appropriate attention during the psychotherapeutic session.

Requests to tape sessions. The request to tape a psychotherapeutic session is relatively uncommon. It is sometimes suggested by obsessional patients who view psychotherapy as a mining operation. The tape is an opportunity for them to dig obsessively for a mythical nugget of wisdom.

The wish to record the therapeutic session can represent other forms of transference or resistance. The motive of the patient in wanting to preserve a moment or all of the psychotherapeutic process must be explored. Allowing the patient to raise this barrier is to encourage the patient to believe that the usual and customary process of psychotherapy is in some way insufficient or that the patient is not capable of using the psychotherapeutic process as it is presented.

Failure to pay. Although the matter of fees has been discussed in considerable detail before psychotherapy begins (see Chapter 5), the issue of money and its meaning to the patient usually appears several times during the psychotherapeutic course. Changes in the patient's financial status may require discussion and fee adjustments. These should be minor issues. Failure to pay at previously agreed times is a powerful message of resistance. This mechanical barrier should be addressed as early as possible and thus requires that the psychotherapist be constantly aware of the account balance of each patient. This barrier can represent dependency issues, transferred anger, or fear of success. The barrier may be a recapitulation of the patient's life-style (or even a family pattern).

Missed appointments. Whether patients "forget" their appointments (for which they should be charged) or cancel appointments with any degree of regularity, the meanings of such behavior can be important for the psychotherapeutic process. More often than not, such barriers represent fear of further exploration. The fear may be related to loss of real-life dependency or to creation of a new dependency within the psychotherapeutic relationship. Forgetting or canceling appointments may be an effort on the part of the patient to "cool" the psychotherapeutic process as experiencing begins to occur during the sessions. Cancellations and forgotten appointments can represent self-sabotage in patients whose neurotic life-styles include fear of success (Pappo, 1983).

Premature termination. Patients who terminate prematurely are more frequently of a different ethnic group than the therapist, are under 35 years of age, are referred by an associated professional person, and have all of their therapy fees paid by insurance. Presenting complaints of early terminators are most frequently family or marital discord. Extensively trained and experienced psychotherapists have fewer patients who terminate prematurely than therapists of moderate training and experience (Greenspan & Kulish, 1985). In some settings, as many as one-third of all psychotherapy patients terminate prematurely. Those who have had previous mental health treatment seem more likely to withdraw from therapy prematurely (Hoffman, 1985).

Premature termination is the strongest barrier a patient can raise to continuing psychotherapy. This barrier precludes a face-to-face discussion between therapist and patient in most instances. Even in those rare instances when the patient announces his or her intention to "quit" during a therapeutic session, the tone of finality is clear. Although resolution of the barrier is possible, in most instances the responsibility of the psychotherapist is to ensure that the separation is made as comfortable as possible for the patient, with the door left open to resume psychotherapy in the future.

Resolving mechanical barriers

Although mechanical barriers to therapeutic progress may superficially seem to lack dynamic significance, these occurrences must be treated as important material for the psychotherapeutic process. Such barriers are communications of patients' fears, wishes, fantasies, manipulations, and other emotional maneuvers. The psychotherapist must not ignore or criticize this behavior. The barrier must be taken as a message, and the psychotherapist must then respond within the context of the psychotherapeutic process. The sequence to be followed in working with patient barriers and impediments is as follows:

- Accept the behavior as a message.
- Where possible, clarify feelings.
- If appropriate, encourage exploration and experiencing.
- Where resolution does not occur, set limits by structuring.
- Follow structuring with additional encouragement to explore feelings.

The following example illustrates these procedures. A 33-year-old school teacher telephoned her psychotherapist after her 6th session of psychotherapy:

Therapist: Hello. . . . Ms. Jones?
Patient: Yes. . . . Thank you for calling back so promptly.
Therapist: How can I help you?
Patient: I'm sorry to bother you, Doctor, but after our session I felt so good and had such high hopes that I was better, then I got my heart palpitations again this morning. I just had to call to ask what I should do.

Therapist: I understand. . . . I'm sure this is uncomfortable.

Patient: Oh, yes. . . . I hate it.

Therapist: I think it is important that you begin your next session, which is the day after tomorrow, with this. Then we can look at it closely and see if we can understand it.

Patient: Yes. . . . Is there anything I can do now? Can you suggest anything to help me?

Therapist: Only that we will work on this when you come in Thursday.

Patient: Oh . . . well . . . OK. Thank you, Doctor.

Therapist: Then we'll look forward to seeing you at your regular appointment time.

Patient: OK . . . well . . . good-by.

Therapist: Good-by, Ms. Jones.

Gently and with good manners the psychotherapist told the patient that the message was received and would be processed during the next session of psychotherapy. At the next session, the patient did *not* bring up the telephone call, but launched into a discussion of the pressures upon her in her fourth-grade classroom. This kind of evasion is not unusual. The patient rarely reraises a mechanical barrier during the therapeutic session. What the patient *does* talk about may be directly associated with the barrier. The psychotherapist brings up the barrier in the following manner, about 20 minutes into the session:

Patient: So, I really don't know what to do. I like my work but those children can be *so* oppressive.

Therapist: So this is a continuing pressure which maintains through the school year?

Patient: It's worse toward the spring . . . and just after Christmas break. That's the time some of us call "Hell Week." (*giggles*) . . . (*long pause*)

Therapist: I wonder if this could be associated with your telephone call?

Patient: Oh! How?

Therapist: You were distressed. . . .

Patient: Well . . . yes . . . I just felt I *needed* something . . . advice or help. . . .

Therapist: I see. . . . you felt bad?

Patient: Yes . . . I had my palpitations. Maybe it was because of the kids.

Therapist: So you called for help?

Patient: (*pause*) I guess I shouldn't have . . . but I was . . . mad. . . . (*long pause*)

Therapist: Many people are disappointed that psychotherapy doesn't work as well as they'd like . . . even psychotherapists.

Patient: Well . . . I'd felt so good for a week . . . then the palpitations . . . I guess I wanted you to tell me what to do . . . or what I'd done wrong.

Therapist: Do you sometimes feel that everything you do doesn't work out?

Patient: (*pause, weeps*) . . . Yes, I do . . . and I try *so* hard.

In this instance, the sequence of *acceptance,* and *clarification of feeling* led to *experiencing* during the session following the telephone call. The barrier raised by the patient was resolved as part of the psychotherapeutic process. It was not necessary for the therapist to set limits or structure the situation.

In the following passage, the psychotherapist brings up the issue of the patient's nonpayment of the fee. The psychotherapist chooses to initiate the discussion about 30 minutes into the session, at a point where the patient seems to have run out of things to discuss. This is long enough for the patient to use the session for any impelling issues, but leaves enough time to explore the barrier raised by the patient.

Patient: So . . . I guess that's about all I've got to say about that. I'll just have to see what develops later. . . . (*long pause*)

Therapist: No particular thoughts or feelings?

Patient: No . . . not right now. . . . (*pause*)

Therapist: I've noticed that you haven't paid the bill I sent several weeks ago.

Patient: (*pause*) Oh . . . well, I guess I've been a little behind in that.

Therapist: Is that a pattern you've noticed?

Patient: What's that?

Therapist: Delaying the payment of your bills?

Patient: I don't think so. . . . Maybe. . . . (*pause*)

Therapist: At the beginning of our work, we set your fee and we agreed that you would keep your accounts current.

Patient: Well, yes. . . . I've just forgotten about it, I guess.

Therapist: Often what you do in psychotherapy reflects your life-style. This may be one of those repetitive behaviors or recapitulations. It is important for you to keep current in paying for your psychotherapy. There are a couple of reasons for this. I mentioned them when you first started but this might be a good time to look at this again.

When you have paid our agreed-upon fee, you know that the therapy belongs to you. You will have no guilt about "owing" or being dependent on the therapist's charity or indulgence. You will also avoid expressing feelings such as anger and disappointment passively by not paying. It is much more helpful to you to express such feelings directly and have the chance to discuss and understand such feelings.

Patient: I guess I just forgot. . . . I'll leave a check today. . . . (*pause*)
Therapist: How do you feel?
Patient: A little embarrassed but also relieved.

In this instance, the patient is not ready to *experience* the basis of his creating a barrier to therapeutic progress. Because the barrier must be resolved, the psychotherapist sets limits by *structuring* and then encourages further exploration.

In the following interaction, a patient presents the psychotherapist with a gift during a session:

Patient: I've brought you something, Doctor.
Therapist: Oh?
Patient: Yes. . . . It's a gift for Christmas. . . .
Therapist: Tell me about it.
Patient: Aren't you going to open it? (*postures disappointment*)
Therapist: First, I'd like to hear how you decided on this and how you feel about it.
Patient: Come, now. . . . Even Freud said, "Sometimes a cigar is just a cigar." (*laughs*)
Therapist: (*laughs*) Yes . . . but in this case you've decided to reward me in some way with a present.
Patient: Not a reward. It's just Christmas and I thought I'd get you a gift. I give a lot of gifts.
Therapist: What did you think when you got it?
Patient: Aren't you going to open it? (*somewhat angry*)
Therapist: OK. (*opens box, removes silk tie*) Very nice.
Patient: What I thought was—you need a classy tie. I don't care for the dull rep ties you wear.
Therapist: So you decided to help me be . . . uh . . . more "classy."
Patient: Sure. . . . No big deal.
Therapist: Gifts reflect important feelings from the giver . . .
Patient: No big deal. . . . Just a season's greeting.
Therapist: All gifts in psychotherapy are important messages. . . . Have you given ties to others?

Patient: Uh . . . well . . . no—usually I get them.

Therapist: Do you enjoy them?

Patient: Usually not. . . . Most people have horrible taste.

Therapist: So you were giving me a unique gift . . . a tie with good taste.

Patient: Well . . . I hope so . . . I also hoped you'd be pleased, not analytical.

Therapist: Yes . . . well . . . I try very hard to be analytical first. . . . I owe you that . . . at all times. Your gift neither pleases nor displeases me. It interests me very much. Are your family gift-givers?

Patient: Not really. They're usually late or they give comic cards. . . . I'm the one that gives . . . (*laughs*) more blessed to give than receive.

Therapist: Sometimes easier. . . . Do you get many gifts?

Patient: (*pause, seems uncomfortable*). . . . No . . . well, the usual mandatory junk from family and employees.

Therapist: You are uncomfortable?

Patient: (*pause*) . . . Yes. . . . I guess it's easier to give than receive. . . . I don't know why . . . now I feel upset. . . . I'm sorry I gave you that tie. . . . No . . . I'm not. . . . I just wanted to please you.

Therapist: My pleasure is in doing good work here and seeing you work in your own best interests. . . . (*long pause*)

Patient: It is *so* hard to lean back and *be*. I always have to be doing something.

The patient then went on to explore his conflicts about relating closely enough to anyone to allow them to try to please him. Toward the end of the session, the issue of the gift itself was resolved as follows:

Patient: I suppose I should take the tie back. . . .

Therapist: Would you like that?

Patient: I'd hate it. . . . I'd feel a fool.

Therapist: One of my teachers, a great therapist, is a very classy guy who loves and wears classy ties. Suppose I send it to him with our compliments and the details of what his good training of me has done for you?

Patient: (*pause*) . . . I like that idea. . . . I guess the idea behind gifts is really what you have to look at.

The psychotherapist must do everything possible to help resolve patient barriers without offending or creating guilt. This is not always possible, but even such negative responses, which can be explored, are more desirable in the patient's best interests than simply accepting gifts.

Patients may move through an emotional resolution of an important topic, and then stop coming to sessions. This behavior may reflect their life-style or "quitting before they get the benefit." It is sometimes necessary to write to the patient, since he or she may write the therapist to "Take me off the schedule—I won't be coming in for a while." It is appropriate for the psychotherapist to write a response:

Dear Mrs. Jones:
I received the note that you left with my secretary concerning the cancellation of your appointments. We will certainly follow your wishes in this matter. I feel I should tell you, however, that this pattern of canceling is associated with progress that you make in your sessions immediately previous to the cancellations. It has happened before. You might be aware from our discussion that psychotherapy is a recapitulation or a small model of the way we deal in our real lives. Your tendency to "quit before you are ahead" is something we have talked about. I believe your cancellation of your sessions may represent your fear of the progress you began to make just before you canceled. If you wish to discuss this, I believe another session would be reasonable. If you prefer canceling your sessions, we will, of course, abide by those wishes. It is my responsibility as your therapist, however, to attempt to provide you with an opportunity for insight into these decisions.
With all good wishes, I am

Sincerely,

Defensive Barriers

Defensive barriers are those raised by the patient to cope with feelings of danger and threat from the psychotherapeutic process. Much as the patient wishes to live a less painful and conflicted life, fear of revelation and anxiety about giving up known, practiced, and predictable neurotic ways result in defensive barriers being raised. The younger the patient, the more likely that defensive barriers will include termination (Taylor, Adelman & Kaser-Boyd, 1985). The process of psychotherapy frequently proceeds slowly because of the inertia maintained by patients. It is more the rule than the exception that patients will, in various ways, attempt to maintain their old neurotic styles while manifestly seeking better ways of living.

Defensive barriers are automatic reactions of the patient. Rarely is planning involved. The patient creates these barriers while he or she believes that all reasonable efforts are being explored to move the psychotherapeutic process forward. Common defensive barriers will be described, as well as some psychotherapeutic techniques to move toward resolution of these impediments. Some of the commonest defensive barriers will be reviewed.

Silence. The messages of silence are fairly explicit. The patient is saying, "Stop the psychotherapy." The reasons can vary: Fear of revelation, anxiety about losing control, and guilt regarding unacceptable feelings and thoughts are common bases. The patient may see in the psychotherapist a favored or unfavored parental substitute, and the silence is a passive response seeking more participation by the admired therapist. Where the silence is a negative message, the patient may be saying, "I am angry and will withhold what you want me to give."

Silence puts the patient in an intolerable bind or conflict: The process of psychotherapy holds hope for a better life, but exploration is frightening. Silence allows the patient to halt the psychotherapeutic process without taking responsibility for the act. In some instances, silence is a power struggle wherein the patient challenges the psychotherapist to "force" the patient to pursue the therapeutic course, thus placing the burden of responsibility for progress or lack of progress on the psychotherapist.

The psychotherapist must be wary of trying to "discover" or, in the worst case, "guess" the nature of the message of silence. The silent patient requires tolerance and positive expectations on the part of the therapist. The psychotherapist must be able to accept long periods of silence with a relaxed and tolerant manner. Pressures to "reveal" will only lead to more guilt for the patient and continued resistance to progress.

Obsessional repetition. The patient who focuses on inconsequential aspects of his or her life, repeating set phrases or routinely describing self-responses in a pedantic, intellectual style, is stalling or slowing psychotherapeutic progress in a manner similar to silence. Words are spoken but little or no feeling or experiencing occurs with the repetition. The obsessional repetition may take the form of *pseudo-experiencing,* where the patient follows a ritual of reporting in words usually associated with emotion, but frequently presented with little or no emotional involvement. The following is a passage from the beginning of the 34th session with an intense, obsessional man of 26 in his fourth series of psychotherapeutic contacts:

Patient: When I arrived at your office today, I noticed I was uncomfortable. I seemed to be breathing more deeply than usual. My muscles seemed tense and I had a kind of pressure on my chest. I didn't know what to expect.

Therapist: You were uncomfortable?

Patient: Not exactly. Maybe scared, or maybe just aware of these things.

Therapist: You've reported these things at the beginning of each session for the past eight sessions.

Patient: (*slight smile*) . . . I don't know why, but I'm pleased you are aware of that.

The patient is somewhat pleased at being "found out" or "noticed." In some way the obsessional focus has been rewarded. No real experiencing has occurred with the obsessional focus. The psychotherapist was gentle and accepting, posing as little threat as possible in attempting to help the patient focus on his obsessional repetition.

Withdrawal, evasion, or cutting off emotion. This defensive barrier often represents or models the patient's usual and customary neurotic mechanism of denial. Frightening ideas or emotions are simply (or intricately) avoided. The barrier to progress is raised by changing the subject, shifting the focus of associations, or insisting on objectifying what is being discussed. This barrier is illustrated in the 40th session by a depressed engineer as follows:

Patient: I believe I had a dream last night. . . .

Therapist: Tell me what you remember.

Patient: Well. . . . I don't really remember it all that well. . . . (*long pause*)

Therapist: Did you have some feelings about the dream?

Patient: You mean "good" or "bad"?

Therapist: Whatever.

Patient: My daughter tells me she dreams a lot. . . . I guess people are different. I don't think I dreamed at all until I started this therapy.

The patient is aware that dreams may be of some importance. He has been structured about this in the past. He brings up the topic and then evades and withdraws, refusing to invest the experience with emotion. The barriers he raises effectively slow the progress of psychotherapy to in some way protect the patient from painful experiencing.

Help-rejecting complaints. Another neurotic life-style which appears as a defensive barrier against moving forward in psychotherapy is presented by the help-rejecting complainer. No matter the sincerity and skill with which the psychotherapist accepts, clarifies, or structures, the help-rejecting patient avoids and evades involvement with the very issues he or she raises. The patient raises a barrier to the very progress being sought in order to be comfortable with the old neurotic safety devices that have been used to avoid the fears associated with impending or imminent experiencing. Little different in focus from other barrier-raising behavior, help-rejecting complaints often hide feelings of worthlessness. The message is frequently, "I don't deserve better than I have." This defensive barrier may appear as follows:

Therapist: You might want to say whatever comes to mind about the dream.
Patient: I don't see what good that would do. I don't even remember all of it.
Therapist: Sometimes just talking about what you remember may bring up something important to you.
Patient: (*shaking head negatively*) . . . I don't know. . . . Most of this stuff just appears silly to me. . . .
Therapist: Not very practical.
Patient: Yeah. . . . (*long pause*)
Therapist: Perhaps there was something else, important to you, that you want to talk about.
Patient: I've told you everything I can think of. . . . (*long pause*) Maybe I'm just the way I am and nothing will change.

The barrier against progress is effectively raised. The patient is prepared to reject any suggestions or support offered.

Achievement-intolerant striving. Some patients alternate intense periods of progress with abrupt barrier-raising to prevent "too much too soon." The mechanisms by which barriers are suddenly raised immediately following progress are many and varied. A series of missed or forgotten appointments following a very productive session with significant experiencing is common. The patient may plead, "I can think of nothing more to say." Previously productive sessions may stir fears of success, loss of dependency, revelation anxiety, or other negative anticipations; the patient must slow or stop progress. This frequently reflects the way in which the patient has dealt with achievement since childhood. Such patients often present histories which include doing well in school at the beginning of the term and then failing examinations, or starting out well in a new job, gaining early recognition and promotion, and then becoming ill or inefficient and disrupting the achievement. Such patients work very hard in their psychotherapy, striving to do whatever is necessary to make progress. As their efforts are rewarded, the barriers appear. They seem to be aware of the pattern to some extent, but appear at first to be helpless in preventing the disruption. A 26-year-old accountant illustrates this during his 20th session of psychotherapy:

Patient: I really missed coming the last two sessions but I was feeling too bad. . . I guess it was the flu.
Therapist: You had to take off work?
Patient: No. . . . I just felt too bad to come here. The fever and aches seem to come and go.
Therapist: This happened after you had two very productive sessions about the relationship between your feelings about your father and your stepfather.
Patient: (*long pause*) . . . I still have a lot of feeling about that. I never realized how guilty I felt about liking my stepfather better than my father . . . but it wasn't my fault. . . . My stepfather was . . . uh . . he was a better man . . . a better father. It makes me uncomfortable. . . . (*long pause*)
Therapist: How did you feel about missing the two sessions?
Patient: Uh. . . . OK. . . . I want to continue working on this . . . but . . . well, I just didn't feel up to coming in.

Resolving defensive barriers

The dynamic nature of defensive barriers allows somewhat wider latitude for psychotherapeutic intervention than mechanical barriers. Defensive barriers are small samples of the patient's usual and customary style of dealing with the anxiety associated with change. The anxiety may be more intense when the change is associated with power and independence than when change is indicative of failure or loss. The raising of the defensive barrier usually signals that the patient must maintain *status quo* or equilibrium in the sense that the old neurotic ways may be distressing but they are known and safe. The sequence of intervention efforts with defensive barriers differs from working with mechanical barriers in that structuring is rarely effective and interpretation is more frequently appropriate. With defensive barriers, the patient is more likely to tolerate and be able to move on to experiencing with therapist interventions which are more intrusive, than he would be with mechanical barriers. The sequence of psychotherapist responses should be:

- Acceptance of the behavior as a message.
- Clarify feelings where possible.
- Interpret the meaning of the behavior where appropriate and encourage experiencing.

The later in the psychotherapeutic process that defensive barriers occur, the more effective probative interventions are likely to be. The following illustrates a therapeutic response to *extended silence* during the 12th session with a 24-year-old bank teller:

Therapist: (*after four or five minutes of absolute silence*) . . . You seem to have little to say today. . . .
Patient: (*no response . . . silence continues*)
Therapist: Silence can be an important message in itself. . . .
Patient: (*no response, looks away . . . appears to be on the verge of weeping*)
Therapist Holding in is sometimes a way of expressing fear or anger . . . or even both.
Patient: (*no response . . . weeps very gently . . .*)
Therapist: Feeling bad in therapy is sometimes necessary in the process of feeling good.
Patient: (*nods and continues to weep silently*)

The opportunity for interpretation did not present itself. In the 35th session, with silence having occurred on a fairly regular basis, the following interaction occurred with the same patient:

Patient: I haven't much to say today . . . (*long pause*)
Therapist: Yet you said you're distressed about your mother-in-law.
Patient: (*nods slightly*) . . . (*long pause*)
Therapist: In our past sessions, silence has been one way for you to deal with troubling thoughts and experiences.
Patient: . . . (*no response*) . . . (*long pause*)
Therapist: You told me that as a child you were forbidden to talk back. . . . Is silence a way of saying you feel angry, but also fear expressing yourself?
Patient: (*no response*) . . .
Therapist: Even when you believe you are in the right? . . . Like with your mother-in-law?

Patient: She *was* wrong. She had no business telling us we shouldn't go to New York for vacation. (*angrily*) She's never been to New York, but she acts as if she knows what's right for everyone! (*cries*)

Therapist: She treats you as your parents did?

Patient: (*nods continuing to cry*)

Therapist: And no matter how much you believe she or they are wrong, you can't say so.

Patient: Yes ... it's like ... like being in jail. ... I have no rights. ... It's been that way since I was little. ... Mother said anger is "ugly."

The psychotherapist accepts the patient's silence as a message, attempts to clarify the patient's feelings, and then interprets her silence as a repetitive style of dealing with anger. The patient accepts this and acknowledges the silence as a recapitulation of earlier defensive reactions.

The psychotherapist must beware of expecting clarifications and interpretations to be accepted by all patients under all circumstances. Some patients accept interpretations or at least consider them with reluctance. Defensive barriers rarely disappear dramatically. Such barriers may lessen, appear with decreasing frequency, or reappear. This is demonstrated in the following excerpt from a session with the *help-rejecting complainer* who, as illustrated earlier in this chapter, refused to free associate to a dream. Thirty sessions later, he was able to remember and report his dreams, but continued to raise defensive barriers as follows:

Patient: I had a *really* strange dream. ... I was sitting in an old-fashioned swing on a porch. My daughter and my granddaughter were on either side of me. We were swinging. My granddaughter—she's six, you know—started to take off her clothes. I said, "Honey, you don't want to do that." When I turned to my daughter . . . expecting her to follow through and tell Debbie to stop undressing, I saw *she* was taking off her clothes! It was really strange. ...

Therapist: How did *you* feel?

Patient: Huh? I felt she ought not to be getting undressed!

Therapist: It was disturbing to you?

Patient: It was just unusual. ...

Therapist: Why don't you just talk about the dream as your thoughts come to you?

Patient: I just told you the whole dream.

Therapist: Try to experience the emotion you felt while the dream was
     going on. . . .
Patient: (*no response, shakes head*)
Therapist: Were you pleased?
Patient: (*pause*) That was strange. . . . I was . . . well . . . almost a little
     excited . . . but . . . (*long pause*)
Therapist: Perhaps guilty?
Patient: Guilty? About what?
Therapist: About feeling excited?
Patient: You guys are all alike! You see sex behind everything. It was
     just a dream.

Although fairly well along in number of therapeutic hours, the patient
is too fearful to take opportunities to experience his inner responses and
move ahead. He does tolerate a carefully presented interpretation, but rejects any further help, raising a barrier to further exploration.

The psychotherapist must be prepared to intervene at the level appropriate to the patient's readiness to move ahead. Psychotherapists who feel
impelled to instruct or to receive acknowledgment of their interpretations, or who insist on the patient looking closely when the patient is
still too frightened to look closely will only encourage more barrier-raising
and delay therapeutic progress. Sometimes it is important to the patient
to respond to an appropriate and helpful interpretation by reassuring
himself or herself that the old barriers can be raised, if necessary. As psychotherapy proceeds, these barriers will drop away as the patient no longer requires them.

Confrontational Barriers

Barriers raised by the patient which force the psychotherapist to consider being judgmental of the patient or the patient's behavior often
reflect a patient's deep anxiety about ambiguity in personal relationships.
The psychotherapist's objectivity and acceptance serve to focus all attention during the therapeutic session on the patient. For some patients this
is very frightening.

Confrontational barriers demand that the psychotherapist play the
role of the "good" or "bad" parent. The patient can deal with this more
easily, albeit neurotically, than with the frightening opportunity for self-
discovery. Confrontational barriers are more likely to appear earlier than
later in psychotherapy. Patients with significant character pathology
may raise these barriers throughout the therapeutic course. (Character
barriers will be explored in Chapter 9.) Confrontational barriers, by their

very nature, require immediate response from the psychotherapist. Some of the more common confrontational barriers raised by patients during psychotherapy are:

Demands for guidance and advice. The usual message of this barrier is "I'm here for help, not to work." Beneath this demand lie deep dependency needs, fears of success, or separation anxiety. During the seventh session of individual psychotherapy, a second-year law student raises the following confrontational barrier:

Patient: I've been coming for two months and I don't see that much has happened.
Therapist: You're disappointed.
Patient: No. . . . I just think you should give one some direct answers. I can't decide whether to drop my Contract course or finish and take a low grade. All you do is say, "How do you feel?" . . . The question is whether to drop Contracts or not. . . . You teach in graduate school. How will it affect my record if I show a "drop"?

Attention to the psychotherapist's staff. This confrontational barrier is most frequently raised by patients who are compelled to test limits in their everyday life in order to allay anxieties regarding such issues as self-worth, rights and privileges, or belonging. A 40-year-old salesman whose presenting symptoms included chronic lateness, forgetting of important responsibilities, and intermittent impotence reports the following during his fourth session of psychotherapy:

Patient: Your receptionist doesn't like me very much.
Therapist: Oh?
Patient: I was early before my last session and I was chatting with her—kidding, you know—but she was very cold and did everything but tell me to shut up.
Therapist: You were offended?
Patient: Well . . . not offended, but certainly she wasn't very responsive. . . . I wanted to ask her to lunch sometime and I was just . . . well, sort of being "friendly" and she gave me some non-sense about being busy or having to get on with her work.

Sometimes the confrontational barrier is raised by the patient making unreasonable or inappropriate requests:

Patient: I asked your secretary if she would like to do some part-time work for me in the evening. I hope you don't mind.
Therapist: Yes. . . . She told me after your last session.
Patient: Does your staff have to tell you everything?

Unreasonable expectations or demands. Although barriers of every sort may carry a variety of implicit messages about patients' fears or needs, unreasonable expectations often reflect the compulsion to achieve mastery or control. Many seemingly successful or self-assured people harbor deep anxieties about the degree to which they are worthwhile. Successful mastery of others is a reassurance of sorts that the person is not as worthless as he or she inwardly believes. The patient may insist on discussing issues with the psychotherapist on the telephone. The patient may stand in the doorway, extending the session after it is over. The patient may approach the psychotherapist on the street and begin to interact therapeutically. Sometimes this barrier is raised very smoothly and rationally, although the confrontation is quite clear. During her 10th session, the second-year law student raised the following confrontational barrier:

Patient: I've applied for a summer clerkship with the Public Defender's Office and I would like to use your name as a reference. I hope you don't mind.

Insistent hostile challenges. Although superficially resembling unreasonable expectations, the barrier raised by the insistent hostile challenge is a more direct, less realistic venture. This barrier is most commonly raised by bright, rather infantile patients. The challenge is frequently a projection of the patient's own style, philosophy, or attitude toward others with whom he or she has become close. Guilt-ridden but assertive patients may raise this barrier as self-exploration becomes uncomfortable.

A 28-year-old guidance counselor with two previous psychotherapeutic experiences raises an insistent hostile barrier at the beginning of the 25th session of his third effort at psychotherapy. During the 19th session, the patient had discussed his intense anger toward the father, a school principal, but admitted that he fantasized a warmer relationship where the father praised and approved him.

Therapist: Well, how goes it?
Patient: (*looking very distressed*) What do *you* care? . . . What the hell do you *really* care? (*with rising volume and animosity*)

Therapist: You feel pretty uncomfortable. . . .

Patient: No. . . . I enjoy this crap! . . . Week in, week out . . . I could do a lot more worthwhile things with my money . . . not that it would make a bit of difference to you! (*almost shouting*)

Seductiveness. Although mild seductiveness may be a defensive barrier, direct declarations of affection and interaction wish or expectancy are confrontational barriers. The barrier usually reflects aspects of the patient's conflicted life-style. As with most barriers raised by patients during psychotherapy, seductiveness places the patient in a no-win situation where the psychotherapist is forced to deal with the patient's conflict in an authoritarian manner. In the following example, a 27-year-old investment counselor raises a confrontational barrier with her psychotherapist by writing a letter to her after the second session. During this session, the patient said she would like to think about whether she was ready for long-term psychotherapy before scheduling sessions regularly:

Dear Mary:

I hope you don't mind me calling you by your first name? "Doctor" is so distant (although it's appropriate and well-deserved). I've done a lot of thinking about continuing in therapy. I'd like to go forth, although we'll have to see how our schedules match at the next session.

One thing concerns me, though, and I ought to tell you about this. I find that I am thinking about you more than a little. It may be that you make me feel good about myself in our sessions, so I think about you a lot to have good feelings. I *want* you to know that I'm fond of you. I look forward to seeing you. I want you to like me, but I'm not sure that's possible—you see so much of the awful side of me. I want to call you, just to talk with you. I don't want you to be angry with me, but I do feel this way. I've written instead of telling you because it's very hard to tell your therapist that you're attracted to her as a woman.

Hoping you understand,

Jane

If the psychotherapist is threatened by the patient's raising a seductive confrontational barrier, the sanctity of the psychotherapeutic setting will diminish or even be destroyed. The psychotherapist's response must not be encouraging, nor should the therapist's reaction be harsh.

Intoxication. The patient who comes to the therapeutic session drunk or under the influence of intoxicating drugs raises a powerful confrontational barrier. In spite of the folklore to the contrary, intoxication lessens or eliminates the individual's capacity to explore, experience appropriately, and integrate new learning. There is no therapeutic value in conducting a session under such circumstances. The session must be terminated and the confrontation evaluated during the next scheduled session. The session should be ended pleasantly but firmly:

Therapist: You seem a bit unsteady today.

Patient: Yeah. . . . Lunch was a little long . . . about three martinis longer than I planned. (*laughs loudly*)

Therapist: You've had quite a bit to drink.

Patient: Oh, Doc! Don't tell me you're going to give me a temperance lecture. (*laughs uncontrollably and dumps the ashtray on the floor as he attempts to put out his cigarette*)

Therapist: I think you'd be more comfortable if you could go home and rest awhile.

Patient: I'll be OK, Doc . . . a couple of cups of coffee and I'll be fine. . . . I could take a nap on your couch. (*laughs uncontrollably*)

Therapist: I'm taking the keys to your car. I'll have the secretary call a cab to take you home.

Patient: Aw . . . don't get mad, Doc. It was just a few extra drinks.

Therapist: When you come on Thursday for your next session, we'll talk about it. Meanwhile don't worry, just get some rest. (*escorting the patient out*)

Resolving confrontational barriers

The confrontational barriers raised by patients during psychotherapy may be dangerous, inconvenient, threatening, or even socially noxious. To respond with criticism or disdain is unacceptable. Such natural but punitive responses by the therapist are psychotherapeutic errors. The sequence of responses most likely to resolve confrontational barriers in the interest of therapeutic progress is:

- Accept the confrontation as an important message reflective of the patient's neurotic life-style.
- Respond with tolerance and acceptance.
- Clarify feeling which emerges in reference to the confrontation.
- Gently but firmly set limits without undue delay.
- Interpret the behavior when appropriate.

This sequence can be seen in the psychotherapist's response to the *demand for guidance* confrontation barrier raised by the law student presented earlier in this chapter:

Patient: All you do is say, "How do you feel?" ... The question is whether to drop Contracts or not. ... You teach in graduate school. How will it affect my record if I show a "drop"?

Therapist: It's annoying that I don't help you or make suggestions in a simple matter like this. ...

Patient: Of course! It wouldn't hurt for you to simply help me a little!

Therapist: Actually, it might. For me to "advise" or "help" you in this real-life decision would be for me to decide you are helpless or unable to make decisions in your own best interests. Furthermore, it would mean I have little expectation that you can learn to trust and depend on your own judgment. I don't see you in that way. You may doubt your ability to learn to make effective decisions, but I have no such doubts. It is much more important that we examine and understand your frustration in making decisions than to simply solve the problem. Problems occur and recur, and will throughout your life. Self-understanding and the solution strategies you learn through your psychotherapy will be useful to you all your life.

Patient: (*long pause*) ... I suppose ... but I still can't decide and I feel terrible. ...

Therapist: This is not a new situation for you.

Patient: What do you mean?

Therapist: You told me earlier that before your first marriage you had strong doubts. You were unsure.

Patient: That's right. ... I should have listened to myself.

Therapist: But instead?

Patient: Well ... I asked my mother what I should do ... and she convinced me I just had the "jitters" and everything would be fine.

Therapist: And?

Patient: It sure wasn't "fine" at all!

Therapist: So ... advice in the face of your own unsureness is not always best for you.

Patient: I guess ... even from my mother. ...

Therapist: Even from your mother ... and your therapist. ...

Patient: (*short silence*) ... I can see that ... but it's sure hard to do. ...

The psychotherapist *accepted* the confrontation barrier as an important message reflecting the patient's behavioral style. The acceptance was tolerant and gentle. Feelings were clarified. A firm but gentle structuring was presented to the patient. Feeling the time was right, the therapist interpreted the confrontation barrier as an example of the patient's pattern of dependency on others' decision-making as being more in her best interest than her own feelings and choices. The barrier is lowered and the psychotherapy proceeds.

In responding to unreasonable expectations or demands, the psychotherapist should follow the same sequence of responses as noted above. The law student demonstrates her abiding dependency needs, raising a confrontational barrier:

Patient: I've applied for a summer clerkship with the Public Defender's Office and I would like to use your name as a reference. I hope you don't mind.

Therapist: You feel a letter from me would help you to get that job?

Patient: Yeah. . . . I guess your recommendation would carry some weight.

Therapist: What would you hope I'd write about you?

Patient: Well . . . you know . . . the usual stuff . . . good, I hope! (*laughs*)

Therapist: You'd want me to weigh and judge you in a letter.

Patient: I suppose so.

Therapist: That would be very different from the way I feel about you. I never weigh and judge you as far as I know. I accept you as a person working very hard to understand yourself. I work with you by creating a safe setting for you to explore the way you're living your life— the pleasant and unpleasant, the rewarding and the disappointing. I don't judge or weigh you. To ask me to write a letter of recommendation is to ask me to stop being your therapist.

Patient: (*pause*) I didn't look at it that way. . . .

Therapist: I realize that this summer job is important to you, but I am duty-bound to remain your psychotherapist—until *you* decide differently.

Patient: Well, yeah. . . . I can see that.

Therapist: But your wanting me to write a recommendation for you is important. Perhaps it reflects some feelings you have about me. . . .

Patient: Sure. . . . I think you're great! That's why I asked. You're an important and respected person.

Barriers raised by patients must be viewed as opportunities to move forward in the psychotherapeutic process. Even hostile challenges can be productive elements of psychotherapy, assuming the psychotherapist is not threatened by the barrier and does not become punitive. In the following segment, the psychotherapist would commit a therapeutic error by responding in a threatened and punitive manner to the hostile challenge barrier raised by the 28-year-old guidance counselor referred to previously in this chapter:

Patient: No. . . . I enjoy this crap!. . . . Week in and week out . . . I could do a lot more worthwhile things with my money . . . not that it would make a bit of difference to you! (*almost shouting*)
Therapist: Well, it's your money and your choice.
Patient: What do you mean?
Therapist: You *choose* to come here, you can *choose* to quit.

Nothing therapeutically good can come of the psychotherapist's meeting confrontation with a counter-confrontation. More appropriately, the psychotherapist followed the sequence of responses which follows:

Patient: . . . . not that it would make a bit of difference to you! (*almost shouting*)
Therapist: This is all frustrating.
Patient: You're damned right . . . all give and take. I give, you take!
Therapist: So it's also very unfair.
Patient: (*pause*). . . . At least you could tell me how I'm doing . . . or what I should be doing.
Therapist: Many people in psychotherapy feel as you do . . . wondering if it's worth not only the money, but the effort . . . and the frustration . . . and the slow progress.
Patient: You can say *that* again!
Therapist: It seems slow . . . and often that is kind of a choice of safety.
Patient: What do you mean?
Therapist: Many people in therapy are very uncomfortable if emotions or new ideas come too quickly. It can raise a lot of anxiety. Nobody *likes* a lot of anxiety and in psychotherapy people can do things to slow the process and relieve the anxiety.
Patient: Yeah? Like what?
Therapist: Sure . . . like "forgetting" sessions, being silent, not talking about their real feelings. . . .
Patient: Well . . . I sure don't pull my punches!
Therapist: That's helpful. . . .
Patient: I expected you to get mad . . . (*pause*) . . . maybe throw me out of therapy. . . . I'm terrified when I lose my temper.

Therapist: So . . . if I "threw you out"?
Patient: (*pause*) . . . (*smiles*) . . . then I'd have more money to spend and
    I wouldn't have to work so hard in here.
Therapist: A kind of relief.
Patient: Yeah . . . yeah . . . but for how long?

Again, the barrier raised by the patient is treated as an important
message. The behavior is accepted, the feelings are clarified, some structuring takes place, but it is the patient who makes the interpretation. The
earlier labile emotional reaction of the hostile challenge seemed to "bleed
out" the patient's tension, especially after the psychotherapist accepted
and clarified the feelings. The patient then went on to develop insight into
his own behavior.

In the case of the seductiveness barrier, raised early in the course of the
psychotherapy by means of a letter, the therapist chose to deal with this
at the beginning of the session immediately following the receipt of the
letter, as follows:

Therapist: Good morning.
Patient: (*softly*) Good morning. . . . (*long pause*)
Therapist: I received your letter.
Patient: Oh! . . .
Therapist: Thank you.
Patient: Oh . . . I'm embarrassed.
Therapist: Embarrassment is a strong feeling we all have at one time or
    another—and psychotherapy moves forward when we look at your
    feelings, especially strong feelings.
Patient: I shouldn't have written that letter.
Therapist: The important thing is for us to talk about your feelings and
    you expressed a lot of feelings in your letter.
Patient: I wasn't sure you knew I was gay. . . . Then I was afraid you
    knew. . . . Most people hide what they *really* feel about things
    like that. . . .
Therapist: I'm sure it's difficult at times.
Patient: (*long pause*) You didn't say how you feel about *me*.
Therapist: When we started, I told you quite a lot about psychotherapy.
    If you'll remember, I said that when we decided on this, that we
    would form an alliance to work in your best interests. I was, and I
    am, committed to this, working hard to understand you, accept you
    as a person, and give you the best skills I can as a psychotherapist.
    Personal relationships in psychotherapy are forbidden by our ethics,

even by the law, since they interfere with the process. I will do everything I can to help make your psychotherapy a productive process.
Patient: That seems so . . . well . . . *cold!*
Therapist: Perhaps it seems that way . . . and can even be annoying.
Patient: Oh, no! I'd never be annoyed with you!
Therapist: It would be all right if you are.

The psychotherapist has responded to this early and difficult patient barrier with acceptance, clarification, and structuring. Interpretations were not made of the hostile-dependent and manipulative aspects of the patient's behavior. The psychotherapist wisely omitted probative responses since therapy was in the very early stages and the patient relatively fragile.

Dealing effectively and therapeutically with instances of intoxication during the psychotherapeutic session is a difficult business at best. The patient's memory for the incident will be spotty or even amnesic in some cases. The psychotherapist should not focus on what was done or what was said unless the patient insists on such a focus. Attention must be directed to the structuring necessary to preserve the psychotherapeutic process. This is illustrated in the session following the incident of intoxication reported earlier in this chapter:

Therapist: Good afternoon.
Patient: Well . . . yes . . . but it wasn't the other day. I don't know what happened—I can usually handle three or four drinks.
Therapist: Intoxication is often puzzling since few people plan or expect to lose control of themselves with drugs or alcohol.
Patient: Well . . . I'm very embarrassed, but I don't think I "lost control." I was a little unsteady.
Therapist: Do you remember what you said and did here last Tuesday?
Patient: (*pause*) Well . . . some. . . . I know I laughed a lot. . . .
Therapist: Memory loss is very common after intoxication.
Patient: Are you saying I'm an alcoholic?
Therapist: No. That would be for you to say if you so thought. What I'm saying is that our work together requires pretty intense communication and concentration. Psychotherapy cannot take place when one partner is under the influence of intoxicating drugs. If you are, we must cancel or reschedule our session.
Patient: I've never had any trouble communicating when I drink and I've never had an accident! At least, nothing major. . . . You mean I can't come to therapy even if I had *one* drink.
Therapist: Not if you expect to have a productive session.

Patient: Are you mad at me, doctor?

Therapist: No. . . . Perhaps you think I should be or expect me to be.

Patient: Well . . . everyone else seems mad about my drinking.

Therapist: So . . . you would expect me to be mad.

Patient: (*long pause*) I don't know what to expect.

Therapist: You feel depressed?

Patient: Yes . . . very depressed.

Therapist: Perhaps drinking eases that.

Patient: It does. . . .

Therapist: And then you feel more depressed aftewards?

Patient: Yes . . . and then I drink again.

Therapist: Pretty discouraging.

Patient: It's all I can do . . . especially on weekends.

The psychotherapist sets limits, structures, accepts the patient's behavior, clarifies feelings, and makes a mild interpretation of the patient's behavioral pattern in using alcohol. No dramatic changes are likely to follow, but psychotherapy can proceed.

PSYCHOTHERAPEUTIC ERRORS

Where there is little or no moralistic component in patient barriers, psychotherapeutic errors are mistakes made by the therapist. These mistakes may be the result of poor training, inexperience, fatigue, neurotic needs, or character deficiencies. They are errors which will exert negative influence on the psychotherapeutic process. Some therapeutic errors destroy the psychotherapy and, in extreme instances, the psychotherapist and/or the patient. Dealing with psychotherapeutic errors places a heavier moral and ethical burden on the psychotherapist than learning the tradecraft to respond to patient barriers. Patient barriers are an expected and perhaps necessary part of the psychotherapy process. Such patient behaviors bring into the therapy setting the neurotic behavior and self-defeating life-styles which are grist for the mill of psychotherapy. Psychotherapeutic errors disrupt or delay the therapeutic process unnecessarily by forcing the patient and the therapist to struggle with the psychotherapist's inadequacies, ignorance, neuroses, and character flaws.

Psychotherapeutic errors fall roughly into three categories: *Errors of Inadequate Training and Experience, Neurotic Errors,* and *Errors of Character Inadequacy.* Each of these areas will be described and illustrated. This will be followed by attention to means of avoiding or, if necessary, rectifying such errors.

Errors of Inadequate Training or Experience

Training to become a psychotherapist follows no absolute, prescribed plan. Credentialing of psychotherapists is an issue which has received considerable attention during the past century, with no conclusions or agreed-upon procedures emerging. Some combination of didactic education, supervision, experience, and/or personal psychotherapy form the most common preparatory methods. Beyond this, specifics vary considerably. Very little attention has been paid to the tradecraft of "doing" psychotherapy up to the present time.

Although the behavioral therapies have developed the most specific procedural training, the extent and quality of supervision has been found wanting (Allen, Szollos & Brownen, 1986). Many psychotherapists develop style and procedures based on their clinical experience, modifying much of what they learned in graduate school and from supervisors. Since each psychotherapeutic alliance is to a greater or lesser extent unique, some flexibility and creativity are required in applying rules and principles of therapeutic tradecraft. On the other hand, there is considerable information regarding psychotherapeutic experience available in print and through training institutions and workshops. There are some "basics." It should not be necessary for each emerging psychotherapist to rediscover the basic principles for conducting the psychotherapeutic session. Some common errors primarily based on poor or inadequate training or education will be considered:

Logistical errors. Poor planning, bad manners, and thoughtlessness can create psychotherapeutic errors. A secretary who is harsh, probative, seductive, critical, or impolite can create a negative effect in the psychotherapeutic process. The psychotherapist's staff and their behavior are the full responsibility of the therapist. At the first sign that patients are in some way being made anxious or reactive by other staff, the psychotherapist must explore and resolve the source of difficulty.

Where records are not kept privately and concealed from general view, the therapeutic process can be affected. No patient is likely to feel secure in psychotherapy if his or her file is openly handled by other staff, or if therapy records are left about outside of the therapy room.

Frequent cancellations or appointment time changes instituted by the psychotherapist are therapeutic errors. Such changes are clearly disruptive of the regularity and consistency necessary for the psychotherapist's first responsibility—creation of the therapeutic session as a sanctuary.

Allowing the patient's account to build beyond four or five sessions is usually a therapeutic error. Delays in payment should be explored and resolved before they become a source of guilt and anxiety for the patient or of resentment for the psychotherapist.

Double-booking, giving the patient an appointment card with the wrong dates or times, giving patients short notice about the therapist's vacation time, and any other procedure which distresses or interferes with the patient's positive expectancy for psychotherapy must be considered an error.

Spoiling the sanctuary. Things the psychotherapist may do which disrupt or spoil the special, safe nature of the psychotherapeutic setting are often based on omissions in education or training. Such errors disrupt the privacy, specialness, and safety so crucial to therapeutic progress. Socializing with the patient, accepting more than one member of a family or close social group for individual psychotherapy, breaching confidentiality or the patient's privilege in any way, or involvement in the patient's life outside of the therapeutic session are all errors which will disrupt the psychotherapeutic process. The psychotherapist must not encourage dependence or even contact outside of scheduled sessions. There should be no discussion of the psychotherapy with anyone other than the patient without the patient's explicit knowledge and permission. Even when such discussions seem necessary and useful, as with relatives concerning the best interests of the patient, the psychotherapeutic alliance is likely to be disrupted.

When the psychotherapist is compelled to give up the therapeutic role for "realistic" reasons, the effect on the patient and the therapy must not be ignored or rationalized. Errors require exploration and resolution.

The presence of family pictures or mementos in the therapeutic setting is likely to disrupt or delay progress. It is difficult for the patient to see the session as devoted to his or her progress when the therapist's mate, children, or hobbies dominate the setting in which the psychotherapy takes place. The psychotherapist's office should certainly be a place that is comfortable and pleasant for the therapist, but not in ways which exclude or threaten the patient.

Overenthusiasm. Although characteristic of novice psychotherapists, errors of overenthusiasm can be found among experienced therapists whose training and supervision were inadequate to begin with and whose efforts to broaden their training have been minimal or nonexistent over the years. The compulsion to "do" during the psychotherapeutic session is difficult for some therapists to give up or curb. Such behaviors as offering advice or "saving" the patient from behavior which is self-rejecting are common errors.

Enthusiastic psychotherapists who never learned better may enter into *Pygmalion mechanics*. In George Bernard Shaw's *Pygmalion* (or in the popular musical version *My Fair Lady*), Professor Higgins, the speech professor, creates a princess from a street urchin. Such is the neurotic appeal to have power and mastery over others that many psychotherapists have become overenthusiastic about helping a patient with a low level of self-esteem or status achieve their "true potential." Noble as such a goal may be, it is a therapeutic error to enter into such Pygmalion mechanics. This is illustrated in the following case where a 24-year-old female patient reports her efforts to write professionally:

Patient: I *really* want to be a writer . . . since I was little. I've worked very hard at it, but I can't seem to find a way to finish the stuff I write or get anyone to read it. That's why I brought you my story, "San Francisco Nights."

Therapist: Yes . . . I read it and it's quite good. It is somewhat reminiscent of William Saroyan's San Francisco themes.

Patient: I've never read him.

Therapist: Oh . . . you must. . . . He is a very influential early new wave writer. I'll give you a list of his stories that focus on the themes in your "San Francisco Nights."

Patient: Oh. . . . That would be good!

Therapist: Also, after you revise and cut it a bit, you should submit it to several literary magazines.

Patient: I just don't know . . . if it's good enough or where to go with it.

Therapist: You can get a book called *Writer's Market* at the library. . . . That's a good way to find out where to submit original writing.

It is unfortunate for the patient that this psychotherapist's literary inclinations did not remind him of Shakespeare's admonition, "What fools these mortals be." The psychotherapist, in his enthusiasm to play Pygmalion, misses or ignores the patient's self-doubts, fears of success, and dependency needs. Clearly a psychotherapeutic error has been committed. The psychotherapist, because of his limited training, focuses on *his* goals and *his* knowledge and *his* enthusiasm.

Other errors of overenthusiasm include participating in the patient's humor, banter, or playfulness. Being "clever" and sociable with patients disrupts the security of the psychotherapeutic alliance. No matter how socially acceptable it may be, humor and banter have angry or competitive bases and it is a therapeutic error to enter into this with the patient rather than accepting and clarifying the feelings involved.

The poorly trained or inexperienced psychotherapist may seek to push therapy forward by presenting probative interpretations before the patient is ready to understand and experience such responses. The following is an excerpt from the third session conducted by a doctoral-level psychology trainee in a university clinic with a 19-year-old male college student:

Patient: This semester I'm having a *lot* of trouble with my professors.
Therapist: Are they all male?
Patient: Male?.... Yeah.... I guess they are. Is that important?
Therapist: It could be.... A lot of males carry over their love-hate of
    their fathers to all male authority figures.
Patient: Huh?

Clearly this student psychotherapist has moved too far, too soon.

Sometimes errors ordinarily based on inadequacy of training, education, or supervision occur repeatedly or in spite of the psychotherapist's education or training which identifies such errors. The creation of these therapeutic errors may constitute neurotic conflicts or character inadequacies on the part of the therapist.

Resolving errors of inadequate training or experience

The process of resolving (or better, avoiding) errors based on inadequate training or experience requires that the psychotherapist be consistently sensitive to his or her training background in respect to current thinking and practice in psychotherapy. Signs of therapeutic error such as early termination, frequent plateaus in the patient's flow of ideas, few referrals from former patients, and a sense of not knowing what is going on with the patient should suggest to the psychotherapist that training inadequacies may exist.

There is probably nothing which can be done to resolve errors of inadequate training which have occurred in the past. The concerned psychotherapist who intends to pursue and develop professional excellence will at this point plan and implement a program of reading, workshops, and supervision to acquire whatever training is necessary to avoid future errors.

In some communities, psychotherapists form study and training groups where issues of method and technique can be discussed and explored in a comfortable, collegial setting. Regular participation in such a group can prevent, as well as resolve, psychotherapist errors based on inadequate training or experience.

Neurotic Psychotherapy Errors

Psychotherapists are human, subject to the same world of stress as their patients. Treatment can be seriously skewed by the neurotic traits of the psychotherapist. The emotional problems of psychotherapists can not only disrupt the process, they can overwhelm and damage the patient (Leo, 1985a). Periods of significant distress are reported by the majority of psychotherapists. When psychotherapists seek help, the vast majority, even behavior therapists, choose dynamic, nonbehavioral personal therapy (Norcross & Prochaska, 1986b).

Neurotic psychotherapy errors reflect the fears, anxieties and inappropriate or inadequate coping mechanisms of the psychotherapist. Just as the neurotic behavior of the patient reflects his or her life-style, these psychotherapeutic errors reflect the psychotherapist's life-style. Many of the mechanisms of defense used by therapists disrupt the psychotherapy without the therapist's conscious awareness. In other instances, psychotherapists may commit neurotic errors and rationalize or excuse their behavior as "only human." True as this may be, therapeutic errors prevent progress and should be identified and resolved in the best interests of the patient.

Some of the more commonly occurring neurotic therapeutic errors will be described.

Becoming too busy to conduct practice properly. As the psychotherapist becomes known and accepted in the community, referrals may abound. To have many referrals is flattering and rewarding. However, there are limits as to the number of patients who can be seen effectively. The psychotherapist who cannot identify and adhere to his or her own limits will become harried, overburdened, and ineffective, burdening patients with serious, neurotically based therapeutic errors. The errors commonly committed by psychotherapists who cannot control their own schedule include chronic lateness in starting sessions, frequent canceling or changing of appointments, forgetting, recapitulation or repetitive themes in patients' explorations, and thinking of other matters while the patient talks.

Overly busy psychotherapists may rationalize that since they are identified as being such superior therapists, the patient undoubtedly profits from the therapeutic contact regardless of how distracted or inattentive the psychotherapist may be.

Becoming angry or inappropriately confrontative. Angry confrontation of patients is almost always a neurotically-based psychotherapeutic error. This type of error reflects the fears and anxieties of the psychotherapist. Such responses can never be helpful and are sure to impede the psychotherapeutic process. When the psychotherapist becomes angry at the patient, it is an invitation to role reversal; the psychotherapist demands that the patient be understanding and helpful. This is illustrated in the following dialogue from the fifth session between a psychiatric resident and the patient, a 27-year-old secretary:

Patient: I'm really annoyed. My husband got drunk at the football game and embarrassed me again. He's always doing that. . . .
Therapist: Does he get drunk a lot?
Patient: Well, not exactly drunk. . . . He has two of those large cartons of beer . . . but he acts . . . so childish!
Therapist: Then he wasn't *really* drunk . . . like falling down?
Patient: I suppose not . . . but he . . .
Therapist: You were exaggerating then? He was just drinking some beer at the football game.
Patient: (*pause*) . . . I suppose you could say that.
Therapist: So *he* was acting perfectly normal, but *you* were angry at him. You *resented* his joking and fun-making.
Patient: (*pause*) . . . Are you angry with me?
Therapist: No! Why should I be angry with you?
Patient: I don't know. . . . I just feel you didn't approve . . . just . . .
Therapist: Well, you did overreact, didn't you?
Patient: I guess . . . if you think so . . . I don't know. . . .
Therapist: Well, it seems to me your husband was only having a good time and you resented it and overreacted.
Patient: So you see me as . . . getting upset about a little thing. . . .
Therapist: Yes, that's a good way to put it.

The moralistic, judgmental attitude is inappropriate for a psychotherapist. Toward the end of this sequence, the patient seems to be responding as a therapist.

Overresponse to threats. Psychotherapy is an opportunity to explore all sorts of behavior which may not be comfortable or socially acceptable. The openness and tolerance created by the psychotherapist encourages exploration and experiencing. When the psychotherapist acts in such a way that the setting appears unsafe or unhospitable, therapeutic progress will slow or cease.

Some psychotherapists are particularly vulnerable to threats presented by the patient. By law, psychotherapists have certain duties to warn (to be discussed later in this chapter under External Barriers). Decisions to cease conducting psychotherapy and intervene in the patient's life should be extremely rare occurrences in the psychotherapist's career. Threats, both direct and indirect, should be viewed as opportunities to help the patient understand and experience. In the following excerpt, a 28-year-old management trainee presents threatening behavior during his 15th session of psychotherapy. The therapist in this simulated example overresponds:

Patient: I'm getting sick of coming here . . . and fed up with you just sitting there and doing nothing. What I'd like to do is just punch you out and walk out of here . . . maybe turn over your damned desk while I'm at it!

Therapist: Well . . . you wouldn't *really* do that would you?

Patient: You're damned right I would! I'm sick and tired of coming here and getting nothing out of it! (*stands up and paces*)

Therapist: I'm afraid you're too agitated to continue this session. You'll have to leave now.

The psychotherapist's anxiety is such that therapeutic responses are not possible. The patient's behavior represents an important aspect of his life-style and it is important that it appear during the therapeutic session. The psychotherapist has committed an error in overreacting. The more appropriate response in the actual session was as follows:

Patient: You're damned right I would! I'm sick and tired of coming here and getting nothing out of it! (*stands up and paces*)

Therapist: You feel very strongly about this. . . .

Patient: (*pacing*) I'm sick of you telling me the obvious. Why the hell don't you tell me what's *wrong* with me!

Therapist: (pause) Do you feel there is something wrong with you?

Patient: (*stops . . . seems confused*) Me . . . I, uh . . . Why the hell do you think I'm here?

Therapist: So that you can feel better . . . about yourself.

Patient: (*returns to chair, throws himself down*) That's a hopeless case!

Therapist: It sometimes feels like a terrible burden. . . .

Patient: You got *that* right. . . . I am nuts. . . . I get these waves of rage but I'm always too scared to say anything . . . I don't know why I did it just now—I usually hold it in. I don't know.

Therapist: Strong emotion can be pretty scary.

Patient: Yeah ... yeah ... (*long pause*) ... You're not mad at me?

Therapist: No. ... This is your place ... and expressing your emotion and feeling strong feelings are what make therapy progress.

Patient: (*pause*) ... When I was a kid, my Dad wasn't home much. He was in the military. When he did come home, I was excited and agitated. I would sometimes yell and carry on and he'd get mad and put me in my room for the rest of the day. He'd say, "You're con-fined to barracks for insubordination." It was the worst kind of punishment. I wanted to *be* with him and I hated him for being away and then keeping me away. I've *never* been able to say what I really felt. (*shaking head*)

Therapist: But today you did.

Patient: Yeah ... but I was terrified. ... I thought you'd tell me I couldn't come here anymore.

Therapist: Like Dad?

Patient: Yeah ... yeah ... like Dad.

The psychotherapist appropriately accepts the patient's outburst, makes efforts to clarify feelings, structures the nature of the therapeutic setting, and then reinforces the patient's spontaneous discovery that the outburst was a recapitulation of a significant developmental experience.

Not setting limits where appropriate. The other end of the con-tinuum from being too harsh, rigid, or authoritarian is indecisiveness and fear of setting out the parameters or limits of psychotherapy when the patient's behavior threatens the structure and sanctity of the process. This error is relatively rare unless the psychotherapist has passive-aggressive needs which create situations wherein the patient is en-couraged to test the limits of the psychotherapeutic milieu. The error of not setting appropriate limits is most likely to appear in the early stages of the psychotherapist's career. In the following example, a 38-year-old physician during his sixth session of psychotherapy tests the limits set by the psychotherapist:

Patient: You can't really understand how difficult my wife can be. No matter how often I tell her how I want things at home, she manages to screw up almost everything.

Therapist: It's pretty distressing.

Patient: You're damned right it is. I want to bring her to my next session so you can *see* how difficult it is.

Therapist: Well, I don't ...

Patient: (*interrupting*) You won't understand what I'm talking about unless you see it yourself. She is not to be believed. I'll bring her Thursday.

Therapist: Well . . . we usually don't . . .

Patient: *(interrupting)* I know it's unusual, but *she* is unusual. . . .

Therapist: Well . . . OK.

The psychotherapist in this constructed example would be overwhelmed by the patient's aggressive manipulation of the structure of psychotherapy. Giving in to the patient's demands would very likely create a major disruption of the purpose and process of psychotherapy. A more appropriate and therapeutic way of dealing with the limit-testing actually happened as follows:

Patient: *(interrupting)* You won't understand what I'm talking about unless you see it yourself. She is not to be believed. I'll bring her Thursday.

Therapist: What would you hope would happen Thursday?

Patient: Huh?

Therapist: If you were to bring your wife here . . . what do you hope she'll do or say?

Patient: Well . . . you'll see what I'm up against!

Therapist: You feel I don't really understand how hard it is.

Patient: Well . . . sometimes it's a thing you have to see. I'm not sure. . . . *(pause)*

Therapist: If I saw your wife's behavior, I would have no doubt about your frustration and stress.

Patient: Yeah . . . it's hard. *(pause)*

Therapist: And depressing.

Patient: Yeah. . . . *(pause)*

Therapist: And perhaps seems like too much.

Patient: You're right there . . . too much. *(pause)*

Therapist: You must have tried many solutions to this?

Patient: Yeah . . . we separated once. . . . That was no good. . . . Then . . . I . . . uh . . . well, I, uh . . . had this, I guess, affair. . . . She found out.

Therapist: That must have been difficult.

Patient: Oh, Brother! You don't know what hell she raised and how she made my life miserable. . . . I paid the price!

Therapist: So none of it has been easy.

Patient: No . . . not easy. . . .

Without panic or rigidity, the psychotherapist focuses on the patient's expressed feeling. The limit-testing mechanism gives way to the patient's need for catharsis and exploration. The error has been avoided and the psychotherapeutic process is maintained. If the psychotherapist finds that he or she is regularly unwilling or unable to set limits to maintain the integrity of the therapeutic setting, it is clear that the errors emanate from unresolved conflicts within the psychotherapist's personality.

Involvement in the patient's everyday life. Although poorly trained or character-deficient psychotherapists may enter into their patients' everyday lives, such behavior can also manifest neurotic needs for power, love, acceptance, or self-punishment. Some of the more common ways that this happens include:

- Accepting invitations to socialize with the patient.
- Responding to patients' requests for advice or guidance on a regular basis.
- Using the patient's goods or services.
- Establishing contact with or responding to the expectancies of patients' families, supervisors, or coworkers.
- Sharing sport or recreational time with patients.
- Joining patients in business ventures.

Although one could argue that such involvements do not necessarily lead to psychotherapeutic errors, each situation has the potential to disrupt or destroy the therapeutic alliance. Such risks represent a psychotherapist's neurotic needs and should be considered therapeutic errors.

Avoidance of appropriate responses. When the psychotherapist avoids an appropriate therapeutic response, the patient is allowed or encouraged to continue in confusion. The commonest errors of this type are those involving patients' efforts to create strong emotional interaction with the psychotherapist. Expressions of love, warmth, and sensuousness toward the psychotherapist can touch on natural needs for such affect. By the same token, expressions of rage, hatred, and threat can call forth the psychotherapist's defensive structure. In each case, therapists should be prepared to accept and respond appropriately to such behavior. Avoidance in responding to positive or negative transference activities of patients is a serious psychotherapeutic error usually emanating from the therapist's anxieties concerning spontaneous emotion. The following excerpt from the 12th session of a 20-year-old college student with her therapist-in-training, a 30-year-old male graduate student in psychology, illustrates neurotic avoidance of appropriate response:

Patient: I wonder if this whole business of dating and all is worth it. . . . I mean, you know . . . it's so immature! Don't you think?

Therapist: Well, possibly. . . .

Patient; You, for instance, wouldn't be like some of those silly boys I see. You're serious . . . and dedicated.

Therapist: (*pause*) . . . I suppose.

Patient: With a person like you . . . I could be . . . I mean . . . *be myself!*

Therapist: Last week you were talking about your father and how often he was gone or busy. Could you tell me more about that?

The student-psychotherapist, apparently uncomfortable with the patient's developing transference feelings, changes the subject. This not only postpones an important aspect of the patient's exploration, but may serve to weaken or even destroy the sanctuary so necessary to the psychotherapeutic alliance.

Ignoring repeated puzzling or inappropriate behavior. Patients in psychotherapy frequently say or do unusual things. While it is an error of technique or a neurotic error to "pounce" on anything which strikes the psychotherapist an unusual, ignoring such behavior which is repetitive may reflect the therapist's anxieties. In the following sequence, a somewhat schizoid male patient, age 31, demonstrates an unusual physical response during his 35th session. This response had occurred several times in previous sessions. His experienced female psychotherapist ignores it:

Patient: (*long pause*) There are things you just *can't* talk about.

Therapist: Too embarrassing?

Patient: (*jerking his head vigorously to the left*) Well . . . maybe.

Therapist: (*long pause, patient continues to jerk*) What thoughts do you have?

Patient: (*continues to jerk*) Uh . . . none very clear. (*long pause, jerking continues*)

Therapist: Have you had any dreams since our last session?

Again, an error occurs as the patient avoids significant behavior, with assistance from the psychotherapist.

Not dealing with depletion or overload. The psychotherapist who overbooks, forgets appointments, is chronically late, or regularly drowses during sessions is entering his or her conflict behavior into the therapeutic environment. The focus of psychotherapy must be on the patient's conflicts, not on those of the therapist. Expecting the patient to accept or "understand" such neurotic behavior may to some extent represent poor or inadequate training. The chronically depleted or overloaded psychotherapist is committing conflict-based errors.

Resolving neurotic psychotherapeutic errors

It is very difficult to reliably differentiate errors caused by inadequate training from those which result from the psychotherapist's character flaws or neurotic conflicts. Because any reaction or response pattern may be a combination of such elements, rigid differentiation is unrealistic. The psychotherapist who commits neurotic errors in psychotherapy is likely to ignore, avoid, or rationalize such errors in order to allay anxiety. Psychotherapeutic errors based on the psychotherapist's conflicts can be identified by one or more of the following signs:

- The behavior is distressing to the patient.
- The behavior is repetitive.
- The therapist feels guilty about what has been done or what has been omitted.
- The patient questions or objects to the repetitive behavior.
- The psychotherapist is consistently uncomfortable with the patient.
- The psychotherapist apologizes or acknowledges the behavior but continues to make the therapeutic error.

Unless the psychotherapist is willing and able to identify his or her neurotic needs, resolution of errors based on the therapist's conflicts is unlikely. The psychotherapist who intends to pursue and maintain competence must develop a capacity to evaluate self regularly. It is clear that the profession of psychotherapy is a stressful one (Norcross & Prochaska, 1986a). When it becomes apparent that neurotic conflict creates therapeutic errors on a regular basis, consultation with an experienced colleague is indicated. This step, no matter how simple and practiced, is viewed with alarm by most psychotherapists. It is often seen as evidence of deficiencies or a mark of failure.

Consultation often leads to an identification and resolution of the source of conflict. Occasionally, such consultation may determine that psychotherapy for the psychotherapist is indicated. When this kind of conflict resolution is called for, entering into psychotherapy as quickly as possible is advisable in the best interests of the patients of the distressed psychotherapist. Psychotherapy with psychotherapists will be explored in the next chapter.

Errors of Character Pathology

Identifying and classifying character pathology, in contrast to neurotic adjustments or behaviors, has been and remains difficult. For the purposes of this section, psychotherapeutic errors based on the therapist's character pathology will be defined as those behaviors by the psychotherapist which the therapist knows are considered unacceptable or forbidden by ethics or law. There is no prescribed list of such behaviors (APA, 1981; Haas, Malouf & Mayerson, 1986). Psychotherapeutic errors based on the therapist's character deficiencies generally benefit a want or need of the psychotherapist at the expense of disrupting or destroying the therapeutic alliance. These errors may have a destructive effect on the patient's personality. Those psychotherapists who are guilty of such errors often rationalize their behavior when discovered or challenged (Holroyd & Bouhoutsos, 1985).

Defaulting on the promise to provide a safe setting and to work in the patient's best interests is the essence of therapeutic error resulting from the psychotherapist's character pathology. Some of the more common errors of character deficiency are considered below:

Intimacy between patient and psychotherapist. For more than half a century, sensuous interaction of any degree has been considered countertherapeutic. When Sandor Ferenczi proposed a new style of encouraging catharsis during psychoanalytic sessions by exchanging "motherly" hugs and kisses with the patient, Freud wrote to Ferenczi:

> We have hitherto in our technique held to the conclusion that patients are to be refused erotic gratifications. You know, too, that where more extensive gratifications are not to be had milder caresses very easily take over their role, in love affairs, on the stage etc. Now picture what will be the result of publishing your technique. There is no revolutionary who is not driven out of the field by a still more radical one. A number of independent thinkers in matters of technique will say to themselves: why stop at a kiss? Certainly one gets further when one adopts "pawing" as well, which after all doesn't make a baby, and then bolder ones will come along who will go further to peeping and showing—and soon we shall have accepted in the technique of analysis the whole repertoire of demiviergerie and petting parties, resulting in an enormous increase of interest in psychoanalysis among both analysts and patients . . . . . . and God The Father Ferenczi gazing at the lively scene he has created will perhaps say to himself: maybe after all I should have halted in my technique of motherly affection *before* the kiss. (Jones, 1957, pp. 163-164)

Freud's prediction has come to be. Between five and 10 percent of psychotherapists admit having had intercourse with their patients. Most of these tend to repeat such behavior (Holroyd & Brodsky, 1977; Holroyd & Bouhoutsos, 1985). The courts have held that the psychotherapeutic relationship creates an emotional transference making it impossible for a psychotherapist to engage in any kind of intimacy with the patient and simultaneously give the patient proper therapy. There is even question as to whether an erotic relationship is permissible after psychotherapy ends (Cummings & Sobel, 1985).

Breaches of confidentiality or privilege. The guarantee of confidentiality and legal protection of patient privilege are, aside from legal exceptions such as duty to warn or duty to report child sexual abuse, honor-bound pledges made by the psychotherapist to the patient. Casual references to patient behavior in social settings or for the amusement of friends or colleagues are therapeutic errors which demonstrate character deficiencies of the psychotherapist. Such behavior may result in the patient being compromised and exposed to scandal. It is clear evidence that the psychotherapist neither respects the patient nor considers the therapeutic alliance a matter of serious professional commitment. Although cavalier disregard of the patient's confidence (or clinical records) may sometimes be rationalized as reflecting inexperience on the part of the psychotherapist or poor administrative controls, the potential impact on the patient and the psychotherapeutic course is so powerful and dangerous that the therapist must be faulted for a lack of awareness and capacity to act responsibly in the patient's best interest.

Lying to the patient. Lies, deceits, distortions, and omissions in professional communication between psychotherapist and patient are errors based on the psychotherapist's deficiencies of character. On the other hand, the patient is not entitled to, nor is the therapeutic process enhanced by, information about or from the psychotherapist which is unrelated to the process. The psychotherapist who withholds information about his or her personal life is maintaining the sanctuary of the therapeutic setting as "the patient's place." Purposely deceiving the patient about such things as the psychotherapist's availability for scheduled appointments, the amount of time which the patient can expect at each session, the security of records, or the therapist's true qualifications represents a serious therapeutic error. Such errors are committed by psychotherapists who know perfectly well they are doing wrong, but choose to endanger their patient's therapeutic process by such behavior.

The following excerpt is from the seventh session of a 42-year-old school teacher who entered psychotherapy for the second time:

Patient: (*long pause*) I'm glad I returned to psychotherapy. . . . I really didn't want to come. . . . I thought about it for six years before I called.

Therapist: It was a hard decision.

Patient: Yes . . . no . . . I mean . . . I knew I needed help, but my experience six years ago was so upsetting. . . . I thought I couldn't go through that again . . . I, uh. (*weeps softly*)

Therapist: It was bad. (*long pause*)

Patient: I was so depressed, so hopeless, then I started with Dr. Jones and I so much wanted to find out . . . to change . . . and maybe I expected too much . . . but I . . . he would cancel appointments at the last minute. . . . I'd be all set to explore something and he or his secretary would call and say, "He's been called out of town" or "There's been an emergency." I could understand that . . . but it was once or twice a month. Pretty soon I began to feel embarrassed . . . that I wasn't *that* important . . . maybe just a silly woman. . . . Then . . . I was holding in and getting more depressed. . . . (*weeps*) . . . One afternoon his secretary called and canceled my appointment. I had a lot to talk about. . . . She said he'd been called out of town. I felt *so* bad. I went out to supper. I saw Dr. Jones at the restaurant. I left. . . . Somehow I felt it was my fault. I wasn't good enough . . . and I wasn't worth his time (*weeps*). . . . (*long pause*)

Therapist: Did you ever discuss this.

Patient: Oh . . . no. *I* was embarrassed. I felt he was justified in avoiding me. I wouldn't talk after that. . . . Soon I quit. . . . (*weeps*) . . . I thought about killing myself. . . . It was hard. . . . I knew I needed help . . . but I just *couldn't* go . . . to him or anyone. So I moved and took a job here. I just *had* to get away.

Therapist: So you saw the lies as some kind of measure of your own lack of worth.

Patient: (*weeping*) . . . Yes. . . . He thought of me the way I thought of myself. . . . He made it true. . . .

Therapist: Were you angry?

Patient: At first . . . but then I blamed myself.

Therapist: That makes it hard to trust this therapy . . . and me.

Patient: Well . . . I hope you aren't offended. I wanted to tell you.

Therapist: I am glad you did. I feel bad about your experience and about anyone who would make things harder for you. It will not happen here . . . but you will have to judge that yourself.

The deceit of the previous therapist was clearly a therapeutic error with significant and potentially dangerous effects on the patient.

Taking cash from the patient to evade taxes. There exists a view among some that doctors prefer to be paid in cash so that they can record and report less income and evade taxes. Unfortunately, some psychotherapists accept and encourage this behavior. A joint venture with the patient to break the law is a psychotherapeutic error because it establishes a close personal and philosophical relationship between psychotherapist and patient. Such a "private" agreement of mutual involvement in crime creates a barrier to the maintenance of the sanctuary of the therapeutic session. In addition, the therapist as crime partner is hardly in a position to set limits and maintain objectivity.

Entering into business with the patient. During the course of psychotherapy, some therapists start business ventures with patients. Such involvement represents a therapeutic error since the maintenance of a certain psychological distance is necessary for the psychotherapist to maintain objectivity and attend to the needs of the patient. The weakening of the therapist's responsibilities in exchange for personal gain speaks for character inadequacies. Business dealings between psychotherapist and patient are countertherapeutic and should be avoided on the grounds of ethical concern and sound judgment.

Accepting gifts from the patient. Patients may wish to give the psychotherapist a gift—to express appreciation, guilt, affection, or other feelings and motives. Dealing with these gestures in a therapeutic manner has been addressed earlier in this chapter. The psychotherapist who is offered, and accepts, gifts from patients regularly is creating therapeutic error by engaging in a relatively intimate social interaction with the patients. This will eventually interfere with objectivity, openness, and the opportunity for patients to experience emotion during the therapeutic process. The psychotherapist who encourages or cannot effectively deal with patient gift-giving has character deficiencies which will create and perpetuate problems.

Avoiding consultation. There are frequent occasions during every psychotherapist's career where errors, confusion, or doubts occur. At such times, the therapist is duty-bound to seek consultation with colleagues to clarify or resolve issues which might be detrimental to the therapeutic setting or to the process and progress of particular patients. When a psychotherapist becomes alarmed or even concerned, such consultation is mandatory.

The following illustrates such a consultation. A fairly experienced therapist became concerned about threats of suicide from a patient who was being seen in long-term individual psychotherapy. She received a note from her patient suggesting that "It is all over . . . there's no use of going on." The patient had made such threats in the past, but the current episode occurred soon after the death of the patient's father. The psychotherapist chose to consult with a colleague who had seen this patient in group psychotherapy in the past:

Therapist: I appreciate your seeing me on such short notice.

Colleague: That's OK. Jane is acting up again, I see from this note.

Therapist: Well . . . I'm concerned. . . . She's threatening to stop therapy. I've still got the gun she bought the last time she felt suicidal. . . .

Colleague: I remember. You did well with her. . . . I'd guess she'll never want that gun back.

Therapist: She uses so much medication for her various real illnesses, she has the means.

Colleague: That's important. . . . What about her family . . . the support system?

Therapist: I felt I had to warn the husband. . . . I told Jane that I would. . . . She had a tantrum but I feel she was relieved . . . but I feel so helpless to deal with her manipulations sometimes.

Colleague: I remember those well when she was in group. . . . I believe she left group because the limits were set too stringently by her fellow group members. That put the whole burden back on you.

Therapist: Yes. . . . I wish she'd continued . . . but now what? I believe she might, given the right circumstances, do it!

Colleague: Yes . . . that's possible . . . and must be a prime concern . . . as it clearly is with you. Have you offered her extra sessions?

Therapist: Yes . . . she's coming again tomorrow . . . but . . . I wonder sometimes if I'm doing Jane any good . . . or doing the right things.

Colleague: Don't we all? . . . This is pretty burdensome.

Therapist: Well . . . it's not just that.

Colleague: But it is somewhat that.

Therapist: Yes . . . but should she be getting other kinds of help?

Colleague: Does she want to be hospitalized?

Therapist: God, no! She hated it the time her husband admitted her years ago.

Colleague: So . . . in effect you're doing everything you know how to do—as well as you can.
Therapist: Well . . . I guess.
Colleague: *I* think you are . . . and I believe the crisis will pass. I think maybe we should talk some about how angry we can get at patients who test us this way.

A decision not to consult might be ascribed to pride, lack of time, or other rational explanation. In simpler terms, if the psychotherapist doesn't do something which is ordinarily in the best interests of the patient, a therapeutic error has probably been committed. Conscious avoidance of correct or appropriate behavior suggests a basis in character pathology.

Resolving character-based psychotherapeutic errors

Defining a therapeutic error as being a result of the psychotherapist's character inadequacies may be problematical when such an error occurs only once, except in blatantly unacceptable behavior such as sexualizing the patient or engaging in illegal acts. When the unethical or unacceptable behavior occurs more than once, it becomes clear that the distortions, evasions, and destructive intentions of character pathology are involved. The destructive "acting-out" which is a hallmark of character pathology rarely occurs only once (Holroyd & Brodsky, 1977).

Those psychotherapists who have created character-based errors in their psychotherapy are unlikely candidates to resolve such errors. A transfer to an experienced, interested, and willing colleague, with full disclosure, is mandatory. Each step of the transfer process must focus on the best interests of the patient. The patient must be fully informed and involved regardless of the liability to the miscreant psychotherapist.

Following the proper attention to the interests and welfare of the patient, the psychotherapist should seek rehabilitation and preventive restraints. This ordinarily would require the selection of two senior colleagues, not personally known to the psychotherapist-at-fault. One should serve as a therapist to deal with the character deficits while the second should serve as a psychotherapy supervisor to ensure that the psychotherapeutic errors are not repeated.

These recommendations are stringent and carry a strong tone of moral indignation, punishment, and rehabilitation. It is suggested that this is appropriate for psychotherapists who endanger their patients by creating character-based psychotherapeutic error. The alternative is to leave the profession.

EXTERNAL BARRIERS TO PSYCHOTHERAPEUTIC PROGRESS

There are circumstances outside the direct control of either the patient or the psychotherapist which raise barriers to therapeutic progress. When these occur, the therapist and the patient must jointly evaluate and agree upon methods of resolution of the interference. Such barriers may begin as external circumstance, but can become a vehicle for neurotic barrier behavior by the patient or therapeutic error by the psychotherapist. Some of the more common external barriers to therapy progress will be considered and then methods of resolution will be addressed.

Legal Issues

Whenever the patient is a party in a legal matter which requires the involvement of the psychotherapist in the proceedings, the psychotherapeutic process will be disrupted or even ended. When deposed by an attorney, subpoenaed for records, or required to testify, the psychotherapist's skill at establishing a sanctuary, maintaining the therapeutic alliance, and intervening objectively and appropriately is nullified. In the face of these pressures and authoritarian actions, efforts to conduct psychotherapy become superficial and futile. Such circumstances occur infrequently, but the psychotherapist must be prepared to recognize and deal with barriers based on legal actions.

Personal injury suits. Should a patient become either a plaintiff or a defendant in a civil suit involving personal injuries of any sort, the patient's consultation with a mental health professional will be of interest to attorneys on both sides of the adversary process. All of the psychotherapist's records are subject to *discovery* (the process before actual trial when attorneys are allowed, even mandated, to seek all possible information which might be regarded as evidence admissible and cogent to the case). Should the patient's mental status be an issue in the suit, guarantees of privilege no longer apply and the psychotherapist will be questioned by both the patient's attorney and the opposing lawyer. Subpoenas for records or for a deposition where the psychotherapist will be questioned about everything he or she knows about the patient are disturbing since they herald a disruption or even the end of the psychotherapeutic alliance.

Family litigation. With over half of marriages ending in divorce and 15 percent of these divorces involving litigation, most psychotherapists can anticipate being called to testify as either a *treating doctor* (providing facts about the patient's diagnosis, therapeutic course, and prognosis) or an *expert witness* (providing opinions concerning the patient's nature, condition, character, and reactions). In some situations, a psychotherapist may have been consulted by both parties in a marital conflict, thus complicating even more the issues of confidentiality and the psychotherapeutic alliance. Psychotherapists prefer to be exempted from participation in such matters, but the law recognizes such preference in only very limited respects. (These will be addressed shortly.)

Duty to warn. The now famous Tarasoff decision* has been affirmed in most states, thus requiring a psychotherapist to warn the potential victim of a patient's imminent intent to do harm. The authorities must also be warned once the psychotherapist determines that the threat of dangerousness to self or others is genuine and has a high probability of occurring in spite of anything the psychotherapist might do to intervene. If the psychotherapist overestimates the danger and warns unnecessarily, a civil suit against the psychotherapist may be brought. If the psychotherapist does not warn and the patient does hurt himself/herself or others, both criminal *and* civil charges may ensue. Aside from the legal quandary, "blowing the whistle" on a patient is bound to adversely affect or destroy the therapeutic relationship. It is fortunate that duty-to-warn issues are rare in the course of a psychotherapeutic practice.

Child abuse. All states require that professionals who discover that their patient has been guilty of child abuse report this to the authorities. Psychotherapists who do this immediately lose their ability to provide the sanctuary necessary to conduct psychotherapy as we have described it.

Malpractice litigation. Psychotherapists are vulnerable to civil (and in some cases criminal) charges by patients, relatives, or others who may be in some way involved with a patient's treatment. Such litigation not only destroys the relationship with the patient involved (as in the case where the patient wishes to continue the psychotherapy in defiance of the wishes of family or guardians) but influences adversely the ability of the psychotherapist to function well with other patients (Fisher, 1986).

Tarasoff v. Regents of the Univ. of Cal., 13 Cal. 3d 177, 529 P. 2d. 553, 118 Cal. Rptr. 129 (1974).

Coping with barriers raised by legal issues

No method of coping with the barriers to effective psychotherapy raised by legal issues is likely to be completely effective in terms of returning the psychotherapy to a pre-incident level of confidence and security for both the patient and the psychotherapist. The end result, at best, will be a period of retrenchment and joint efforts to return to an acceptable level of confidence and sanctuary. More likely, the psychotherapeutic relationship will have to be terminated and the patient encouraged to begin again with another psychotherapist.

In order to anticipate as well as deal with legal issues in psychotherapy, the therapist should be well informed and prepared. A certain amount of preparatory study should be done by all practicing psychotherapists (Blau, 1984a; Fisher, 1986; Sales, 1981; Shapiro, 1984). These materials should be read and understood *before* legal issues arise in order to prevent precipitous or inappropriate action by the psychotherapist. Assuming that the psychotherapist understands the fundamentals of the legal process, the following actions are recommended when legal barriers occur.

- The psychotherapeutic process should cease and the legal issue should be addressed directly and realistically.
- In cases of apparent dangerousness which seems imminent and not preventable, the patient must be faced with the psychotherapist's duty to warn. If the patient does not withdraw from the intent to hurt self or others (such as refusing to give the therapist a lethal object involved in the intent), the psychotherapist must contact the patient's family, the object of the patient's threat, and, where appropriate, law enforcement officials to intervene and prevent the dangerous behavior. If the patient has an attorney, he or she should also be informed of the situation.
- In those circumstances where it becomes apparent that the patient has been engaging in child abuse, the patient should first be encouraged to inform the appropriate health agency, thus "turning himself (or herself) in." If the patient refuses or delays, the psychotherapist must inform the appropriate authorities.
- Where the patient remains in psychotherapy while others file malpractice charges, the psychotherapist should review the situation with the patient and with the patient's attorney as early as possible after the issue arises. The patient should be reassured that the psychotherapist will protect, as far as the law allows, all confidential information that has been shared between patient and therapist.
- The psychotherapist should contact his or her attorney as soon as an issue arises in order to have competent legal advice as to the

therapist's rights, obligations, privileges, and options in the matter at hand.

- The psychotherapist should ensure that all notes, tests, messages, consultations, and other material in the patient's folder are organized and clearly identified. These, as well as appointment book notations, are likely to be subpoenaed. Copies of material such as pages from the appointment book should have all references to other patients removed. The originals should *never* be turned over to anyone without the approval of the therapist's attorney.
- In most cases, opposing attorneys will want to examine *all* notes, tests, work-up sheets, and reports. Copies should be prepared and available before deposition.
- Prepare an up-to-date résumé or *curriculum vitae*. The attorneys for both sides will request this. Be prepared for questions concerning education, training, certification, and other qualifications.
- If the psychotherapist's case file contains information which has no bearing on the legal proceedings, a *motion for protective order* should be requested before the material is made available to an opposing attorney. Such a motion will require the psychotherapist to meet with a judge in chambers. If the judge agrees that the information is of no relevance to the case, he or she will "seal the record," which in effect will prevent that information being revealed during the litigation.

It should be clear from the above that when legal issues affect the patient, the psychotherapist, or both, psychotherapy cannot proceed. At best, the sessions will focus on intellectual aspects of the case or catharsis for both patient and therapist. The anxiety and threat that are so much a part of adversary legal proceedings can destroy a psychotherapist's effectiveness. Should the patient wish to continue psychotherapy during the course of legal proceedings, even referring to another psychotherapist is unlikely to be helpful since the new psychotherapeutic consultations will be subject to the discovery process. At best, counseling and support can be provided to the patient.

Relatives

The process of psychotherapy frequently raises the anxiety of those who relate closely to the patient. Although significant others in the patient's life may generally support the psychotherapy process as being in the patient's best interests, fears of being found at fault or discomfort at changes in the patient's personality can stir the anxieties of friends and relatives.

This can become a therapeutic barrier when any of the following occurs:

- The friend or relative counsels the patient that the process of psychotherapy is harmful, without value, or unnecessary.
- The interested party calls or writes the psychotherapist asking questions, revealing information about the patient, or offering advice or criticism.
- A significant person threatens to remove support, financial or otherwise, if the patient continues in psychotherapy.
- A significant person in the patient's life offers or suggests a "better" treatment or a more "effective" psychotherapist.
- A relative calls or writes the therapist with a demand to cease the psychotherapy, threatening suit, ethical charges, or bodily harm.
- Relatives of the therapist meet patients socially or in business contacts and allow themselves to interact with the patient—on either a friendly or unfriendly basis.

Even though the patient and the psychotherapist may be blameless for these external impediments to therapeutic progress, the responsibility to acknowledge and remove the impediments falls squarely on both parties of the therapeutic alliance. To avoid the issue is to solidify the barrier to progress. In the following example, the patient's mother called the psychotherapist, offering to tell "things he wouldn't tell you" and asking that the therapist not reveal to the patient that she had called. The dialogue of the telephone call was as follows:

Therapist: This is Doctor Jones.

Relative: Doctor Jones, I'm Tommy Green's mother.

Therapist: How do you do, Mrs Green.

Relative: I hope it's all right to call you. I've been so worried. Tommy is such a delicate boy and has had so many problems . . . many of which I'm sure he hasn't told you. . . . (*pause*)

Therapist: Yes, Mrs. Green?

Relative: Well, as his mother, I thought we should talk so that I can help, tell you some things that would help you understand Tommy. Of course, I wouldn't want him to know I called—you'll respect my confidence, won't you Doctor?

Therapist: First of all, I'm sure your son will understand your concern for him and I think you should tell him that you called and offered to help. I, of course, am duty-bound to tell him you wished to help.

Relative: Oh Doctor! No! He'll be furious!

Therapist: Perhaps he will understand that you have a mother's concern.

Relative: Oh! You mean you'd tell him? Oh, my! I don't know!

Therapist: It would be best that you tell him of our talk.

Relative: I guess I shouldn't have called.
Therapist: It's natural for you to be concerned.

The therapist is courteous, supportive, but firm. During the next session, the psychotherapist reported to the patient (a 36-year-old married computer programmer) his mother's call:

Therapist: I must tell you that your mother called me on Monday offering to help with your therapy.
Patient: Oh?
Therapist: Yes. . . . She felt there were things she could tell me about you that would never tell me and would help in our work.
Patient: Do you think that would help?
Therapist: No. . . . Do you want your mother to bring up those things in your life that she thinks are significant?
Patient: I hope you told her off!
Therapist: No. I was polite and suggested she tell you she called.
Patient: She didn't . . . but she told my sister, who told me. I was wondering if you would tell me.
Therapist: At the beginning I told you I would be as open as possible. Sometimes this is hard to believe.
Patient: I guess I'm not sure I can trust anyone.

Had the psychotherapist not revealed the mother's efforts to involve herself, the sanctuary might have been lost. The effectiveness of the therapeutic efforts would certainly have been diminished.

Coping with barriers raised by relatives

The first order of business, as always, is the preservation of the psychotherapeutic sanctuary. The therapist must avoid action that is not in the best interests of the patient. The basic rules are as follows:

- The patient must be told of all contacts by others.
- All responses to such contacts must preserve and protect confidentiality.
- Barriers raised by relatives of the patient are usually associated with repeated incidents of conflict in the patient's life experience. The psychotherapist should make every effort to help the patient understand the roles and needs of all parties associated with the conflict incidents. Clarification and interpretation should be used to enhance the patient's experiencing as the barriers are discussed during the therapeutic sessions which follow the barrier incident.

Medication

In an era of biological psychiatry, psychotropic medications are readily available to almost all patients in psychotherapy. The effects of such medication often fall far below the hopes of psychiatrists and the expectancies of patients. Although some degree of behavioral control can be expected from the use of psychotropic medications, negative effects which constitute barriers to psychotherapeutic progress can be expected. Experiencing is slowed significantly. Thus, the most important patient reactions, necessary for the therapeutic process to occur, are disrupted or eliminated (Karon, 1986). The effects of psychotropic medication in significant numbers of cases may be neurological changes of a deteriorative nature (Breggin, 1983).

Coping with the barriers raised by medication

The psychotherapist cannot ethically or rationally forbid a patient to use psychotropic medication. When the issue is introduced, either as a question or a statement of intent by the patient, the psychotherapist should make every effort to ensure that this barrier be as limited and unobtrusive in the psychotherapeutic process as possible. It is the psychotherapist's responsibility to help the patient face and deal with certain specifics with regard to the use of psychotropic drugs during the course of psychotherapy.

- Patients should inform their physicians that they are actively engaged in psychotherapy and that reduction or elimination of the psychotropic medication may be desirable.
- Psychotropic medication can have detrimental side effects and harmful long-range sequelae. The patient has a responsibility and right to understand the effects of the medication.
- Should the patient decide to continue to use medication, it is the psychotherapist's responsibility to set limits and even terminate the therapeutic process should it become clear that medication is interfering significantly with the patient's capacity to use the psychotherapeutic process in his or her best interests.

In the following case, a 32-year-old postal worker suffering a postdivorce depression reports that he is having continuing problems with depression and can't keep his mind on things being discussed in psychotherapy:

Patient: It's not getting any better. . . . I've increased my Xanax but it doesn't seem to help.

Therapist: How long have you been taking this medication?

Patient: On and off for two years.

Therapist: How does it affect you?

Patient: I don't know—sometimes it helps and sometimes it seems to make things worse.

Therapist: I think we should talk about your using medication to feel better. How often do you see your physician?

Patient: Oh...I haven't seen him for about two years....I just renew the prescription.

Therapist: I'm going to suggest a couple of things. First, you should know that psychotherapy proceeds best when you experience emotion during our sessions. Since most psychotropic medications restrict emotions, when you use them you are working against your own progress. I'd like you to make an appointment with your physician. You're probably due for a general check-up. Tell him you are in psychotherapy and that you'd like to proceed without medication. See if he has any objections. If you want him to talk with me, I'd be happy to do so. I also think you should ask your physician for detailed literature about your medications or you can look them up in the PDR, the Physician's Desk Reference, at the University Library. The more you know about what you're doing, the more you can work in your own best interests.

Patient: Do I have to give up all medications?

Therapist: That's something for you to decide with your physician. I can only tell you that it is generally agreed by psychotherapists that psychotropic medications hinder the therapeutic process more frequently than they help.

Patient: I don't know....

Therapist: You're concerned about giving up the Xanax.

Patient: Yeah....I've been using them so long....I don't know... maybe I'm addicted....

Therapist: All the more reason to see your physician.

Patient: Yeah....I guess I'll do that....

The patient had a complete physical. Some mild hypertension was discovered. His physician prescribed a wellness and fitness program of diet and exercise. The patient stopped taking psychotropic medication. The depression lifted and psychotherapy proceeded.

Illness

Significant illness, in the self or in important others, has major implications for the stability and efficiency of the psychotherapeutic process. Should either the patient or the psychotherapist become seriously ill, the process will be affected.

When illness is not life-threatening, various negative emotional responses still occur (Guy & Souder, 1986b). The patient may be fearful, guilty, angry, or in other ways reactive. These responses are also common and to be expected when a person important to the patient becomes ill. The psychotherapist should not be surprised or disdainful when patients exhibit strong emotional reactions to the illness or death of pets. An enormous amount of affection, interpersonal expectancy, and identification can be invested in animals (or even objects such as one's house or automobile).

The psychotherapist's illness usually evokes anxiety about desertion, a response already in the experience of many patients. If, as sometimes unfortunately happens, the psychotherapist's illness is disabling or terminal, the effects are usually devastating for the patient.

Where the patient becomes ill, psychotherapy will be disrupted as the patient faces real issues of survival and mortality. The expected end result of psychotherapy is for the patient to live independently, effectively, and with increased quality of life in such areas as productivity, health, use of the environment, friendships, self-acceptance, parenting, and loving. Illness threatens all qualities of life.

Coping with barriers raised by illness

In the case of a psychotherapist's debilitating or terminal illness, the psychotherapist must make every effort to help patients transfer to another psychotherapist. The mechanics of transfer are simple. Resolving the emotional conflicts caused by the anticipated desertion is problematical. The psychotherapist must first accept the reality that he or she *is* deserting the patient. When possible, the psychotherapist must help the patient focus on this issue, deal with the consequent turbulent emotion and help to transfer to another psychotherapist with a minimum of residual guilt, rage, and regression. This may be difficult or impossible should the psychotherapist's condition limit physical or emotional capacities to carry out these "final" responsibilities to the patient. Where this is not or cannot be done, the burden of conflict resolution will fall entirely on the patient and the replacement psychotherapist—if indeed the patient chooses to continue psychotherapy.

The sequence of interventions to be followed by the psychotherapist where issues of illness emerge is as follows:

- The realities and expectancies involved in the illness, whether it is the patient, the psychotherapist, or a relative who is ill, must be brought out in detail at the earliest session after the issue becomes known.

- Every effort should be made to help the patient experience all the emotional responses which emerge in respect to the illness situation.
- Where grieving and loss are anticipated, they should be brought out openly.
- Additional sessions scheduled closely together can sometimes help working through illness barriers.
- In those unfortunate instances where the patient suffers a terminal illness, the psychotherapist should move the relationship from traditional psychotherapy to the therapeutics of death and dying (Shneidman, 1973). If unable to do this for any reason, the psychotherapist should arrange for another professional to help the patient with issues of termination. This is a very poor second choice to the patient's psychotherapist doing this important work.

In those instances where the patient is seriously ill but not in a life-threatening situation, visits to the patient in the hospital are not likely to be helpful in maintaining the therapeutic sanctuary. A letter, a telephone call, or a very brief visit is sufficient to reassure the patient that the psychotherapist is optimistic about the patient's recovery and that therapy awaits when the patient is fit and ready.

Vacations and Work Schedules as Barriers

Disruptions in the regularity of psychotherapeutic sessions are barriers regardless of the realities involved. Patients take vacations, as should psychotherapists. Some therapists stop seeing patients during the entire month of July or August. Other psychotherapists prefer shorter vacation periods spread throughout the year.

Most patients are threatened to a larger or lesser degree when they become aware that the psychotherapist has a private life which excludes those being treated.

Patients may cancel vacation time as a demonstration of positive transference. Those patients who are anxious about progressing and revealing too quickly in psychotherapy, however, may take every opportunity to cancel sessions.

Psychotherapy is particularly difficult for those patients whose work requires shift duty or emergency demands. Canceling and rescheduling of regular, patterned appointment times disrupts the therapeutic course to an extent dependent on many factors. Schedule changes are more disruptive if frequent. If schedule changes occur at a point in the therapy that is particularly stressful for the patient, regression from experiential focus to intellectualization by the patient can be expected.

Anticipating and dealing with barriers raised by vacations and work demands

Whereas many of the external barriers addressed previously occur with relative rarity, vacations and schedule changes can be expected during every psychotherapeutic course. This should be anticipated and included during the structuring given by the psychotherapist during the first session. An excerpt from a first session illustrates this:

Therapist: During the course of our work together, we may have to deal with interruptions in our appointments. As I've said, regularity of sessions is important for best therapeutic progress. One or both of us will probably take vacations during the time we're working together.

Patient: Not too many I hope. (*laughs*)

Therapist: Of course. . . . There will be times, however, when we can't meet at our regular time. Sometimes there will be a chance for substitute sessions. At other times we'll just cancel. I will give you as much advance notice as possible. I take a week off about four times a year, often in conjunction with a professional meeting or seminar.

Patient: We usually take off two weeks in July. Also, . . . yeah . . . we go to my parent's home for a week during Christmas.

Therapist: In each case, we'll talk about it in advance and try to work out the best schedules we can for you.

In those situations where a patient cancels appointments regularly, it may be necessary for the psychotherapist to bring the issue forth, as in the following case of a 35-year-old female accountant who had canceled five of the previous 10 scheduled sessions:

Patient: I won't be able to be here next Tuesday. We have a review committee meeting.

Therapist: Um-hm. . . .

Patient: I guess we'd better cancel. I'll be out of town the rest of week.

Therapist: Mmm . . . in the past two months you've canceled about half of your appointments.

Patient: Well, yes . . . but I've had these things I must do.

Therapist: You are active and busy.

Patient: I really don't like to cancel or change . . . but . . . well, I've been coming here for six months and I'm still tense and agitated.

Therapist: If you felt better, perhaps it would be easier to come to your sessions more regularly.

Patient: Well, I . . . it's sort of confusing. . . . I am *so* pressured at work.

Therapist: We will do whatever *you* choose. I must tell you, as I did when we started, that regularity of sessions is in your best interests. The therapy process moves ahead more efficiently when we can meet at the times we agree on for your regular appointments.

Patient: It's so hard to be pinned down to a specific time. . . .

Therapist: Has this always been so?

Patient: (*long pause*) I've had a lot of trouble here. That's why I mostly do audits. I have trouble keeping regular appointments. I don't know why.

Therapist: Psychotherapy is a miniature of your life-style. It's not surprising that problems of your everyday life appear here. . . . That's the way it should be. When these things happen here, we can talk about them . . . look at them . . . understand them better.

Patient: I'd sure like to know why I can't keep appointments. That's caused me some heartache in my social life.

Therapist: Now that it's happening here, we can explore it.

Shortly after this session, the patient chose a different hour for her psychotherapy and the regular cancellations ceased.

External barriers to psychotherapeutic progress almost always include emotional issues and neurotic life patterns. Resolution of barriers should be considered as opportunities for the patient to increase self-understanding.

WHEN ERRORS OR BARRIERS MAINTAIN

The general procedure for dealing with problems and barriers to psychotherapeutic progress follow a general formula:

- The psychotherapist must identify the problem or the barrier.
- Where the problem is a result of psychotherapeutic error, the therapist must resolve the error as quickly and efficiently as possible in the patient's best interests. Steps involved for the psychotherapist may be self-evaluation, reading, consultation with experienced colleagues, psychotherapy, or transfer of the patient.
- In dealing with patient barriers or external impediments, the se-

quence of steps to resolution may include tolerance and acceptance, identification of the barrier, clarification of the patient's feelings, interpretation of the dynamics of the situation, confrontation, guided fantasy, or structuring.

Should none of the usual techniques result in resolution of barriers within a reasonable period of time, there are other steps which may be taken to move the therapeutic process forward. These range from mild to drastic, and should be initiated only when the psychotherapist is relatively certain that such actions are in the patient's best interests.

Increasing the Frequency of Sessions

When the psychotherapist decides that the plateau in progress is not temporary and efforts at resolution seem of little help, increasing the frequency of sessions somtimes helps the patient "break through." This is most likely to be helpful when the patient has demonstrated a pattern of being most active and experiencing more toward the end of each session.

Review of Assessment

It is sometimes helpful for the psychotherapist to review the initial psychological assessment. Aspects of the structure of the patient's personality may be found which explain or clarify the difficulties which are impeding progress. This review can be a joint venture between the therapist and the patient.

Supervision or Consultation

Psychotherapists who hesitate to use supervision or consultation limit their potential as professionals. To conceive of a career in the practice of psychotherapy without need for self-exploration, collegial review and sharing or frank advice on complex issues would be a reflection of neurotic self-aggrandizement, naiveté, character faults, or at best supreme self-confidence. The ability to identify needs for consultation is a psychotherapeutic skill equal to any other in working for the best interests of the patient.

Most psychotherapists report that a single consultation with an experienced colleague is sufficient to generate insights as to how to resolve a knotty problem which has not yielded to usual and customary techniques.

Psychological Evaluation

Even though the patient has had a psychological assessment before beginning psychotherapy, there may come a time when progress ceases and no clear solutions emerge after all of the procedures above have been tried. In such a situation, it is advisable to refer the patient to a colleague very experienced in the evaluation of personality dynamics for help in identifying important areas for therapeutic focus. The following illustrates such a procedure:

A 32-year-old female librarian stopped psychotherapy after 150 individual sessions. She was much improved in respect to anxiety and depression, which had been debilitating. She still expressed ambivalence about her ability to relate to men. She returned after eight months, requesting a continuation of psychotherapy. After several sessions, it was clear that neither the psychotherapist nor the patient was able to understand what prevented further exploration and experiencing. The patient was referred to a senior colleague for psychological evaluation. The report follows (names and other identifying information are fictitious):

PSYCHOLOGICAL EVALUATION
(PSYCHOTHERAPY)

NAME: Jones, Mary   DATE OF EXAMINATION: 1/3/86
BIRTHDATE: 12/1/54   AGE: 32-1
EDUCATION: 16+   OCCUPATION: Librarian

REFERRAL

Jane Coe, Ph.D. refers Ms. Jones. Ms. Jones has been in psychotherapy with Dr. Coe for some period of time. Referral is for the purpose of evaluation of progress, discovery of the basis of her current ambivalence toward her marriage, and recommendations for completing psychotherapy. Dr. Coe includes a detailed assessment which was done in 1979. Full Scale intelligence was found to be at the 80th percentile (Verbal at the 88th). Personality analysis found Ms. Jones to be a "loner," with mixed sexual identification. Fixation and conflict with a suspicious, critical, and stubborn mother were noted. Psychotherapy was recommended.

On interview, Ms. Jones indicated that she would like to know what areas in her emotional life contain unresolved conflict. She is very interested in knowing the nature of her ambivalence toward her husband. She would like to know how to "move off center." She would like to know why she is very ambivalent about having children.

Ms. Jones had about 150 sessions of individual psychotherapy with Dr. Coe. She has had three sessions of group therapy and three joint sessions with her husband with a marriage counselor.

The current marriage took place in 1981. It is her second marriage, and there have been many ups and downs. She has no children.

EXAMINATION PROCEDURES

Rorschach Examination.

RESPONSE TO EVALUATION

Ms. Jones is a blond woman of about 5'4" in height, weighing about 125 pounds. She has blue eyes. She speaks in a clear and articulate manner. She is forthright. Emotional response is relatively flat. She rarely responds with humor, or any change from a very serious expression of self. She is cooperative throughout.

RESULTS OF EXAMINATION

A. *Formal Aspects*

The record is characterized by 30 responses, with no significant difference between chromatic and achromatic cards. An F percent of 33 suggests that ego controls are modest. Twelve populars versus two originals suggest that Ms. Jones seeks the "safe" socially acceptable course in most decision making.

The profile is unbalanced somewhat to the left suggesting that Ms. Jones still functions more in her inner life than in her outer life. The separation between the two is rather rigidly maintained. M sum C is 7:4, indicating that she is not living-out some of her strong needs for human contact.

There is one D-W plus three Contaminations in the record. This suggests that at one time Ms. Jones was quite capable of flagrant episodes of inappropriate behavior.

The number of Additionals suggests that Ms. Jones has made some rather significant changes, particularly in her perception of the inner self and the development of ego controls. There are also indications that she has learned to face some of her most frightening inner thoughts and ideas during the course of the therapeutic venture.

The Psychogram has a certain degree of balance. Although Ms. Jones may complain of being uncomfortable at times and suffering inner tension, she is actually able to manage in the real world.

B. *Personality Composite*

(1) *Interpersonal activity.* With people, Ms. Jones tends to be very reactive to emotional stimuli. Her primary response is to back off. She will try to consolidate herself and deal with such stimuli intellectually. Should the stimulation continue, she will tend to constrict. Her response to the environment and to people is quite variable. It can range from rigid focus on tiny details to sweeping holistic response to a variety of stimuli, making for an unusually good ability to see the overall picture. She can be quite creative at times. She does suffer periods of extreme tension and stress.

(2) *Early identifications.* There are indications that the sources of her distress in life lie in confusion in the early identification. She apparently understands this more than ever before. The mother is still the cardinal figure in her life. The picture of the mother is that of an impulsive, energetic, and sometimes amoral person, a frightening but attractive figure who has a dominant force in this woman's life. Apparently the mother kept a certain psychological distance from the child, but demanded obedience and respect. She frightened the child and is the primary source of Ms. Jones' earliest and deepest anxieties.

The father is seen tentatively as a love object. She perceives him as malevolent, capable of being bestial, but still somewhat attractive and potentially warm. She may have seen him in her growing years (and perhaps today) as a predatory male.

(3) *Sources of anxiety.* The earliest sources of anxiety would appear to be from the mother, who in some way, directly or through a substitute (religion?), evinced a suggestion of "mysterious power." This power implied that any kind of strong emotion, expression of impulse, or trusting of the inner self is likely to be extremely dangerous. This resulted in a deep anxiety as to whether one really had permission to be a woman. Although this started quite early there apparently was a great deal of trouble between 9 and 13 years of age having to do with the growth of the body image leading to severe preadolescent problems. Certainly she reached adolescence with the feeling that the world is a dangerous place and that any emotional stimulus is to be looked upon with great suspicion.

In respect to the father, there are intense mixed feelings. In some ways she sees men as takers, without feelings of warmth or sensitivity that are trustworthy. They are seen as predatory, and she sees herself as being in grave danger of losing grace and control if she should allow herself to be attracted to a predatory male (who would be most attractive to her). In this she sees her own sexual impulses as lewd and lascivious.

As a result of these considerable pressures in her early life, she has mixed feelings about her sexual identification, seeing disadvantages in both male and female roles.

There is a growing ancillary anxiety about the idea of changing therapists.

(4) *Primary outlets and defenses.* Intellectual defenses include an automatic response of constriction whenever emotional stimuli occur in a close environment. This results in Ms. Jones focusing on detail, withdrawing, and, if the emotional stimulus continues, deteriorating in her reality-testing. She protects herself against too much creativity by focusing on the mundane. She prefers to pacify her tension and to deny anger. Fantasy is a source of much relief, although she distrusts the fantasy if it becomes too emotional.

She apparently is beginning to see herself as a person able to overcome many adversities. She still attempts to separate intellect from emotion. She sometimes has bizarre fantasies about the power of other people.

In the midst of fragmentation, she can suddenly pull herself together and be creative, angry, oppositional, and reality-oriented. Creativity is becoming a more frequent channel for the appropriate direction of anxiety.

C. *Changes from the Therapeutic Experience*

The indications are that a number of significant changes have occurred as a result of psychotherapy. These would include:

1. Ms. Jones seems to be able to be more open about bizarre and frightening ideas than she probably has ever been before.
2. There is evidence of increased but flexible ego control.
3. She is beginning to shape her explosive feelings into more positive and external directions.
4. She apparently can experience a wider range of fantasy without panic than has been possible in the past.
5. There apparently is a greater confidence in herself that she will overcome barriers in the future.
6. Ms. Jones is apparently able to allow more sensuality to emerge.
7. Her periods of depression are less insidious and more understandable to her.

D. *Barriers to the Full Utilization of Emotional Energies*

Ms. Jones is still not able to achieve her intellectual and emotional potential. The following barriers seem to interfere with this emergence:

1. If emotional stimuli from the environment and from other people are persistent, she still tends to withdraw and become confused.
2. She still has deep repressions regarding sexuality in relationship to the parents.
3. She experiences very painful tensions at times when these repressions are approached by situations in life.
4. She has a moderate burnt-child reaction to revealing the inner self.
5. She is still terribly frightened of rejection by the mother or mother surrogates.
6. There are indications that early religious training forms a part of the constraining repressions.

E. *Directions and Focus for Continuing Therapy*

Ms. Jones is probably in a better situation now for the purpose of finishing psychotherapy than she ever has been before. The focus of attention by her therapist and by Ms. Jones should be:

1. The issue of father and males. She sees them as unreliable, stupid, lustful, insensitive, and dangerous. As a result of this, she has an enormous conflict about any impulses she has involving males, and about pregnancy.
2. The pregnancy anxiety is also related to the deep anxiety regarding the mother as a model and as a competitor. There are certainly powerful repressions that occurred early in her life regarding childbirth and sexuality. These should be explored.

3. The above items account for the ambivalent sexual identity and should be discussed in that respect.
4. The difficulty in being naturally creative is associated with the fear of sexual expression and this should be the topic of interpretive activity in the sessions.
5. It may be helpful to encourage Ms. Jones to be very free and expressive about her fantasy life which contains all the material necessary to resolve the above conflicts. Guided fantasy might help her to move into this important area.

Prognosis at this point would appear to be quite good.

Ellery Smith, Ph.D.
Consulting Psychologist

The results of the evaluation were reviewed several times by the psychotherapist and the patient. The plateau ended almost immediately as the patient began to discuss and experience the areas of concern and conflict upon which the evaluation focused.

Adding Group Psychotherapy

Referral of a patient to group psychotherapy with another therapist while continuing the individual therapy can enhance the experiential and integration stages of a patient's psychotherapy process. During group psychotherapy, the patient becomes involved with a variety of people at various levels of closeness and conflict. Such interactions stir the patient's personality and conflicts representative of the patient's life patterns are likely to occur. These experiences are then available in both group and individual sessions for exploration and evaluation.

Transfer to a Psychotherapist of the Opposite Sex

When progress lags and the plateau in therapeutic progress is not ended by various efforts of the psychotherapist and the patient, a transfer to a psychotherapist of the opposite sex may be helpful. This transfer may be temporary or permanent, a decision which must be made by the patient. Such a transfer can help a patient explore transference and resistance issues concerning the first psychotherapist as well as other conflicts which may have become associated with the initial psychotherapeutic setting or process.

All of these barriers, errors, and resolution processes have been presented in a simplistic and discrete manner. In the operational world of psychotherapy practice, things are rarely simplistic. Psychotherapists' errors can interact with or invite patients' neurotic barriers. Patient behavior can also invite psychotherapeutic error from the unwary, inexperienced, or disturbed psychotherapist. Success in the psychotherapeutic process sometimes leads to regression or early termination. At all times, the psychotherapist must weigh and judge interventions to be used and the appropriate moment for such responses. The weakening and repair that goes on in all psychotherapeutic alliances is a reflection of the skill and commitment of the psychotherapist, as well as of the degree of disturbance experienced by the patient (Lansford, 1986).

The process of conducting psychotherapy is clearly a complex task requiring professionals of intelligence, good training, experience and integrity.

CHAPTER 9

Special Situations in Psychotherapy

The considerable variety of mental disorders and the almost limitless expressions of these disorders based on individual differences place a handicap on psychotherapists of limited experience. Therapists of extensive background and training, including specialized supervision, can treat a fairly broad spectrum of personality and behavioral disorders. Special or "unusual" situations in psychotherapy about which inexperienced psychotherapists are confused or frustrated occur less frequently as the psychotherapist gains experience and extended skills from thousands of hours of practice and continuing education.

It is unlikely that any psychotherapist is equipped by training and experience to provide competent clinical services to *all* the various patients and conditions likely to be seen in a broad professional practice. Some psychotherapists restrict their practice to patients of a certain age, and or socioeconomic, educational, or experiential background. Many psychotherapists refuse to see patients who are deeply disturbed or who suffer character pathology. Psychotherapists who know and understand their limitations are probably better able to serve the needs of the patients with whom they work than psychotherapists who believe they can be effective with "anyone."

Even the most experienced of therapists will be confronted by situations which, by their intensity or unusualness, demand modification or even abandonment of usual and customary psychotherapeutic style and procedures. These special situations place a particularly heavy demand for tolerance, ego, strength, and patience on the psychotherapist.

Though modification of technique or principles may be in the patient's best interests, such modifications may so change the relationship between psychotherapist and patient that a return to dynamic psychotherapy is difficult or impossible.

This chapter is not presented as a means of training psychotherapists to deal with all of the situations described. For those therapists who wish to provide services for schizophrenic patients, suicidal patients, criminals referred by the courts, character disorders, and other unusual problems, special education, training, and supervision are necessary and available. An overview of a number of special psychotherapy situations likely to be encountered in practice will be presented, as well as references for those who wish to read further.

PATIENTS WITH COMPLEX PERSONALITY STRUCTURES OR BACKGROUNDS

These patients bring to psychotherapy views of life or styles of responding which are impediments to the establishment of a traditional dynamic alliance. Effort by the psychotherapist to develop the three essential tasks—sanctuary, sensitive awareness, and appropriate intervention—may be thwarted by the patient's personality barriers or lifestyle. Modifications of psychotherapeutic style, attitudes, or procedures are necessary if the patient is to be properly served.

The Schizophrenic Patient

Early, poorly controlled studies suggested that drug treatment of schizophrenia equaled or exceeded the effectiveness of any kind of psychotherapy (Tuma, May, Yale & Forsythe, 1978). Later, more rigorous research showed that even a modest amount of dynamic psychotherapy (averaging 70 sessions over a 20-month period) produced significant changes, such as lessened thought disorder, less time in hospital, and ability to live a more satisfactory life in a wide variety of ways. These effects became more marked the longer the patient was followed after therapy. Thus, individual psychotherapy proved to be less costly than other treatment methods for schizophrenia in the long run (Karon, 1963; Karon & Vanden Bos, 1970, 1972, 1974, 1976).

Schizophrenia is a term applied to a wide variety of behaviors. Generally, people so labeled suffer mental deterioration characterized by withdrawal, defects in communication, and changes or reductions in the ability to perform conventional social behaviors.

The nature of the schizophrenic patient. The schizophrenic patient is terrified. Whereas neurotic patients may be anxious about a wide range of mild to severe stimuli, the schizophrenic experiences terror about the most mundane daily events of life. The drastic defense mechanisms of withdrawal, strange thinking and communication patterns, inappropriate affect, hallucinations, and delusions are usually desperate efforts to deal with continual, chronic, overwhelming terror. Unfortunately, these mechanisms which give the schizophrenic patient very temporary safety tend to make their problems of everyday living worse.

Most of those who "break down" and are labeled "schizophrenic" have suffered subtle and unsubtle rejections from superficially normal parents who are nevertheless pathogenic in character. Such parents are unable to meet the dependency needs of their children throughout early development. Perhaps of greater etiological importance, such parents do not allow their children to attach themselves to more giving, tolerant, dependency-accepting persons outside of the family. This creates the personality structure of an individual unable to interpret and tolerate the stresses of everyday life with ordinary and useful mechanisms of defense.

Psychotherapists who cannot treat schizophrenics. Such conditions have traditionally been considered extremely serious and even, by some, hopeless. Many psychotherapists refuse to treat schizophrenic patients. The blame is unfairly placed on the patient for being too disturbed or "untreatable" or better served by medication. These equivocations often represent a lack of education or training on the part of the therapist. These attitudes may reflect the psychotherapist's own *pathogenesis* (Vanden Bos & Karon, 1971). Pathogenetic psychotherapists are those whose dominance needs preclude a therapeutic or other close relationship which brings the dependency needs of another in conflict with the therapist's needs. The pathogenic psychotherapist must satisfy his or her needs without regard for the needs of the patient.

Some common manifestations of pathogenesis in a psychotherapist include manipulation of the patient, denial of the manipulation, ignoring the patient's expressed needs, and not allowing the patient to express negative feelings. The psychotherapist is usually unaware of his or her pathogenesis and may proclaim strong and abiding interest in the patient's welfare. Recommendations for electroconvulsive therapy, medication, or institutionalization are often well-meant but destructive forms of such concern.

The psychotherapeutic treatment of schizophrenic patients. As in any psychotherapeutic venture, the establishment of a sanctuary must be the first order of business. With the schizophrenic patient, considerably more tolerance, patience, and support are necessary than with patients suffering neurotic life-styles. Since at first few schizophrenic patients can communicate effectively and form a therapeutic alliance, the first obstacle the psychotherapist must overcome is his or her pessimism in respect to the apparent lack of trust, interaction, and progress which characterizes early sessions with schizophrenic patients. With sufficient safety, tolerance, and support, the real experiential life history of the schizophrenic will gradually appear to account for the severe, unadaptive life-style which brought the patient to treatment.

Over time, there gradually will emerge a picture of pathogenesis in the family background. In many cases, the psychotherapist will find that the patient's parents, more often the mother, met their own dominance needs at the expense of the child's normal dependency without regard for the importance of the child's needs. In many cases it becomes apparent that the parent enacted the role of a dependent, demanding child, while the child was expected to respond as a strong, supportive, parent-like figure. As the story emerges through the patient's peculiar language, delusions, or hallucinations, the psychotherapist will often see that one parent was consistently destructive and the other weak or benign, unable to be emotionally useful. The outer picture of such parents is more than likely "nice folks" who have always been puzzled by their child's odd behavior. In addition, it is likely that the psychotherapist will discover that the parents, in one way or another, prevented their child from making more helpful and rewarding attachments to better-adjusted figures outside the family circle.

To reach a stage of such understanding and progress, the psychotherapist must be prepared to relate to and communicate with the schizophrenic patient in unorthodox ways. The approach must include extreme gentleness and a willingness to admit error and to ask questions. No expression by a schizophrenic patient must be seen as meaningless or unimportant. The schizophrenic cannot afford to communicate clearly according to his or her own life experience. Months may go by without any clear or direct statement from the patient that psychotherapy is being helpful. Often the schizophrenic patient appears to be without affect, when actually terrified.

Hallucinations should be treated as dream material. Their structure is identical, but simpler and more direct. The conscious expressions and statements of the schizophrenic patient are dominated by the unconscious. As the patient becomes more aware of the sanctuary of the psychotherapeutic setting, constantly supported by the therapist's strength, warmth, support, and protection, the content of the hallucinations and

delusions can be compared with what the patient views as terror-
ridden reality.

In conducting psychotherapy with schizophrenic patients, the psychotherapist must be prepared to reassure the patient constantly that the
setting is safe and the psychotherapist is willing and able to offer protection. The psychotherapist must provide an identification model of
strength, concern, and reliability clearly different from and safer than the
models to which the patient was exposed during the developmental years.
Explanations and structuring about how psychotherapy works must be
more detailed and frequent than for neurotic patients. When a schizophrenic patient does not appear for a regular appointment, the psychotherapist should telephone to find out why the patient didn't appear and
to demonstrate continuing concern and support (Karon, 1976).

No one psychotherapeutic style is successful in working with
schizophrenic patients. The approach presented here is one style which is
compatible with the principles of psychotherapeutic tradecraft presented
in previous chapters. Experience is even more critical for sustained or
consistent success in working with schizophrenic patients than for psychotherapy with less disturbed patients. Working with a supervisor with
much experience specific to this difficult and special patient group can be
helpful in sustaining the motivation to work with schizophrenics whose
capacity to give effective responses and clear feedback is very slow to
develop during the psychotherapeutic course (Karon, 1976).

The Borderline States

Early efforts to describe borderline states were generally unsatisfactory. Patients who were considered not quite psychotic but certainly more
fragmented in ego structure than neurotics were sometimes called
"pseudoneurotic schizophrenics" or "prepsychotic," implying that except for an obvious break with reality, a psychosis was not present. Some
suggested the term "borderline," but this was generally rejected as im-
precise (Knight, 1953). Although diagnosis and description of borderline
states remain somewhat ambiguous, it is generally agreed that the disorder falls between the neuroses and the psychoses on the dimension of
ego strength.

Advances in the study of borderline states through the use of psychological tests have given a more complete picture of this complex condition. Intellectual functioning is much more intact than is found in psychotic patients, albeit "I don't know" responses may hide fragmentation.
The content and formal organization of thought and language reveal lap-
ses in logical thinking. There are episodes of language disorganization and

slippages in reasoning. Language is used in idiosyncratic ways but not distorted as extensively as in schizophrenia. Occasional fluid language episodes make it appear as though the borderline person is free associating. Logical connections between ideas seem loosened.

Reality testing and perceptual organization are relatively intact. Reality is accurately perceived at first and then may be endowed with fantasy or bizarre interpretations, which the borderline patient is able to recognize as fantastic or unusual. The ability to regulate emotional arousal is impaired. The borderline patient overreacts, underreacts, or moves back and forth between these extremes. Labile shifts in moods, emotions, and needs are frequent and rapid. The borderline patient can shift rapidly from formidable, threatening anger to soft, childlike dependency. The borderline patient struggles to maintain rigid control and then suddenly collapses under a flood of emotion. Sexual, dependency, and aggressive feelings appear in childlike, egocentric form. Direct gratification is almost irresistible.

The defenses of borderline patients are a patchwork of faltering attempts to balance stress. Regression and intellectualization alternate rapidly. Attempts to reduce tension and stress are often frantic. Gross denial inappropriate to obvious realities is common. Projection and threats of violence are frequent. When repression fails, the borderline patient fluctuates rapidly between grossly inaccurate perceptions of himself or herself as well as of significant others, shifting emotions, and contradictory ideas. This condition has been called *splitting*. Adherence to conventional values and rules falters (Kernberg, 1975; Berg, 1983; Wilson, 1985).

Psychotherapeutic treatment for the borderline patient. The psychotherapist treating borderline patients must be prepared to tolerate an enormous variety and range of emotional and intellectual fluctuations. These unstable defenses are maladaptive and the psychotherapist who is inexperienced in this area can become discouraged or frightened by the patient's wide and wild jumps from denial to dependency to omnipotence, then devaluation and primitive idealization. Many psychotherapists speak of a nagging, subtle fear that they experience during therapy with borderline patients. They see no sense of humor in the patient in spite of the ranging, poorly controlled emotion. Therapists report that borderline patients "get under their skin." This may represent psychotherapists' response to the enormous rage which constantly penetrates the borderline's controls. These uneasy feelings on the part of experienced psychotherapists constitute a diagnostic indicator that special efforts must be made to keep the borderline patient working within the limits of the psychotherapeutic process (Berkowitz, 1983).

All of the tradecraft presented in previous chapters applies in the psychotherapy of borderline patients. The essential difficulty for the psychotherapist lies in maintaining an appropriate, relaxed, and involved psychotherapeutic neutrality without becoming disturbed by the patient's wild affective and organizational shifts. It is psychotherapeutic error to become cold, aloof, or remote when the patient's behavior is threatening. By the same token, the psychotherapist must not leap into the patient's maelstrom of emotion and try to "straighten things out." The patient is used to the wild fluctuations and may be less anxious about these than the inexperienced psychotherapist. The psychotherapist must maintain the sanctuary of the psychotherapeutic process and be prepared for a long, arduous process of sensitive awareness, constant resetting of limits, and appropriate interpretive intervention.

Of perhaps primary importance is for the psychotherapist to understand and tolerate the extremes of primitive anger, ominous threats, manipulation, and overwhelming need for gratification of dependency needs presented by the patient during most of the psychotherapeutic course. The demands that the sanctuary of psychotherapy be perfect, total, and constant can be trying to even the most experienced psychotherapist. Even when the psychotherapy is well advanced, sudden and unexpected fears of abandonment can be expected to occur.

To work effectively with such patients, psychotherapists must avoid changing their style to accommodate the patient's fluctuations, carefully avoid countertransference, face issues with the gentleness and support used with schizophrenic patients, and maintain psychotherapeutic neutrality without aloofness. It is clear that special training, supervision, and consultation are vital in order to provide appropriate psychotherapy for borderline patients.

Character Disorders

This general grouping of disturbances includes a variety of conditions characterized by the individual's failure to reach socially acceptable levels of adjustment. A prominent moral tone is noted in many of the diagnostic labels which have been used to describe these maladjustments. The labels include *Psychopathic Deviant, Sociopath,* and *Antisocial Personality Disorder.*

Common characteristics of character disorders include glibness and charm, a grandiose sense of self-worth, low frustration tolerance, and a tendency of boredom. The person who suffers a character disorder tends to be unwilling or unable to accept personal responsibility for clearly asocial or antisocial behavior. A history of delinquency, impulsivity, and early behavior problems can be expected. Poor control of temper, a lack of emotional depth and empathy, and little or no remorse or guilt are recurrent response patterns. Lying, deception, and lack of sincerity are characteristic of the severe forms of character disorder (Cleckley, 1976; Hare, 1985; Schroeder, Schroeder & Hare, 1983).

Patients with character disorders who seek psychotherapy are most frequently motivated by threat or opportunity. Treatment mandated by the courts represents a significant source of referral of patients suffering character pathology. Within the prison setting, mental health services represent an opportunity for prisoners with character pathology to demonstrate that they are making efforts to repent and be rehabilitated, in order to become eligible for early release.

Once antisocial life-style is established, the emotional needs and resources for psychotherapy are no longer available to the individual, and a genuine seeking of help is rare. As character-disordered individuals reach middle age, they sometimes "burn out" and become uncharacteristically depressed and anxious. These circumstances sometimes motivate the individual to seek psychotherapy.

A less asocial form of character pathology is found in the *narcissistic personality disorders.* Such individuals present a grandiose style suggesting importance or uniqueness. Their fantasies are full of unlimited success. A driving need for admiration, attention, and approval is characteristic. These individuals share with the more extreme character disorders a lack of empathy and a tendency to exploit others. Close relationships are rare, but those which are developed are characterized by exploitation and vacillation between aggrandizing and devaluating the other person. There are wide fluctuations in self-esteem and mood. Reactions to even the slightest rejection or insult include rage, withdrawal, grandiosity, and somatic symptoms (Kohut, 1977; Lazarus, 1982; Reich, 1960). The tendency to "act-out" by expressing anger, resistance, dependence, or sexual needs in socially questionable ways is strong. These episodes of acting-out are inevitably self-destructive or dangerous to the individual (Lapkin, 1985).

Those character disorders who defend their behavior, their choices, and their acting-out, and who are relatively comfortable, without anxiety or depression, are very poor candidates for psychotherapy. The patient with character pathology who sees the aberrant behavior as not under control and as an interference with life-style and goals, or who are deeply distressed by the consequences of their behavior, are more amenable to psychotherapy.

Psychotherapy with character disorders. Those individuals who are alienated from society and culture by choice, who prey upon and profit from the weakness, gullibility, or warmth and acceptance of others, are poor risks for traditional dynamic psychotherapy. A lifetime style of deceit, manipulation, shallowness, superficial charm, and lack of emotional depth will be brought to the psychotherapeutic setting. The insufficiency of distress and need usually precludes the development of a therapeutic alliance. The character disorder is usually unable to experience within the context of psychotherapy. The sanctuary is not accepted or believed. Compulsive manipulation characterizes the patient's approach to the opportunity to reveal the self in a safe setting.

In those cases where a character-disordered person seeks help and may be "burning out," the psychotherapist must establish a series of rigid ground rules to help determine whether the patient is able to use psychotherapy effectively. Fees must be paid in advance. Limits regarding phone calls, appointments, relations with staff, confidentiality, and other procedural matters must be clearly explicated, repeated where necessary, and unfailingly enforced by the psychotherapist. At the same time, the psychotherapist must remain supportive, empathetic, genuine, and willing to help create and support the therapeutic alliance. The avoidance of moral judgments concerning the patient's past behavior is critical. At the same time, the therapist must not—explicitly or implicitly—condone or support current or planned asocial behavior. These requirements are extremely demanding, even for the most experienced psychotherapist.

Should a patient suffering a character disorder become seriously involved in a psychotherapeutic effort, the therapist can expect a deterioration of the rigid manipulative, charming, shallow life-style. Deeply disturbing depressive symptoms, somatization, and despair develop rapidly. Suicidal ideas and efforts are not uncommon. Short periods of hospitalization in a supportive and protective residential treatment setting are sometimes necessary if the decompensation is extreme. Tolerance, acceptance, and availability on the part of the psychotherapist must maintain during such episodes.

Psychotherapy with narcissistic personality disorders. Where the narcissistic patient claims to be out of control and unable to modify asocial or self-destructive behavior, psychotherapy should be conducted as it has been presented in previous chapters. The expected response in this group is shame and distress experienced by the patient in respect to episodes of acting-out.

Those patients who defend their behavior, feel no acute pressure to change, and reject the concept that their behavior is self-destructive must be treated in a different manner. Many psychotherapists reject or feel rejecting toward such patients. The patient who defends narcissistic acting-out but who nevertheless seeks psychotherapy is in need of help.

With such patients, the psychotherapist must in every respect avoid judgmental or moral attitudes toward the patient, well beyond what is required with patients suffering neurotic difficulties. The psychotherapist should be curious and inquiring rather than intellectualizing and interpreting. The psychotherapist must attempt to understand and express awareness of the adaptive or balancing value of the patient's behavior (Roth, 1985). In this sense, the psychotherapist must communicate to the patient that he or she understands the value the patient has derived from behavior which is not accepted by others or which is self-destructive to the patient. Thus, rage, alternative sexual life-styles, and grandiose ideas must be seen by the psychotherapist as strivings for growth, mastery, and balance by the patient.

Extra sessions, some flexibility regarding payment, and constant reassurance are necessary if psychotherapy is to proceed with narcissistic patients. Often the psychotherapist must resist repetitive pressures from the patient's family or friends to intervene in the patient's life and set limits or interpret social expectancy. Throughout, the psychotherapist must express respect and appreciation. Interpretation should be minimal in such cases. Active listening and support of the patient's wish to accomplish allow patients to experience and discover their fallibilities and real potential (Fields, 1985; Kohut & Wolf, 1978; Lapkin, 1985).

It should be clear at this point that psychotherapy with patients who suffer from any form of character disorder is at best very demanding and stressful for the psychotherapist. Experienced psychotherapists who are interested in and willing to work with patients suffering character defects will see only one or two such patients at one time. A full caseload of such patients may be impossible for most psychotherapists to tolerate and serve effectively. Those psychotherapists who are experienced with patients who have character pathology expect the therapeutic course to be long, with many starts and stops, as well as wide fluctuations in the patient's emotional stability.

The Psychotherapist as Patient

Although many mental health professionals undergo psychotherapy as part of their early training, this section is primarily addressed to the issue of treating professional-level psychotherapists who seek help for themselves. Acknowledgment of such a need by a psychotherapist is, at best, difficult. Though tolerant of patients' emotional distress, many mental health professionals see such circumstances as evidence of technical inadequacy or personal weakness. Recent attention focused on impaired professionals has helped many psychotherapists to seek help (Turkington, 1986).

Barriers to a smooth psychotherapeutic course tend to be raised by both the psychotherapist and the psychotherapist-patient. With the usual patient, the psychotherapeutic session has traditionally been held *in camera,* a secret place where the psychotherapist's style and procedures are known only to the patient. The patient plays a fairly dependent role and is ordinarily naive in the lore and practice of psychotherapy. What they see is usually all they know of the process.

Faced with a patient who practices the same profession, the psychotherapist may feel threatened by potential evaluation and criticism, and may fear discovery, revelation, or analysis of his or her own feelings. It is possible for the psychotherapist to feel guilty about being in the "healer" role while a colleague suffers. Such barriers can become therapeutic errors unless resolved early and satisfactorily.

Barriers to progress raised by the psychotherapist-patient are likely to be more frequent and less malleable than therapeutic errors initiated by the psychotherapist. Feelings of shame, guilt, inadequacy, and depression, though expected of a patient, are intensified in the psychotherapist-patient who often fears or expects criticism or rejection for failure as a professional. Such attitudes can lead to abject passivity or aggressive defensiveness, neither of which makes the already difficult task of psychotherapy easier—for either the patient or the therapist. Some common barriers raised by psychotherapist-patients will be considered briefly.

Challenges to technique. Rarely does the psychotherapist-patient directly challenge the psychotherapist. It is more likely that the patient's discomfort will be manifested by identifying or labeling the therapist's responses. Sometimes innocuous-appearing questions express the patient's discomfort in the unaccustomed role. In the following example, a psychiatrist in her 12th session of psychotherapy raises a challenge to technique:

Patient: I can see why I was depressed . . . the stress, overwork, and then John acting as he did . . . it was too much.
Therapist: So, John's announcing he was leaving tipped a precarious balance.
Patient: Oh . . . you're clarifying my feeling! It's funny to be on the other end of it. I'm not sure that's really what happened. I'm really concerned as to why I let it happen. I hope you don't think I was blaming it entirely on John.

The complexity of the patient's anger, anxiety, and defensiveness is apparent. These responses almost always occur early in the psychotherapy and seldom represent a serious threat to progress.

Obfuscating intellectualizations. Again, this barrier tends to appear in the early sessions of the therapeutic course with psychotherapist-patients. Not very different from other patients who try to avoid experiencing painful or frightening material, the patient-psychotherapist adds an element of "shared knowledge" to deny uncomfortable feelings. In the following segment, a 35-year-old psychologist intellectualizes during his eighth session, as follows:

Therapist: So, your boss is a real pain for you, emphasizing details instead of appreciating your general contributions to the hospital.
Patient: It's typical, I'm sure—a dominance/submission conflict. He's an authority figure whether I respect him or not. I suppose I have the usual oedipal ambivalence toward him.
Therapist: Such as?
Patient: Oh, you know, kill father, marry mother, and all of that.
Therapist: Mm. . . .

No special techniques are necessary in dealing with this form of intellectualization. These responses should be treated as any patient's efforts to avoid experiencing painful or embarrassing issues.

Arranging supervision. A not uncommon way for the psychotherapist-patient to evade self-exploration is to use the therapy session to discuss his or her own cases. This encouragement of the therapist to play the role of colleague or supervisor is a subtle way of expressing dependency needs or compulsions to manipulate the therapist. Except for psychotherapist-patients suffering character pathology, this barrier is most frequently raised early in the course of the psychotherapy. This represents a complex issue. Psychotherapist-patients are very likely to be concerned and reactive regarding their interaction with their own patients and such concerns are proper topics for psychotherapeutic focus. The psychotherapist in such a situation must strive to maintain the experiential focus on the psychotherapist-patient's personality and emotional responses. The role of evaluator or therapy supervisor should be avoided.

Socializing professionally. It may be much more difficult for the psychotherapist-patient's therapist to avoid all contact outside of the therapy session than it is with other patients. The psychotherapist and psychotherapist-patient may share membership in professional societies or attend the same professional meetings. Maintenance of the appropriate psychological distance is vital and should be a mechanical barrier which the therapist and the patient bend every effort to maintain so as to ensure no interference with the patient's progress through psychotherapy. This may require a certain contrived or studied avoidance during professional meetings, but the maintenance of the psychotherapeutic sanctuary may require such behavior. Structuring should address this issue before psychotherapy begins.

Involvement in the patient's professional growth or rehabilitation. A relatively common reason for a psychotherapist to seek psychotherapeutic help results from ethical, educational, or legal sanctions which require treatment before the psychotherapist-patient is allowed to begin or continue professional practice. Circumstances imply or state explicitly that the psychotherapist-patient's professional future is to one degree or another dependent on the outcome of the psychotherapeutic process. With greater attention currently being paid to the "impaired professional," psychotherapists should be prepared to deal with the complexities of conducting therapy under such special burdens.

The onus of a therapist being forced to make value judgments on a patient which are likely to have serious effects on the patient's life is probably going to interfere with any dynamic psychotherapeutic process. Judges, ethics committees, and training institutions may expect both interim and final evaluations of the patient (Larke, 1985).

Psychotherapists should from the beginning refuse to make such value judgments. Efforts should be made to convince the referring authority that an external audit by an uninvolved, objective professional or board of professionals should be assigned the evaluative task, allowing the psychotherapist to function fully and exclusively as the provider of treatment. Absent this possibility, the psychotherapist should from the beginning assure the patient that the only evaluative statement which will be made will simply state that the patient has or has not committed himself or herself to a serious involvement in the therapeutic process. Even this very conservative evaluative role may interfere with establishing an effective therapeutic alliance.

Sending patients to the psychotherapist. Although not a barrier exclusively raised by patients who are also psychotherapists, this form of transference, gift-giving, or identification is more commonly demonstrated by psychotherapist-patients. Such a possibility should be discussed before psychotherapy begins since it is far simpler to deal with this barrier before it occurs, as opposed to analyzing and resolving the issue after the fact.

This issue of referrals is of particular importance when working with psychotherapists who suffer narcissistic disorders. Such patients may refer others in an effort to win favor or feel worthwhile. Later the patients may become threatened, fearful, and competitive as they fear the person who was referred might be receiving better (or worse) treatment than they themselves.

Psychotherapy with the patient-psychotherapist. The tradecraft of creating the psychotherapeutic process is not conceptually different when treating patients who are professional psychotherapists. Barriers to effective psychotherapy which are expected with a patient who practices as a psychotherapist should be anticipated and prevented insofar as possible. Issues of potential importance, misunderstanding, or conflict should be raised by the psychotherapist and concord or agreement reached with the patient before psychotherapy begins. Structuring should be carefully planned. The following issues should be discussed during initial meetings:

- *Professional collegial disengagement.* It should be gently but firmly made clear that during the course of the psychotherapeutic process the therapist will sever all current and avoid all future collegial interactions with the psychotherapist-patient. Should this be embarrassing or impossible, the psychotherapy should be conducted by someone else.
- *Fees.* Most mental health professionals choose to provide some form of adjusted fee as a demonstration of professional courtesy. The psychotherapist's position in the matter of fees should be presented and discussed preliminary to the first session of psychotherapy. All questions should be answered or resolved. An agreement as to the fee arrangement must be reached prior to beginning psychotherapy. It should be clear, as in all cases, that the issue of fees and payment is always open to exploration during the psychotherapeutic course.
- *Limits.* Initial structuring should include such issues as professional socializing, referral of patients, requests for supervision, recommendations and other issues unique to the situation, as well as the psychotherapist's philosophy, style, and limits regarding these matters. The psychotherapist must present these limits in a sensitive and reasonable manner. There should be no implication that the therapist "expects" the therapeutic course to be made difficult by the patient.

Psychotherapy with psychotherapists should not be conducted much differently than psychotherapy with any other patient. Unfortunately, the uniqueness of a therapist working with a colleague-patient and vice versa probably offers more opportunities for both barriers and therapeutic errors to occur. Special concern for and regular review of procedures and interactions in this kind of therapeutic alliance are strongly recommended (Fleischer & Wissler, 1985).

Psychotherapy With Minority Clients

Minority cultural and ethnic groups are underrepresented among the clients of psychotherapists in western society. Traditional racism and xenophobia influence referral and intake styles. A tendency for majority psychotherapists to view racial and cultural differences as deficits has been all too common (Greene, 1985; Mays, 1985). Language, manners, and customs which differ from the psychotherapist's may be confusing. Asian-American clients, for instance, tend to view physical and mental health more synonymously than westerners. Feelings of rage may be diverted, disguised, or expressed in ways unfamiliar to one who is not aware of the strong cultural imperative regarding such emotions in the early development of many persons of Asian or Pacific background (Sue, 1981). These and other factors result in reluctance to seek psychotherapy and early termination where the psychotherapist and patient differ significantly in cultural or racial experience and status.

Racial bias and prejudice are particularly powerful barriers or bases for psychotherapeutic error. Both the therapist and patient are subject to the inner perceptions which result in distrust and power struggles (Hall & Maloney, 1983). Rigid or narrow perspectives on the part of the psychotherapist can result in misinterpretation of individual and family experiences reported by the minority group patient (Jones, 1985).

The burden of creating a safe and supportive psychotherapeutic environment falls squarely on the psychotherapist. Some psychotherapists are unable or unwilling to explore those factors which make psychotherapy with racial and cultural minorities different in significant ways from psychotherapy with patients culturally or racially similar to the therapist. These therapists should not offer services to minority clients who differ significantly from the therapist in background.

These problems exist beyond the more extreme and obvious differences in culture and race between psychotherapist and patient. Similar difficulties can arise between psychotherapist and patients whose life experiences differ in geography, education, religion, and political philosophy. Almost anything in the personal experience, background, or attitude of a patient which differs from that of the psychotherapist can result in barriers or psychotherapeutic errors.

For a psychotherapist to maximize the potential of the therapeutic experience, the fundamental tasks of the psychotherapist must be pursued seriously and conscientiously. The sanctuary must be maintained. Sensitive awareness must not be tempered with preconceived ideas and narrow cultural values. Appropriate intervention must include an awareness by the therapist of goals and aspirations which may be unique to the minority patient. Before beginning psychotherapy with a patient of cultural or racial background different from that of the therapist, certain steps or procedures can be helpful:

- The psychotherapist should explore his or her closely-held beliefs concerning people of the patient's cultural or racial background.
- The psychotherapist should consult with an experienced colleague of the patient's background for advice and recommended reading, and to establish a potential consultation/supervision liaison.
- The psychotherapist should focus on these issues during the first session or the session preceeding the start of psychotherapy. The psychotherapist should tell the patient that every effort will be made to understand the patient's minority status and that the psychotherapeutic process will be conducted with an appreciation of the enhancements and tribulations that accrue to persons of race or background different from the majority environment in which they live.
- The psychotherapist should reveal any prejudice or bias he or she has experienced and identified in respect to the patient's cultural or racial background and enlist the patient's help in identifying and resolving any such prejudices which emerge during the course of the psychotherapeutic process.

Interim reevaluation of personal values, goal-setting for the patient, and subtle forms of bias should be undertaken by the psychotherapist on a regular basis during the course of the therapeutic process. This is, of course, what the psychotherapist should be doing with every patient.

CATACLYSMIC EVENTS

As with most of the special situations presented in this chapter, cataclysmic or catastrophic events are relatively rare in the course of psychotherapy. Such occurrences do happen and the longer a psychotherapist practices, the higher the probability that one or more of these rare events will occur. An understanding of cataclysmic events and ways of dealing with these within the context of the psychotherapeutic venture is necessary to the competent practice of psychotherapy.

Catastrophic events always disrupt dynamic psychotherapy. Inherent to the tradecraft and philosophical conceptualization of dynamic psychotherapy are certain givens: The patient has a drive, a wish, a striving for a better quality of life, the various abilities or skills to seek this, and time to develop self-awareness, integration, and independence through the therapeutic process. Catastrophic events disrupt or destroy one or more of these elements. In each of the major cataclysmic events to be addressed, the psychotherapist must make careful and very difficult decisions involving the patient's best interests. Such decisions can include drastic steps such as terminating the therapeutic course, changing professional roles, and referring the patient to other therapists.

During the course of psychotherapy, patients may experience a wide range of stressful or very stressful events. Death of family members, loss of job, academic failure, divorce, and legal liability are just a few of the life events that occur. These can usually be dealt with effectively using the tradecraft of dynamic psychotherapy as it has been presented in previous chapters. Modest modification of these principles may be useful when the patient is a victim or bereaved (Pennebaker & O'Heeron, 1984; Barnes & Prosen, 1985; Rando, 1985; and Rubin, 1985). Events involving the death or disability of the patient or the psychotherapist will be considered cataclysmic events in this section.

Suicide

Over 40,000 people commit suicide each year in the United States. In addition, a good many deaths resulting from vehicular accidents are probably suicidal ventures. Self-termination regularly ranks between the fourth and seventh most frequent causes of death in the United States. Comparable figures are reported throughout the world.

In contrast, suicide is a relatively rare event for patients undergoing psychotherapy. Although literally all psychotherapists are concerned with the phenomenon of suicide, very few have reported the experience of having a patient in ongoing therapy commit suicide.

An understanding of the psychological, cultural, and social aspects of suicidal behavior helps to clarify the rarity of the event in psychotherapy. Such understanding is vital for all practicing psychotherapists so that they can maximize the therapeutic environment's potential to prevent and, where necessary, intervene in suicidal ventures by patients in psychotherapy.

The nature of suicidal behaviors. Views of self-destructive behavior are necessarily subjective, even when such views are supported by demographic and statistical data, academic background, clinical experience, and personal contact with self-destruction and death.

The most current views of Shneidman (1985) would appear to offer the psychotherapist the clearest current view of the nature of the human desire, threat, or act to self-terminate. Schneidman's *aphorisms* or truths form a basis for preventing the occurrence of suicidal behavior. Should the patient express suicidal ideation and intention in spite of preventive efforts, these aphorisms are vital in understanding the rationale and techniques required of the psychotherapist for effective intervention. (The following definitions are abstracted from the original, and critiques of oversimplification are properly directed to the current author.)

- *The common stimulus in suicide: Unendurable psychological pain.* Persons who seriously consider terminating their lives seek to escape unendurable psychic pain or anguish. The act of suicide is to end consciousness, anticipating relief from the pain. The level of pain or anguish which triggers suicidal behavior is unique to the individual. The concept of ending one's life results from an inner-felt necessity to do *something* to stop the unendurable anguish.
- *The common stressor in suicide: Frustrated psychological needs.* No matter how disturbed or pathological the act of suicide may seem to an observer, to the intender the act seems logical as a way of dealing with thwarted or unfulfilled needs. There are usually a number of such frustrated needs. The act of suicide may be committed to avoid criticism, humiliation, shame, or blame. The act may represent vindication or revenge. In treating a suicidal patient, the basic rule is to address the frustrated needs and the intolerable anguish. If this reduces the psychological discomfort, suicidal behavior is less likely to occur.
- *The common purpose of suicide: To seek a solution.* Suicidal efforts are not random acts. The behavior is performed to get out of a problem or a bind. The individual has come to believe that it is the only thing to do to make the best of a bad situation. The solution is drastic, but the issues are intolerable to the individual.
- *The common goal of suicide: Cessation of consciousness.* The purpose of the suicidal act is to end unendurable psychological pain. It is a way out.
- *The common emotion in suicide: Hopelessness/helplessness.* When individuals feel their situation is hopeless and that they are helpless to change this, suicide is considered. Additional feelings of shame, guilt, and frustrated dependency may be present, but the basic emotion common in suicidal persons is the impotence of hopelessness/

helplessness. When this state continues, there is a tendency to "give up" and believe that ending consciousness is the only way of changing things. With hopelessness/helplessness there is also an overpowering feeling of loneliness.

- *The most common internal attitude toward suicide: Ambivalence.* Those individuals who have reached the state of yearning for suicide still yearn and hope for intervention and rescue.
- *The common cognitive state in suicidal thinking: Constriction.* Individuals seriously contemplating self-termination have a kind of tunnel vision in which the range of options or choices consciously available are narrowed to two—to live or to die. The more constricted the thinking, the more lethal the suicidal thoughts are likely to be. Rescue or remediation must focus on the pathological constriction. To save someone from suicide, one must broaden the individual's options.
- *The common interpersonal act in suicide: Communicating intention.* About 80 percent of those who commit suicide present clear clues to the impending lethal event. These signals of distress may be consciously or unconsciously generated. The distress signals can be expressed helplessness or pleas for response or opportunities for rescue. Common statements of suicide intenders include: "I'm going away," "You won't be seeing me," "I can't endure it," or "I've found a solution for all my problems." The intender may give away prized possessions or act in a manner very different from usual behavior. The cry for help can come in any form.
- *The common action in suicide: Egression.* The act of suicide allows the sufferer to escape the anguish and distress, terminating the pain. The suicidal action can be intentional, subliminal, or subintentional. Such actions are sometimes labeled "natural," "accidental," or "impulsive."
- *The common consistency in suicide: Lifelong coping patterns.* The life history of the suicidal person will show previous episodes of disturbance which includes constriction and dichotomous "either-or" thinking. Habitual patterns of threat, pain, pressure, failure, perturbation, and constriction are consistent with a vulnerability to suicidal ideation and action.

Hopelessness has been found to be the major variable linking depression to suicidal intent (Petrie & Chamberlain, 1983). The psychotherapeutic setting, properly created and maintained, tends to prevent a significant degree of hopelessness as the patient and therapist work together to maintain an expectancy of improvement (Patsiokas & Clum, 1985).

Suicidal threat during psychotherapy. Psychotherapists' increasing concern about suicidal ideas and threats by patients reflects recent attention to a variety of legal liabilities. A psychotherapist may become the defendant in civil actions charging malpractice, not only in cases where a suicide occurs, but even when a patient is injured in any manner in connection with suicidal gestures of limited lethality. Most of such actions have been filed against hospitals and mental health professionals whose contact with the patient has been for diagnostic or short-term treatment purposes (Knapp & Vandecreek, 1983). In such situations, decisions by the courts suggest three criteria in assessing the liability of the mental health professional in cases of suicide by a patient:

1. *Foreseeability.* No liability has been found where the suicidal behavior has occurred suddenly and unpredictably. When a treatment plan overlooks, ignores, or neglects clear suicidal tendencies, the professional may be found liable.
2. *Reasonableness of judgment.* When a professional treats disturbed patients, it is reasonable to expect the professional to take extra precautions and plan more carefully with severely depressed patients. Courts have been flexible in recognizing that there are a variety of acceptable precautions available to mental health professionals. The more obvious the patient's suicidal intent, the greater will be the court's expectancy that the therapist will take this into account in proceeding cautiously.
3. *Thoroughness.* Once a patient is determined to be suicidal, the courts have ruled that the therapist is responsible for notifying or supervising others as to the requirements of the treatment plan which has been developed to deal with the suicidal patient.

These decisions and guidelines are clearly more applicable to residential treatment centers and hospitals than to outpatient psychotherapy. Even though there have been very few civil actions involving suicide of a patient in psychotherapy, the principles remain the same. A reasonable standard of care is required and psychotherapists have fared extremely well in the few cases where actions have been filed against them charging malpractice or neglect in cases of suicide (Schwitzgebel & Schwitzgebel, 1980).

The psychotherapist's good faith efforts and skill in establishing, maintaining, and enhancing the therapeutic environment and alliance are usually sufficient to divert or diffuse the patient from deep and disruptive experiences of hopelessness, helplessness, constriction, and perturbation.

The psychotherapist who is faced with a patient presenting a suicidal threat must openly acknowledge that behavior to the patient, evaluate its significance, and respond appropriately.

Acknowledgment should be an ongoing part of the psychotherapist's ordinary activity during the session. The significance or potentiality of a suicidal threat or implication should be evaluated in respect to signs which are suggestive but not necessarily predictive of suicidal potential (Pope, 1985):

- Direct verbal warnings of intention to commit suicide must be taken seriously.
- Over 80 percent of completed suicides were preceded by a prior attempt.
- The presence of significant depression increases suicidal risk.
- Hopelessness is expressed by the patient.
- Intoxication, usually from alcohol, contributes to suicidal lethality.
- Men are more likely, in a ratio of between three and five to one over women, to commit suicide.
- The risk of a lethal suicidal act increases with age.
- Those who live alone tend to be at higher risk.
- Those who have experienced spousal, paternal or maternal bereavement within the past five years are at higher risk.
- Patients who are unemployed are at greater risk for suicide than those who are working.
- Illness and somatic complaints, as well as eating or sleeping disorders, are associated with increased risk.
- Patients with a history of poor impulse control are more likely to be at risk.
- Patients who tend to think in a rigid, narrow, constricted manner are more likely to consider suicide as an "only" alternative to their problems and anguish.

There are many possibilities and the signs noted above are general guidelines. The psychotherapist's knowledge and sensitivity about the patient and the therapeutic process must stand as the final judgment and evaluation of the significance of any signs of suicidal risk.

Once the psychotherapist decides that suicidal risk is present and significant, response is mandatory. Time is of the essence. Suicidal crises seldom last more than 72 hours. The most helpful interventions decrease perturbation and loneliness while broadening constrictive thinking. For the patient being seen in psychotherapy, the following options can be used without seriously disrupting the therapeutic course:

- *Increase the frequency of sessions.* During a suicidal crisis, the therapist may insist on seeing the patient more frequently—even two or three times a day for a day or so. The psychotherapist must play a more directive role in such circumstances. Fantasies of the suicidal act should be encouraged.

- *Focus on options.* Although contrary to appropriate tradecraft in dynamic or analytic psychotherapy, during a suicidal crisis the psychotherapist should question the motives, decision, and methods considered by the patient. The patient should be encouraged to bring any lethal objects or substances to the session so as to reduce easy access to instruments of suicide. These should be retained by the psychotherapist for "safekeeping." Alternative possibilities for dealing with intolerable conflicts should be suggested and discussed. The patient's assets and potential must be explored.
- *Express and communicate concern and support.* In a relatively direct manner, the psychotherapist must indicate to the patient that the psychotherapeutic alliance is a caring and concerned environment. Realistic potentials for improvement and the lessening of psychological pain must be presented. Here, again, the psychotherapist must take a much more direct stance than usual in communicating support and encouragement.

The following excerpts illustrate some significant aspects of a suicidal crisis presented by a 33-year-old investment analyst in his 40th session of individual psychotherapy. He was depressed, had lost his job when his company merged, and was grieving the loss of his wife four months after their divorce:

Patient: It's hopeless. . . . (*long pause*) I can't go on.
Therapist: You feel really bad.
Patient: (*no response*). . . .
Therapist: What do you find yourself thinking?
Patient: (*shakes head and begins to weep*)
Therapist: Too much to bear?
Patient: (*nods head, says nothing, continues to look down and weep quietly*)
Therapist: Tell me your thoughts.
Patient: (*long pause*). . . . I bought a gun. . . . I can't go on.
Therapist: When did you buy the gun?
Patient: (*pause*). . . . Two weeks ago. . . . Last night I loaded it . . . but I couldn't . . .
Therapist: That's good. I'm glad you didn't. We can work this through . . . together.
Patient: (*shakes head negatively*)
Therapist: It seems hopeless, but there are other possibilities.

Patient: I can't think of any. . . .

Therapist: I will help you to find other things that can ease the pain.

Patient: It hurts *so* much. (*weeps loudly*)

Therapist: I want you to come in for another session today. Can you come at 5:00?

Patient: I don't know. . . .

Therapist: I want you to have another session today. There are some things we can do to make this better.

Patient: (*shrugs shoulders*)

Therapist: We will explore some things that will lift the burden. Will you be here at 5:00 ?

Patient: Uh . . . yeah . . . I guess.

Therapist: What will you do from now until then?

Patient: I don't know.

Therapist: I think you should get something to eat. . . . something you like . . . and then come back at 5:00.

Patient: OK. . . .

Therapist: I'd like to see the gun you bought. Could you please bring it at 5:00?

Patient: I don't know . . . maybe.

Therapist: Good! Then we'll work together on these things and look at other possibilities.

The psychotherapist had his secretary call the patient at home to remind him of the 5:00 appointment. The patient didn't arrive until 5:25. The following then took place in the special session:

Therapist: I was concerned when you weren't here at 5:00.

Patient: I was sitting out in my car. . . . It's so hard to do *anything*.

Therapist: Did you go to the movies?

Patient: Yes, but I walked out in the middle. . . . I couldn't keep my mind on it. . . .

Therapist: Did you bring the gun?

Patient: (*pause*) No. . . . I forgot.

Therapist: Well . . . let's talk about the pain.

At this point the patient reviewed his job loss, the broken marriage, the futility of life, and his feeling there was nothing to look forward to in life. The psychotherapist was supportive and responded with clarification of feelings, but made no efforts at interpretation or confrontation. The patient cried again, and expressed some anger. The session ended as follows:

Therapist: I think we've worked hard today and we made a good start. We can whip this thing if we continue to work together. Your next regular session isn't until next week but there are a number of important things we should be talking about. I'd like to see you tomorrow—twice ... at noon and at 5:00 again. Can we do this?

Patient: Twice?

Therapist: Yes. ... You once talked about wanting to teach someday. We should talk about that. You also talked about wanting but not wanting to be with people. I have some ideas for you about that. We need to spend more time together at this point.

Patient: Well ... I ... OK. ...

Therapist: So, we'll meet at noon tomorrow. Will you bring the gun, please?

Patient: OK. ...

The next day the patient came at noon and did bring the gun he had purchased. The psychotherapist helped the patient fantasize his suicidal thoughts and intentions. The psychotherapist suggested the patient drive to the local university and explore the possibility of teaching as an adjunct instructor in his specialty of stocks and bonds. The patient did this and found there was a possibility of part-time teaching. The psychotherapist asked to keep the gun until some future time when the patient might wish to have it back (he never asked for the gun back). The suicidal crisis was past. Psychotherapy continued. Group psychotherapy with another therapist was added to the patient's program of individual therapy. No further suicidal crises occurred. The patient finished psychotherapy about two years later.

The psychotherapist was concerned for the patient. He chose to work through the crisis within the context of the psychotherapeutic process. This was a choice based on experience and the psychotherapist's understanding of this specific patient. In some very rare instances, the psychotherapist may decide that the suicidal crisis is too volatile to be contained and that measures external to the psychotherapeutic environment are indicated. When this happens or when the psychotherapist loses confidence in the intensified psychotherapeutic environment to handle the crisis, more direct measures are necessary in the patient's best interests and for the patient's protection. Under such circumstances the following procedures are warranted:

- *Hospitalization.* The purpose of hospitalization is to support and protect the patient during the suicidal crisis. If the patient is unwilling to accept this option, the psychotherapist must decide whether to initiate an involuntary commitment. Most state laws require that it be demonstrated by a weight of evidence beyond reasonable doubt (or, in some states, with clear and convincing evidence) that the patient is "dangerous to himself or others." Should the patient object to the involuntary procedure, the issue must be taken before a local judge who will decide if involuntary commitment is appropriate. Should the patient decide on voluntary hospitalization, the psychotherapist should participate actively in selecting the most appropriate setting and treatment staff.

- *Social network support.* When the psychotherapist decides that the suicidal crisis requires measures beyond intensified psychotherapy, significant relatives, friends, and coworkers must be contacted and urged to express support and caring. This must be done carefully and, when possible, with the full knowledge and understanding of the patient. Although breach of confidentiality and consequent legal liability may be involved, the psychotherapist must balance these considerations against a responsibility to participate in the protection of the patient.

- *Use of the telephone.* Calling the patient and encouraging the patient to call the psychotherapist at any time during a suicidal crisis are important aspects of intervention. Unhelpful as telephone consultation may be in dynamic psychotherapy, it is a crucial symbol of caring, support, and broadened options during a suicidal crisis. The patient is able to say, "In addition to living or dying, I can call my therapist." Telephone contact with the more significant members of the patient's social network may also be necessary or advisable.

Once the psychotherapist decides that the suicidal crisis cannot be resolved within the psychotherapeutic framework, the sanctity of the therapeutic setting and the special nature of the psychotherapeutic alliance cease to exist. The psychotherapist becomes a part of the patient's real life and support system. The psychotherapist acting in such a manner, necessary as it may be, communicates a lack of trust in the patient's judgment and assumes a dominant, directive role.

It is questionable as to whether the relationship can ever return to the status that existed before the psychotherapist "took over." Once the suicidal crisis is over, the psychotherapist should structure subsequent sessions so that psychotherapist and patient focus on the roles each played. Issues of dependence, resentment, learned helplessness, and recapitulation of early life patterns and expectancy should be addressed in depth. If an appropriate level of interaction cannot be reestablished, referral to another psychotherapist may be necessary or advisable. If such a transfer is necessary, extreme care and caution must be exercised by the psychotherapist to prevent referral from being seen by the patient as desertion or rejection. The complexities of these procedures, though necessary, are probably countertherapeutic. It is fortunate that such crises are rare during the course of properly conducted psychotherapy.

The Dying Patient

Equally as rare as the suicidal crisis during the psychotherapeutic process is the likelihood of a patient's developing a terminal illness. If such an illness develops and is of predictably short duration, the purpose of the psychotherapy to enable the patient to live more effectively is lost. Those illnesses with fairly optimistic prognosis (more than one year) can be treated as any major stress faced by the patient during the psychotherapeutic course.

Where death is imminent—several months to a year—the psychotherapist must modify the psychotherapeutic approach and setting. Psychotherapy's purposes include learning to live well. The terminal patient must learn to die well, with dignity. The dying patient must come to terms with the inevitability of death if daily life is to be given the best value possible (Cutter, 1974).

Anxiety and distress concerning one's own death appears to be universal (Conte, Weiner & Plutchik, 1982). The diagnosis of a terminal illness brings enormous fear and conflict to the fore. Kübler-Ross (1969) has proposed five stages of reaction to the fear and awareness of imminent death. These may be conceptualized briefly as follows:

- *Denial and isolation.* Most terminal patients reacted with denial either when informed of their illness or shortly thereafter as a way of balancing the painful reality of imminent death.
- *Anger.* Denial as a defense mechanism fades rapidly as the patient perceives the deterioration which usually accompanies a terminal state. The denial is replaced by feelings of anger, resentment, rage, and envy in respect to those who are healthy. The focus of the patient's attention is "Why me?"
- *Bargaining.* This stage is usually quite brief. It follows the failure of anger to change things. The patient seeks to exchange promises, vows, supplications, or pleadings for additional time—a postponement of the inevitable.
- *Depression.* As the terminal illness progresses and the patient begins to experience more symptoms, the anger and bargaining are replaced by a sense of great loss. Burdens of treatment, income loss, and family disruption contribute to a depression based on sadness and guilt as well as on the impending loss of everything.
- *Acceptance.* Given sufficient time before death as well as help in working through the previous stages, the patient can reach a stage

where feelings can be expressed and integrated into dying as the final act of life.

Not all thanatologists (those who study death) agree with Kübler-Ross's conceptualization of termination. Edwin Shneidman, Professor of Thanatology at UCLA, suggests that people face death in a variety of ways. The stages above may or may not occur. When these stages occur, they may appear in various combinations and orders. Death is a part of the developmental style. People tend to replicate their life-style and manner in termination. As Shneidman (1973) observes, "People die as they have lived."

Psychotherapy with the dying patient. Conducting death and dying therapy with terminal patients is a mental health specialty requiring special training and personal commitment (Cutter, 1974; Feifel, 1959). A somewhat modified approach is necessary when the patient develops a terminal disease during the course of therapy. An alliance has been established and the psychotherapist, as well as the patient, faces the impending termination with apprehension and a sense of personal loss.

The patient always has the option of terminating psychotherapy. If the psychotherapist is to continue to provide therapeutic service during the terminal phase of the patient's life, this must be an agreement mutually acceptable. If the psychotherapist doesn't have the emotional resources to work effectively with a dying patient, this should be determined as early as possible and other supportive arrangement implemented.

Should patient and psychotherapist agree to continue the relationship, the psychotherapist must be prepared to cast aside much of the professional tradecraft associated with proper constraints and psychological distance so necessary to the course of psychotherapy with the physically healthy patient. It is impossible to be therapeutically helpful to a dying patient from a distance. It is proposed that the following are the salient aspects and requirements for psychotherapeutic work with a dying patient:

- *Facing reality.* Once the psychotherapist and patient decide to continue working together, both must know as much as possible about the stages and concomitants of the patient's illness. Permission must be obtained for the psychotherapist to consult with the physicians who will be treating the illness. Treatment, stages of deterioration, palliative medications and their effects, and other matters should be discussed in detail. Most physicians are more than happy to have help with a dying patient. Conferences may be held with the patient present as well as just between the psychotherapist and the physician.

The nature, course, and effects of the terminal illness must be an open matter between psychotherapist and patient. The psychotherapist should encourage open discussion and catharsis.

- *Therapeutic stance.* The therapeutic alliance must be strengthened and the patient must be able to count on the psychotherapist for fairly unremitting support. More frequent sessions, hospital visits, and home visits may be necessary. This places a considerable logistical and emotional burden on the psychotherapist. A certain amount of hand-holding, patting, and hugging is a necessary part of psychotherapy with the dying patient. It is usually necessary for the psychotherapist to become much more transparent and sharing than is possible with other patients. The psychotherapist's views and fears regarding illness and death should be shared with increasing openness. Clarification, reflection, and interpretation continue to be valuable tools in the encouragement and processing of experiential responses by the patient. These must now be used more supportively than before illness and death became the key aspects of the patient's future.

  Psychotherapists who have conducted therapy with a dying patient report feelings of guilt regarding their own survival, feeling impotent to change the course of events, charging professional fees, and other matters. The psychotherapist must do everything possible to ensure that these natural issues do not overburden the therapist or the patient. Reading (Cutter, 1974; Feifel, 1959; Shneidman, 1973, 1980) is helpful. Consultation with experienced colleagues is mandatory. This is hard, draining work, and the psychotherapist needs support.

- *The patient's family.* In order for a person to die with dignity, cooperation and support from family, friends, and relatives are of signal importance. The patient's support network needs help. This may be provided entirely by the patient's psychotherapist, although it is probably more efficient and less stressful to have collegial help from one or more other professionals who practice in the specialty of death and dying.

  Issues of hospitalization versus home treatment, medication, and treatment choices affect everyone close to the patient. Family sessions can be very helpful in such matters. Having a second therapist to deal with the family on these issues is particularly helpful when issues of *unfinished business* stir up threat and conflict.

- *Unfinished business.* This refers to very strong emotions, positive or negative, toward family which have never been faced with the significant parties. The psychotherapist must encourage the dying patient to face, accept, and resolve strong residual guilts and resentments.

"It no longer matters" is a specious argument—it does matter. Support and encouragement should be used to help the patient conduct unfinished business. Where this causes negative reactions in the family, group meetings may be helpful to bring feelings into the open and resolve the long-standing conflicts. This will benefit the dying patient and the surviving family members. In most cases, all parties will report a sense of relief and a new openness.

The following is from an individual session with a 58-year-old woman in the terminal stages of cancer. She had been in psychotherapy for three years before her inoperable terminal illness was diagnosed. The psychotherapist and patient had worked through issues of rage, fear, and anticipated terminal course and treatment. In the session reported below, she reported unresolved feelings toward her husband and two sons:

Patient: I guess it's natural . . . but I always resented their excluding me on a lot of things. . . . They'd go off and talk and if I asked, they'd just look at each other and say, "Nothing". . . .
Therapist: So it was hard to be the only female in the home.
Patient: Yeah (*laughs*), even the dogs were always males. . . .
Therapist: Did you tell them?
Patient: No. . . . Wouldn't have done no good. They always hang together.
Therapist: Ever felt like telling them?
Patient: Yeah . . . a lot.
Therapist: Why not now?
Patient: Now? . . . . I couldn't do that!
Therapist: Why?
Patient: Well . . . you know . . . with me on the way out and all . . . I would . . . no . . . but it would be nice.
Therapist: How about if I was there?
Patient: What do you mean?
Therapist: We could have a family session—everybody tell everything.
Patient: Oh my gawd! Wouldn't that be something!

After another session of individual therapy, the patient reported that she had brought up the issue of her resentment about being excluded. She said that the husband and the older son had simply denied, with some heat, that the exclusion had occurred. The younger son, however, thought that this had probably happened and a loud, angry interaction among the three men of the family ensued. The father stopped this abruptly, reminding them that they must "respect" mother's condition. The patient decided on a joint session. Something similar occurred, with the father attempting to calm everyone in due deference to the mother's illness. The following took place:

Mother: You always do that.
Father: What dear?
Mother: Shut off the discussion and somehow blame me.
Father: (*looking with blank innocence at the therapist*) I'm only trying to make things pleasant!
Therapist: Has this sort of thing gone on a lot in the past?
Son #1: Oh . . . every once in awhile.
Son #2: Actually, every time there is any disagreement involving any heat.
Father: Well . . . fighting in the family isn't right. We must stick together, especially now.
Mother: You're doing it again!
Father: What do you mean? (*angrily*)
Mother: You close down discussions before we can get our feelings out . . . and then lay the blame on good old Mom.
Father: Now dear . . . all this excitement . . . it can't be good for you.
Mother: Oh, go play in traffic!
Father: What! (*pause*) When you talk like that, you put everyone off.
Son #1: Speak for yourself, Dad. I think she's right.
Father: Now see here!
Son #2: No . . . you see here. You've always accused mother of being "pushy," but actually you're the one who maneuvers things around to come out the way you want.
Son #1: Bill, that's not exactly fair. I don't know that we should be washing the family laundry in front of Dr. Jones.
Mother: Or in front of each other. This family hates open emotion.

At this point the father became emotional and made a series of accusations, followed by the patient making counteraccusations. All joined in and a good bit of unfinished business was brought up by all parties. Some shouting and then crying took place. At the end there was a sense of relief expressed by all. The younger son set the tone of resolution at the end of the session by saying, "This should have happened a long time ago, but it's great that it's happened now." All agreed.

Aftermath. After the patient dies, the family of survivors may seek help with their bereavement. Unless the psychotherapist is trained in bereavement counseling and wishes to practice in this specialty, referral to an appropriate bereavement center or counselor is indicated. It may be impossible or, at best, very difficult, to become a competent psychotherapist to a survivor of one with whom death and dying therapy has been done.

Psychotherapy with patients experiencing cataclysmic events is very draining for the psychotherapist. These events, fortunately, happen rarely in the course of a psychotherapist's practice.

By no means have all the special or unusual situations which can occur in a lifetime of psychotherapeutic practice been addressed. The methods and procedures presented can be adapted to other unusual situations. All of the fundamentals apply.

CHAPTER 10

Ending Psychotherapy

Termination of psychotherapy should be the patient's final integrative act of the therapeutic course. Early termination, the cessation of therapy before a significant amount of experiencing and integration take place, is a relatively common occurrence in psychotherapeutic practice. Early termination and integrative ending of psychotherapy will be considered in detail.

EARLY TERMINATION

Termination by the Patient

There are many reasons why a patient may wish to end psychotherapy before significant changes in perception of self occur. This can take place at any time during the psychotherapeutic course. Some of the more frequent types of early termination by patients will be addressed:

The patient moves. The patient may be required to end or interrupt the psychotherapeutic course by a family move, new job opportunity, or desire to live elsewhere.

Every effort should be made to review the anticipated termination during a therapeutic session. It is generally helpful for the patient to explore feelings about the disruption of psychotherapy.

During the final sessions, the psychotherapist can help the patient decide on whether psychotherapy should continue in the patient's new setting. The psychotherapist should offer to recommend several psychotherapists in the community to which the patient is moving. Where the psychotherapist knows no one in the new community, the patient should be referred to a professional person in the new community who is likely to know of the psychotherapeutic options available. The psychotherapist should be willing to write a letter of referral to such a point of contact, with the patient's permission, making it easier for the patient to establish a new setting in which to continue psychotherapy.

An example of such a letter follows:

April 15, 1987

Melanie Smith, M.D.
2116 Elmwood Drive - Suite 201
Madison, WI 53714

Dear Dr. Smith:

As I mentioned to you in our recent telephone call, Dr. William Allen of Chicago recommended you to me as knowledgeable of the opportunities for psychotherapy in your community.

My patient, Mr. Charles Jones, will be resettling in Madison next month. I have suggested he make an appointment to consult with you about continuing the psychotherapeutic course he began with me in the Fall of 1986. He's done quite well and would like to complete therapy.

Once Mr. Jones has selected his therapist, I will forward a copy of his psychological report and a summary of our therapy work.

We appreciate your willingness to help in this transfer.

Very truly yours,

James M. Doe, Ph.D.
Psychotherapist

All correspondence or transfer of records should be sent only with the patient's written permission.

Family barriers and interference. The patient's participation in psychotherapy is not always approved or well received by the patient's relatives, friends, and mate figures. The patient's decision to explore the self and perhaps to make life changes can be very threatening to those who have known and needed the patient "as is." Some patients respond to these pressures by terminating psychotherapy. In the following excerpt from the 14th session of a 26-year-old radio announcer, termination of therapy takes place at the request of his fiancée:

Patient: I've decided to stop therapy . . . for a while at least.
Therapist: Tell me about that.
Patient: Well, . . . Things aren't really changing. . . . I still get discouraged . . . feel I lack direction. Mona says that all this will be gone if I just settle down and plan for our marriage and our life together. She and my mother both agree that I don't need psychotherapy—just a stable family life.
Therapist: So it would please them. . . .
Patient: Yeah . . . but, . . . well, . . . it makes sense to me.

Such announcements can threaten the psychotherapist. Under no circumstances should the therapist present arguments as to the fallacies of thinking in the fiancée's and mother's position. Such behavior places the patient in the untenable conflict of choosing between family and psychotherapy. Such a choice may be important or even useful, but *only when brought forth by the patient*. For the psychotherapist to create the conflict and ambivalence would be a therapeutic error. The patient's decision should be explored gently. If little or no ambivalence is found, the decision should be supported, with opportunities left open for a return to psychotherapy in the future. This is illustrated by a portion of the same therapy session in which the broadcaster announced his decision to terminate psychotherapy:

Therapist: Well, it seems that you're pretty comfortable about stopping therapy at this time.
Patient: Yeah. . . . It makes sense and I think it will work out. My mother told me she had gone for help once . . . many years ago . . . but she found that things worked out when she made some decisions and carried them through. I guess I'll try that.
Therapist: We'll cancel the rest of your appointments then. If, in the future, you'd like to continue, call me and we can set things up again. If, in the future, you'd like to try another psychotherapist, I'd be happy, if you request it, to forward your records and a summary of what we've done.
Patient: Yeah. . . . I'm glad the door isn't closed behind me.

Therapist: People in therapy sometimes feel like trying it on their own. If it works out—fine. If not, they can always return and continue.
Patient: I appreciate that . . . and what you've done for me.
Therapist: Well . . . what we've done, we've done together.

The patient is free to leave without guilt or ambivalence. The patient is furthermore encouraged to know he can return to psychotherapy should he wish to do this in the future.

Financial issues. Circumstances which constrict the patient's income may precipitate temporary or permanent termination of psychotherapy. The financial stress may be a rationalization on the part of the patient in order to quit therapy for deeper emotional reasons. If not, the psychotherapist's philosophy of fee-setting will determine, in most situations of this sort, whether termination takes place.

Where the psychotherapist has a fixed fee schedule, with no exceptions, the psychotherapy is terminated until the patient is able to afford the therapist's expected fee. When this happens, the patient should be referred to an agency or clinic setting where treatment may be continued. This may be a very disruptive experience for the patient, representing rejection and another failure experience in the patient's life.

The best circumstance, in cases where the patient cannot afford the psychotherapist's regular fee, is a system whereby fees can be adjusted to reflect the patient's altered financial status. Setting fees based on income has been discussed earlier. When patients face a financial crisis (or, for that matter, an increase of income), the fee for psychotherapy should be discussed and a new fee set jointly by psychotherapist and patient.

Panic resulting from progress. As has been frequently noted, some patients may become threatened and anxious as they make progress in psychotherapy. The "flight into health" which results in premature termination of the psychotherapy is one form of such panic. In some instances, the patient may simply call and cancel all further appointments. Occasionally, a patient may terminate by writing to the therapist. The longer a patient has been in therapy, the more likely that termination will be announced during a therapeutic session.

When a patient ends psychotherapy by telephone or letter, the psychotherapist should write to the patient, accepting the decision. The following elements should be included in the letter:

- Acknowledgment that all future appointments are cancelled as the patient requested.

- Supportive comments to lessen the patient's guilt.
- Encouragement to continue in the future (if appropriate).
- An offer to be available for the patient to continue in the future or to transfer records to another psychotherapist should this be that patient's wishes.

Termination by the Psychotherapist

Termination of the therapeutic course by the psychotherapist should be a relatively rare phenomenon. Ordinarily this is the patient's decision, as part of the integrative phase of psychotherapy. The decision to end the therapy made by the therapist removes this power from the patient. In short-term, time-limited psychotherapeutic ventures, the therapist, together with the patient, may limit the length of therapy, setting termination at a specific date or a predetermined number of sessions (Lamb, 1985). Such procedures are usually required by university clinics, community mental health centers or cost-containment insurance systems. Such procedures would be more accurately described as crisis consultation, counseling, or behavioral management than as psychotherapy.

In the course of dynamic psychotherapy, as described in previous chapters, termination by the therapist may occasionally be necessary. Some of the usual bases are described below:

Illness of the psychotherapist. Psychotherapists become seriously ill at times, and decide to end their professional careers. When this occurs, it is of vital importance, where physically and emotionally feasible, for the therapist to allow the patient to express feelings such as grief, rage, or diappointment about this disruption. For some patients this may represent a recapitulation of earlier desertions by significant family figures.

The psychotherapist moves. This sort of termination occurs more frequently among psychotherapists in agency or university settings. Career moves are less frequently found among independent practitioners, who tend to settle in one community for the majority of their professional careers.

Retirement. Even independent practitioners eventually end their professional practice. In contrast to termination because of illness or a career move, the psychotherapist who intends to retire is in a better position to take no new cases and allow most or all current patients to reach the end of their psychotherapeutic course in the usual integrative style.

Psychotherapeutic contraindications. Whereas the previously cited reasons for the psychotherapist to terminate psychotherapy might be termed *natural,* or *life-change* bases for ending therapy, there are a number of other situations which can arise in psychotherapy which may require the psychotherapist to terminate.

- *Countertransference* situations can develop. In these, the psychotherapist develops strong positive or negative feelings toward the patient. If these cannot be resolved in a satisfactory, timely manner as has been described in previous chapters, the therapist must terminate the psychotherapy. Not to do so would compound the therapeutic error.
- *Intolerable limit-testing* by the patient can be a reasonable basis for the psychotherapist to terminate therapy. The patient may cancel sessions with such frequency as to prevent meaningful therapeutic interaction from taking place. The patient may refuse to pay agreed-upon fees. Occasionally, a patient may attempt to intrude upon the psychotherapist's private life in spite of previous structuring and agreement as to the limits on interaction outside of the therapy session. To prevent such behaviors from worsening the patient's condition, the psychotherapist may have to terminate the psychotherapy.

Procedures for termination by the psychotherapist

As much as possible, the procedures by which the psychotherapist terminates the therapy should be in the patient's best interests. The psychotherapist should initiate the discussion of termination with a fairly detailed structuring. This structuring should include:

- *Reasons.* A simple, straightforward, undefensive statement of why the termination must take place in the patient's best interests.
- *Time line.* Whenever possible, the psychotherapist should suggest that several sessions be devoted to termination and its effects on the patient.
- *Options.* Termination should be specific to the relationship between psychotherapist and patient, leaving open the opportunity for the patient to continue with another psychotherapist.

Following the psychotherapist's announcement and structuring, every effort should be made to encourage the patient to respond emotionally to the termination announcement. Catharsis is vital if the psychotherapist is to be helpful to the patient in exploring future therapeutic possibilities. The psychotherapist should be extremely supportive and helpful in the following areas:

- *Clarification.* Although the therapist has presented reasons for termination during the initial structuring, clarification and discussion of these reasons may be helpful after the patient has responded emotionally.
- *Control and transfer of records.* The psychotherapist should indicate to the patient that records of their psychotherapy will be kept in a proper confidential manner. The length of time such records will be kept should be specified. The patient should be told that if another therapeutic venture is started by the patient, records will be forwarded to the new therapist, with the patient's permission.

NORMAL THERAPEUTIC TERMINATION

Although psychotherapy seems like an endless process for some, it does proceed through known stages to a conclusion. The patient explores, experiences, and integrates. In a sense, the patient becomes his or her own psychotherapist.

Termination Signals

No two patients terminate psychotherapy in exactly the same manner or sequence. The therapist and the patient are both generally aware that intellectualization has practically disappeared, while more of the patient's statements during the session are integrative. Some of the things which happen during the psychotherapeutic session which lead to discussion of termination include:

Plateaus. More and more the patient has periods of silence or long pauses during the session. These differ from depressive plateaus in that the patient seems quite content and the psychotherapist senses tranquility rather than stress.

Positive attitudes. More and more of what the patient says about himself or herself is positive. Comments indicating personal satisfaction and self-acceptance show a marked increase when compared with the beginning and mid-stages of psychotherapy.

Relations with children. Those patients who have regular contact with children and adolescents, either their own or others', often notice an increase in positive responses by the children toward them as the psychotherapeutic process moves toward termination. The following is reported by a 34-year-old woman during her 75th session of psychotherapy (five sessions before she terminated):

Patient: Something strange ... not exactly strange, but new, has happened. I got a call from my nine-year-old niece. She just wanted to talk. ...

Therapist: This was unusual for her?

Patient: Yes. I usually see her when I visit my sister ... but, well, I've never been very comfortable around her. She called and just "talked" for a while. Then she said, "You're neat—I love you, Aunt Jane." I realized that we'd started to talk with each other during our recent visits. It felt *very* nice.

Children are sometimes the first to sense strength, self-assurance and emotional stability developing in the adults around them.

Tolerance of others. As patients move toward completing therapy, they tend to report a tolerance, understanding, or sometimes forgiveness of figures in their lives who have been sources of stress or heartache. Family, former friends, ex-mates, and others are discussed with less bitterness and acrimony. Among patients who have used denial as a primary defense style there may be a reversal, with the patient for the first time during the therapy accurately describing the faults or negative traits of significant others. Even in such cases, the descriptions are more in the form of tolerant acceptance of reality rather than vengeful bitterness.

Growing ability to set realistic limits. The development of the ability to set reasonable limits in situations which previously caused the patient to give in or withdraw can herald an approach to the termination of psychotherapy.

Focus on the future. At the beginning of psychotherapy, most patients avoid discussing their own futures. Focus is usually on the past or on fears of the future. As psychotherapy nears completion, patients tend to describe themselves in positive ways in respect to future stresses, challenges, and opportunities. In the following segment from the seventh session of psychotherapy, a 36-year-old housewife discusses herself in relation to the stresses of family life.

Patient: It's been a wearying job. I can't seem to do everything I should ... and what I do I don't do well. I wonder if I should ever have married ... and I'm really not sure I should have had kids (*weeps softly*). ... I've done a bad job.

Therapist: You feel guilty.

Patient: Ever so much so. ... I haven't seemed to be able to do what's needed. Last week they got into an awful fight while my husband was taking a nap. He was furious with me. I just couldn't manage things.

A year and a half later, the following took place during the patient's 80th session.

Patient: Next year I plan for us to vacation without the kids. They've been more and more responsible and we can leave them for two weeks. My husband was a little reluctant, but I've persuaded him to try a couple of long weekends. In two weeks we're going to the mountains to see the leaves change color.
Therapist: You're looking forward to these trips.
Patient: Yes. I'm looking forward to a lot of things. My husband and I seem a lot more interested in . . . well . . . ourselves, lately.

Five sessions later this patient terminated psychotherapy.

Tolerance of symptoms. The end of psychotherapy does not always bring an end to all symptoms. Even when symptoms remain, however, the patient seems to accept and tolerate these as psychotherapy moves toward completion. In the following, a 46-year-old patient describes his fear of crowds and large groups during the 95th session of psychotherapy:

Patient: I still don't care for parties or group events. I'm not in a panic as I used to be. Instead of never going to such things, I go late and leave early. I pick people I know and chat or really listen to them. If they leave, I stay there and just smile, watching the crowd. I've learned that smiles and nods are acceptable communication in these cattle gatherings.
Therapist: You still don't like it.
Patient: No . . . but I'm not really afraid anymore.

Termination anxiety. As the psychotherapeutic course moves toward completion, most patients sense this and become anxious about losing the source of their hard-earned gains. As they consider temination, they often express unsureness and ambivalence, questioning whether it is time yet to be on their own. The patient is not alone in experiencing termination anxiety. The impending loss of the rhythm and pattern of the psychotherapeutic process also affects the psychotherapist. No matter how carefully and well countertransference has been handled, most therapists feel some tension as they realize that the psychotherapeutic venture is reaching its conclusion (Martin & Schurtman, 1985). This is a natural separation anxiety, to be expected between two people who have formed a very close alliance. They have worked hard and well together and must accept as one of the fruits of their labor, a disengagement and dissolution of the alliance.

Procedures for Terminating Psychotherapy

The patient should lead in terminating psychotherapy. One of the goals in most psychotherapeutic ventures is the development of independence. Choosing to end psychotherapy is a major step for the patient in acting independently.

The psychotherapist can be helpful in this final integrative act. When the patient first addresses the possibility of termination, the psychotherapist should encourage experiencing by the patient. Fear, hesitation, anticipation, and grief are common patient reactions to the awareness that psychotherapy has been successful. The psychotherapist's role at this point is to encourage exploration and to clarify feelings. Once the patient has brought out ideas, hopes, and fears regarding termination and seems to generally be prepared for this step, some structuring by the psychotherapist is appropriate. Some or all of the following concepts should be included in the structuring:

- It is all right to think and talk about ending psychotherapy. This is one of the expected outcomes.
- The patient doesn't have to be symptom-free, perfect, or "sure" in order to stop coming to psychotherapy.
- A "trial period" is an acceptable way of deciding whether it is time to terminate.
- A return for one or several sessions after the trial period to evaluate the patient's experience is perfectly acceptable.
- Should the termination decision prove to be premature, the patient may return to psychotherapy at any time.

Some patients may wish to terminate by "cutting down" sessions to once a month or so. Usually this represents unresolved dependency, but in some instances this may be an appropriate way to end the psychotherapy.

Post-termination Events

Contact with the patient may or may not end with termination. Some patients return to psychotherapy to resolve issues avoided during their initial therapy experience. Some patients return, usually for a brief series of sessions, to deal with traumatic or other stressful events in their lives. No matter how complete the psychotherapy has been, most patients consider the psychotherapist a reliable and trustworthy resource for helping them deal with critical issues following termination.

Nontherapeutic contacts. A certain number of patients attempt to establish social or business contacts with their psychotherapist. This should be discouraged. There is no way of knowing, with certainty, when the patient may need the psychotherapist in the future. In addition, the special, intense alliance formed during psychotherapy results in attitudes of trust, confidentiality, privilege, and legal responsibilities which are inappropriate as a basis of friendship. The same is true of entering into business relationships with former patients. Psychotherapists who find that former patients become friends or business associates during or after psychotherapy should seriously examine their dependency and dominance needs with a senior colleague or psychotherapy supervisor. Such posttreatment relationships can be destructive to both patient and psychotherapist.

Letters of recommendation. Following the completion of psychotherapy, some patients may request letters supporting some sort of application or accreditation procedure. Where the request is in some way connected with the patient's status as an individual who has completed personal psychotherapy, an appropriate letter can be written. Most commonly, such letters are requested by former patients entering graduate programs requiring personal psychotherapy for entrance or graduation, as well as in cases where involvement in psychotherapy has been ordered by the courts or the ethics committee of a professional organization.

Letters should be brief, carefully correct, conservative, and written with the patient's full knowledge and approval. So-called "confidential" letters of evaluation should not be written by a psychotherapist about a former patient.

Character references for jobs or special appointments or awards should not be written by therapists for former patients. Such documents require judgment of the former patient, a role inappropriate for the psychotherapist.

Investigative requests. When a former patient applies for certain professional schools, licensing, or employment in sensitive government agencies, revelation by the applicant of former psychotherapeutic treatment frequently requires investigation. This may be done by mail or by a visit from an investigator to determine the former patient's emotional status before and after psychotherapy.

No information should be provided without the patient's full knowledge of the interrogation and written permission for the psychotherapist to respond.

With the former patient's informed consent, the psychotherapist's responses should be brief, specific to the questions asked, and as much as possible without personal detail. When possible, a copy of the written interrogatory or a tape of the interview should be made, with a copy for the patient and one for the patient's file.

Correspondence. Occasionally former patients will write to tell their former psychotherapist of triumphs or tragedies which followed termination of therapy. Replies should be courteous and brief. Psychotherapy should not be reinstituted by mail. If the correspondence (or phone call, in some cases) suggests that the former patient is in chronic distress, a return to psychotherapy may be suggested.

Contact by former patients is a relatively rare event for most psychotherapists. Sensible, brief, friendly response within ethical and legal constraints is the appropriate guideline for the psychotherapist.

The Closing Note

When termination has been completed and the psychotherapeutic course is done, the psychotherapist should devote an hour or so to review for himself or herself the entire experience. An attempt should be made to summarize and evaluate the salient aspects of the experience. The value in such an exercise lies in the opportunity for the psychotherapist to review the therapeutic alliance, the quality of the psychotherapeutic tradecraft, barriers, errors, and outcomes. It is a time to review what has been done and what might be done better in the future. Some of the aspects of psychotherapy which can be covered in a closing written note include:

- The original problems and those which emerged.
- The early course of psychotherapy.
- Experiencing and the mid-stage of the process.
- Integration and resolution.
- Barriers.
- Errors.
- Outcome.

The following closing note was written for the psychotherapy file of a bank officer who was 46-years-old when she began and 48 when she terminated psychotherapy after 100 individual and 55 group sessions.

PSYCHOTHERAPY CLOSING NOTE

NAME Jones, Mary E.   *Date Began* 1/17/82   *Date Ended* 5/12/84
SESSIONS: 100 INDIVIDUAL   55 GROUP   *Closing Note* 8/15/84

Ms. Jones began psychotherapy about two years after her husband's death in an automobile accident. Her persisting grief, depression and withdrawal were her presenting symptoms. As psychotherapy progressed Ms. Jones identified the loss of her husband as symbolic of earlier disappointments, unresolved resentments, and guilt.

She began slowly. At first she focused on her job dissatisfaction and her conflict with her grown children. She responded to early interpretations of the dynamics and meanings of her symptoms with somatization and withdrawal (missing sessions).

After Group once per week was added to her weekly individual sessions, she began to experience more affect during her sessions. She began to report dreams and to review her interpersonal contacts and her symptoms as symbolic of her life experiences and developmental stresses. She worked through buried rage and guilt toward a deserting father and the deceased husband.

As she came to know and respect herself in psychotherapy, she began to identify her patterns of anger-suppression and guilt operations at work and with her family. She began to assert herself and stabilized her previously turbulent relationships with her sons. At work she began to expect (and in fact received) acknowledgment of her worth and promotion.

Her focus on her husband's death, job and family conflicts, and somatic complaints early in the therapeutic course effectively prevented deeper self-search and experiencing. It was probably a therapeutic error to hold off suggesting Group until her 54th session. She found the security and models in Group which encouraged her to risk exploration of her fantasies.

Ms. Jones left her job as bank teller and accepted a position with another bank as a vice-president. She was extremely pleased with her success here, describing it as "selling my wares for their true worth for the first time in my life."

This kind of closing note is also useful in the event the patient returns to psychotherapy in the future or requests a review of the psychotherapeutic course to be sent to a new therapist. Whether the patient and psychotherapist should conduct a similar review during their last session is a matter best left to the patient. Again, the patient leads.

The psychotherapy case records can be kept for as little as six years and then destroyed. This is the generally accepted minimum for mental health agencies. Some psychotherapists keep case records during the entirety of their professional careers. Whatever the choice in this matter, the style should be explained to the patient at the beginning and at the end of psychotherapy. Safeguards should be established to destroy or transfer the records in the event of the psychotherapist's retirement or death. Except in certain specific legal proceedings, the records are the property of the psychotherapist, but the confidentiality of such records must be maintained in perpetuity or until the records are destroyed.

PART III

Renewal

CHAPTER 11

Stress, Overload, Burnout, and Renewal

The practice of psychotherapy can be stressful. Although generally less stressful than some other professions such as law enforcement, nursing, and teaching (Farber, 1985), the work of the psychotherapist can nevertheless be very demanding. It is impossible not to share in some manner the stresses and striving of patients.

SOURCES OF STRESS FOR THE PSYCHOTHERAPIST

Responsibility of the Role

Psychotherapists are affected by both the realistic and the implied burdens they carry in the role of "healer." Levels of successful performance in this role are difficult to identify, to achieve, and to maintain. Self-expectancies of psychotherapists are usually quite high, increasing the potential for perceived failure and disappointment (Freudenberger, 1985; Guy & Souder, 1986a). Psychotherapists tend to be idealistic folk and may at times expect even more of themselves than do their patients (Suran & Sheridan, 1985).

The Expectancies and Demands of Patients

Along with the patient's personal commitment to the psychotherapeutic process comes the patient's expectancy for the psychotherapist's total skills, energies, and attention. As part of the alliance, the psychotherapist is expected to share the patient's conflicts, pain, and confusion, at least empathetically. The patient's anger must first be tolerated before it can be traced and understood. Demanding dependencies must first be experienced by the psychotherapist before they are identified, interpreted, understood, and resolved by the patient. Although manipulations and limit-testing are not seen as personal attacks, the psychotherapist is nevertheless the object of such behavior. A certain stamina is required and the psychotherapist's efforts are not always rewarded by patient progress (Guy & Souder, 1986a).

The Pressure of Logistics

The conditions under which a psychotherapist conducts a practice can create stress. Those who see patients in an independent practice setting are at significantly less risk for emotional exhaustion than those psychotherapists in an institutional setting or a split institutional/part-time independent practice.

Patient flow and income vary considerably for the psychotherapist in the independent practice setting, yet a relatively small number in this setting consider it stressful (Farber, 1983, 1985).

Some of the pressures of a psychotherapeutic practice are found in any modern organization providing human services, whether the organization is public or private. Non-supportive clerical and administrative staff can create pressures and barriers for the psychotherapist. Inadequate physical surroundings, deficient record keeping and security of records, a poor telephone answering service, and disruptive colleagues or associates are all possible sources of stress which the psychotherapist can expect to find in a lifetime career of professional practice.

Personal Contingencies

The psychotherapist's work can be very consuming. At times there is little emotional energy remaining for family, friends, or outside interests (Farber, 1983). More than three-quarters of psychotherapists report that in the course of their professional careers they have suffered significant problems involving personal relationships. More than one-half of all psychotherapists studied by Deutsch (1985) indicate they have suffered depression related to the stresses of their professional work. The most significant instigating events for interpersonal stress reported by psychotherapists were troubled relationships, dysfunctional marriages, and impending divorces. Job-related stresses ranked second. These distressing experiences are apparently somewhat less frequently found among psychotherapists than among members of the lay public (Norcross & Prochaska, 1986, a, b).

The social life of most professionals is plagued by assertive or manipulative friends and acquaintances seeking advice, direction, or assurance. The psychotherapist is seen by most acquaintances and friends as a fairer mark than physicians or dentists—not only as a source of counsel and advice, but as a handy target for jokes and sarcasm. These social experiences are distasteful and stressful for most psychotherapists and tend to restrict the range of social contacts open to them.

OVERLOAD AND BURNOUT

Burnout is an ever-present hazard for the psychotherapist. A ruinous experience for a professional person, it tends to be found most frequently in those occupations where idealism and self-expectations cease to be met by the work. Symptoms include significant loss of motivation and energy. There is a numbing of feelings and the victim becomes socially isolated. Specific signs in the workplace include a marked increase in clock-watching, somatic complaints, decrease in work efficiency, cynicism, and depression. The condition is most likely to occur after 10 or more years of practice. Personal disenchantments, failed relationships and financial reversals can increase the psychotherapist's vulnerability to burnout. Any professional is at risk for burnout when expected difficulties at work are significantly exceeded. Working conditions which are stressful and clinical situations which "go wrong" or work out badly are also common triggers for burnout reactions (Freudenberger, 1985; Suran & Sheridan, 1985). Among psychotherapists, it has been found that those in the independent practice setting are less at risk for burnout than those who do psychotherapy in an institutional or agency setting. The greater the number of hours spent with patients the greater the vulnerability to burnout (Farber, 1985).

The Prelude to Burnout-Overload

Psychotherapists move toward burnout as they experience *overload*. Overload occurs when rest, relationships, recreation, and other supportive activities are insufficient to balance disappointments, goals and aspirations not met, and excessive demands of a heavy psychotherapeutic practice. Poor education, training, or supervision during the apprentice years can make a psychotherapist more prone to overload.

In the earlier years of practice, the psychotherapist is usually at a peak of idealism and energy. With increasing age (and often with growing success and reputation), the psychotherapist is less equipped to "give all" without overload developing (Guy & Souder, 1986b). The signs and symptoms of overload include:

- Sleepiness during the psychotherapeutic session.
- Drifting attention.
- Being late for therapy sessions with increasing frequency.
- Annoyance with patients.
- Overzealous relief at the end of the work day.
- Feelings of relief when a patient cancels.
- Sardonic or humorous references to patients.
- Psychophysiological responses.
- Increased irritability with staff, family, and patients.
- Disillusionment with the work of psychotherapy.

The more frequently and intensely such signs and symptoms occur, the more vulnerable the psychotherapist is to burnout.

Burnout

Most psychotherapists who experience burnout are unable to function effectively. Part of burnout is unremitting loneliness, extreme cynicism, and depression. The psychotherapist has become dysfunctional. Sleeplessness, deteriorated personal relationships, and withdrawal are common to the burned-out psychotherapist. Some should not be at work and many are unable to go to work. Since the mental health of psychotherapists is instrumental to their work (Deutsch, 1985), it is highly questionable for the burned-out psychotherapist to see patients while in that state.

Rehabilitation of Burnout

The psychotherapist who is unable to function professionally because of burnout must seek help. This may prove difficult for some. The role change from helper to help-seeker may distress some needful psychotherapists.

A skillful colleague should be consulted. Cognitive focusing should be the approach, with emphasis on the following issues:

- *The culminating behavior*. What was the psychotherapist doing or *not* doing which clearly indicated that he or she was impaired?
- *The essential source*. The impaired psychotherapist should attempt

to identify imbalances in such areas as expectations versus outcomes and energy versus demands of patients, family, and activities.
* *The overload buildup.* Once the burned-out psychotherapist identifies the sources of the impairment, it is important to review how the overload was allowed to occur and recur.

This sort of help can be obtained on an individual basis or in larger communities in a group setting (Freudenberger, 1985).

As the therapeutic intervention takes place, the burned-out psychotherapist should consider other rehabilitative steps:

* *Stop practice for at least two weeks.* During this time the burned-out psychotherapist should go off to a totally new setting for a few days. Catharsis with both a therapist and a close other person is very important. As much physical activity as the burned-out psychotherapist can tolerate safely can be helpful. Reading for pleasure during this time is a worthwhile diversion. Exploring new activities or interests is recommended.
* *Return to a smaller case load.* The impaired psychotherapist must cut down on patient hours if rehabilitation is to take place. This can be done by giving the patients a choice between less frequent meetings or transfer to another psychotherapist.
* *Begin deterrents to overload.* A regular physical fitness schedule is vital to help prevent future overload. Weekly recreational activities should be scheduled. Development of new professional skills or applications should be explored. A return to a total focus on psychotherapeutic activity should be avoided.
* *Complete medical evaluation.* As part of a renewal program, the burned-out psychotherapist should begin with a clear understanding of his or her physical condition. Modification of unhealthy eating, drinking, smoking, or other self-destructive habits should begin.
* *Schedule preventive maintenance.* There are things which the psychotherapist can do to prevent recurrence of burnout. These must be planned and carried out on a regular basis. These procedures are addressed in the next section.

Burnout is a seriously debilitating experience which must be faced, stabilized, and reversed as early on as possible.

PREVENTING OVERLOAD AND BURNOUT

Fortunately, psychotherapists appear to be less prone to overload than other professionals. Psychotherapists may possess a larger repertoire of coping strategies to deal with overload. They tend to emphasize rewarding interpersonal relationships, catharsis, helping relationships, and contingency control as ways of dealing with stress. Psychotherapists are less likely to depend on such unhelpful defenses as medication, self-blame, and wishful thinking. Psychotherapists are also more likely than other professional or lay persons to reevaluate and modify their environment (Norcross & Prochaska, 1986a).

Prevention of overload should not be left to chance. Preventive maintenance can be planned to ensure that overload doesn't develop. The recommendations which follow consider two major areas of the psychotherapist's life where stress may be prevented or balanced:

In the Workday and Workplace

There are many things which the psychotherapist can do to ensure that supportive staff and the work setting reduce sources of stress. These measures can also support the comfortable and efficient practice of psychotherapy.

Staff. Clerical and professional staff should be people the psychotherapist generally likes and respects. Such attitudes tend to be mutual and mutually supportive. Colleagues, clerical staff, and administrative personnel with whom the psychotherapist has conflict can be prime sources of stress and overload. Efforts should be made by the psychotherapist to create an open and mutually respectful staff interaction through careful selection, training, and maintenance of communication and positive supportive attitudes. Colleagues and staff should know they are important to the success of psychotherapeutic activity.

Case load and working hours. Every experienced psychotherapist knows how many hours of clinical work and how many particularly difficult patients constitute a full load. Stress builds rapidly as these natural and individual limits are exceeded. These limits will sometimes be exceeded in the normal course of a busy psychotherapeutic practice. The psychotherapist should monitor such overloads and take active steps to balance them when they occur. This should be followed by preventive measures such as planning additional recreational and renewal time.

Consultation. Every psychotherapist should develop close professional and personal relationships with several compatible colleagues. Such relationships serve as mutually supportive safeguards among psychotherapists to help each other deal with perplexing or stressful situations which arise during the course of every psychotherapist's professional career.

Professional development. The practice of psychotherapy profits from scientific and professional developments. Keeping in touch with such developments can be a helpful adjunct activity in preventing overload.

Professional meetings. Regular attendance at regional, national, and international meetings of other mental health professionals is useful in a number of ways. The regular routine of seeing patients is interrupted. Opportunities to see what other professionals say and do abound. Such meetings are opportunities to develop a network of colleagues with whom the psychotherapist can consult in the future. There are many opportunities, formal and informal, to exchange ideas, share concerns, and socialize with other psychotherapists.

Continuing education. With the advent of licensing, certification, and other procedures, renewal of credentials generally requires evidence that the mental health professional seeks to maintain competence through participation in continuing professional education.

Programs of advanced professional education are made available by large numbers of individuals and continuing education consortiums. Mental health professionals' mail is seldom without announcements of workshops and symposia covering a wide range of topics. Psychotherapists who attend several of these a year, on a regular basis, are probably enhancing the quality of their practice. Attendance at such workshops, as with attendance at professional meetings, helps avoid overload and burnout.

Reading. Reading in the professional literature provides an almost unlimited opportunity for the practicing psychotherapist to evaluate and enhance professional skills. Journals and books covering theory, new developments, and practice issues in mental health are readily available to the practicing psychotherapist. Setting aside a regular time to read professional literature is a simple but powerful way of disrupting the buildup of overload. All professionals agree that keeping up is important, but not all do so.

Local professional groups. The journal club or the monthly case conference is a long-standing tradition in the mental health professions. Meeting with colleagues on a regular basis to discuss current research and treatment topics of mutual interest, or to present unusual case material, can enhance practice skills and help prevent overload. Meetings such as these can include lunch or dinner, serving as an opportunity for both personal and professional sharing with colleagues.

Personal Life

Difficulties in personal relationships make up the single most frequently cited cause of distress among psychotherapists (Norcross & Prochaska, 1986a). A supportive and satisfying personal life away from the professional setting helps to prevent the buildup of stress which leads to overload. The psychotherapist can do specific things to ensure a balanced and healthy personal life:

Family. Setting aside time to spend with family on a daily, weekly, monthly, quarterly, and annual basis is a way of preventing the press of a busy practice from consistently relegating these important interactions to incidental "if and when" times. Such planning tends to reduce conflict and tension within the family.

Health. A program involving regular exercise, emphasizing general body tone and cardiovascular fitness, should be a part of every psychotherapist's life. Eating properly with an eye to balanced nutrition should be an essential aspect of the psychotherapist's schedule. Regular and sufficient sleep cycles and rest periods are important. Simplistic and basic as such things may be, they are powerful preventive measures for avoiding overload.

Recreation. Much of what the psychotherapist does involves intellectualization and "holding in." To balance this, the psychotherapist should develop recreational pursuits which allow "letting go," being creative, having fun, and in other ways balancing the restrictions and limitations placed on the individual who practices psychotherapy as a life's work. Chess, card playing, sports, and other such activities allow a certain amount of competitiveness, aggression, and risk. Escapist reading, travel, theater, scuba diving, backpacking, boating, mountain climbing and white water rafting are opportunities for the psychotherapist to experience fantasies and unfulfilled childhood dreams in a productive way.

The opportunities to avoid overload and burnout are almost endless. Awaiting the time when one "needs" such preventive measures is unwise. A balanced life is necessary for the psychotherapist to practice vigorously and effectively. This balance should be planned and developed in the beginning stages of the psychotherapist's professional career.

Epilogue

A few last words in epilogue. The tradecraft of psychotherapy presented in these pages represents a dynamic but practical approach to the conduct of the psychotherapeutic process.

For most of those who practice psychotherapy as a profession, the work is fulfilling. There is a sense of helping and contributing.

Throughout the history of psychotherapy as a treatment method, concern has been expressed that the process is long, costly, and sometimes inefficient. All too true. Hopefully, future research and evaluation will provide better tradecraft.

However, as the modern world proceeds to become awash in technology and efficiency, self and individuality seem to be moving toward extinction. Fun and the pursuit of excellence are still admired, but less frequently achieved. The psychotherapist remains as one of the few resources whereby the individual may work to repossess or activate personal quality and potential.

References

*ADAMS, S. & ORGEL, M. (1975). *Through the Mental Health Maze*. Washington, D.C.: Health Research Group. 2000 P St. N.W., Washington, D.C. 20036.

ALLEN, G. J., SZOLLOS, S. J. & BROWNEN, E. W. (1986). Doctoral students' comparative evaluations of Best and Worst psychotherapy supervision. *Professional Psychology: Research, and Practice, 17,* (2), 91–99.

AMERICAN PSYCHOLOGICAL ASSOCIATION (1981). Ethical principles of psychologists. Washington, D.C.: American Psychological Association.

*APA DIVISION OF THE PSYCHOLOGY OF WOMEN. (1982). *Women and Psychotherapy: A Consumer Handbook*. Washington, D.C.: Federation of Organizations for Professional Women. 2000 P. Street N.W., Suite 403, Washington, D.C. 20036.

ARNDT, W.B., FOEHL, J.C. & GOOD, E.F. (1985). Specific sexual fantasy themes. *Journal of Personality and Social Psychology, 48,* (2), 472–480.

ASERINSKI, E. & KLEITMAN, N. (1953). Regularly occurring periods of eye motility and concomitant phenomena during sleep. *Science, 118,* 273–274.

*BANDURA, A. (1969). *Principles of Behavior Modification*. New York: Holt, Rinehart and Winston.

BARNES, G. & PROSEN, H. (1985). Parental death and depression. *Journal of Abnormal Psychology, 94,* (1) 64–69.

*BAUER, G.P. & KOBOS, J.C. (1984). Short-term psychodynamic psychotherapy: Reflection on past and current practice. *Psychotherapy, 2,* (2), 153–170.

*BECK, A.T. (1976). *Cognitive Therapy and the Emotional Disorders*. New York: International Universities Press.

BEGLEY, S. (1985). A boost for the Freudians. *Newsweek,* Jan. 7th, p. 64.

*BERG, M. (1983). Borderline pathology as displayed on psychological tests. *Journal of Personality Assessment, 47,* (2), 120–133.

Note: Starred references are recommended as providing a picture of the past century of development of current psychotherapies. (These are also recommended reading for beginning psychotherapists.)

BERKOWITZ, M. (1983). Know your borderline: Countertransference as a diagnostic tool. *Psychotherapy: Theory, Research and Practice, 20,* (4), 405–407.

*BERNSTEIN, A. (1965). The psychoanalytic technique. In B.B. Wolman (Ed.) *Handbook of Clinical Psychology.* New York: McGraw Hill.

BLAU, T.H. (1950). Report on a method of predicting success in psychotherapy. *Journal of Clinical Psychology, 6,* (4), 403–406.

BLAU, T.H. (1969). The professional in the community views the nonprofessional helper: Psychology. In Grosser, C., Henry, W.E. & Kelley, J.E. (Eds.) *Nonprofessionals in the Human Services.* San Francisco: Jossey-Bass.

BLAU, T.H. (1984a). *The Psychologist as Expert Witness.* New York: John Wiley & Sons.

BLAU, T.H. (1984b). Foreword in Kaslow, F. (Ed.) *Psychotherapy with Psychotherapists.* New York: The Haworth Press.

BOTTARI, M. A. & RAPPAPORT, H. (1983). The relationship of patient and therapist-reported experiences of the initial session to outcome: An initial investigation. *Psychotherapy: Theory, Research, and Practice, 20,* (3), 355–358.

*BREGGIN, P. (1983). *Psychiatric Drugs: Hazards to the Brain.* New York: Springer.

*BRENNER, D. (1982). *The Effective Psychotherapist.* New York: Pergamon Press.

BROWN, B.B. (Ed.) (1975). *The Biofeedback Syllabus.* Springfield, IL: Charles C Thomas & Co.

BROWN, J.B. & HART, D.H. (1977). Correlates of females' sexual fantasies. *Perceptual and Motor Skills, 45,* 819–824.

BUDMAN, S.H. & GURMAN, A.S. (1983). The practice of brief psychotherapy. *Professional Psychology: Research and Practice, 14,* (3), 277–292.

BUGENTAL, J.F.T. & BUGENTAL, E.K. (1984). A fate worse than death: The fear of changing. *Psychotherapy, 21,* (4), 543–558.

CAMPBELL, D.E. (1979). Interior office design and visitor response. *Journal of Applied Psychology, 64,* (6), 648–653.

CATTELL, R.B. (1983). Let's end the duel. *American Psychologist, 38,* 769–776.

CLECKLEY, H. (1976). *The Mask of Sanity* (5th Ed.). St. Louis: Mosby.

CONTE, H., WEINER, M. & PLUTCHIK, R. (1982). Measuring death anxiety. *Journal of Personality and Social Psychology, 43,* (4), 775–785.

CUMMINGS, N. & FERNANDEZ, L.E. (1985). Exciting future possibilities for psychologists in the marketplace. *The Independent Practitioner, 5,* (1), 19–22.

CUMMINGS, N. & SOBEL, S. (1985). Malpractice insurance: Update on sex claims. *Psychotherapy, 22,* (2), 186–188.

*CUTTER, F. (1974). *Coming to Terms With Death.* Chicago: Nelson-Hall.

DEKRAAI, M.B. & SALES, B.D. (1982). Privileged communications of psychologists. *Professional Psychology, 13,* (3), 372–388.

DEKRAAI, M.B. & SALES, B.D. (1984). Confidential communications of psychotherapists. *Psychotherapy, 21,* (3), 293–318.

DEMENT, W.C. & KLEITMAN, N. (1957). The relation of eye movements during sleep to dream activity. *Journal of Experimental Psychology, 53,* 339.

DENT, J.K. (1978). *Exploring the psycho-social therapies through the personalities of effective therapists.* DHEW Publication No. (ADM) 77–527. Washington, D.C. U.S. Government Printing Office.

DEUTSCH, C.J. (1985). A survey of therapists' personal problems and treatment. *Professional Psychology: Research and Practice, 16,* (2), 305–315.

*DOLLARD, J. & MILLER, N.E. (1950). *Personality and Psychotherapy: An Analysis in Terms of Learning, Thinking and Culture.* New York: McGraw-Hill.

DUGGER, J.G. (1975). *The New Professional: Introduction for the Human Services Mental Health Worker.* Monterey, CA: Brooks/Cole Publishing Co.

DULLEA, G. (1983). Therapists' decor: Do the patients count? *Style, The New York Times,* July 4, 1983, p. 16.

EPSTEIN, S. & SMITH, R. (1957). Thematic apperception, Rorschach content, and ratings of attractiveness of women as measures of sex drive. *Journal of Consulting and Clinical Psychology, 21,* 473–478.

EVERSTINE, L., EVERSTINE, D., HEYMANN, G., TRUE, R., FREY, D., JOHNSON, H., & SEIDEN, R. (1980). Privacy and confidentiality in psychotherapy. *American Psychologist, 35,* 828–840.

EYSENCK, H.J. (1978). An exercise in mega-silliness. *American Psychologist, 33,* 517.

*FABRIKANT, B. (1984). History of psychotherapy. In Corsini, R.J. (Ed.) *Encyclopedia of Psychology,* Vol. 3, pp. 184–186. New York: John Wiley & Sons.

FARBER, B.A. (1983). The effects of psychotherapeutic practice upon psychotherapists. *Psychotherapy: Theory, Research, and Practice, 20,* 2, 174–181.

FARBER, B.A. (1985). Clinical psychologists' perceptions of psychotherapeutic work. *The Clinical Psychologist, 38,* (1), 10–13.

FARBER, B.A. & HEIFETZ, L.J. (1981). The satisfactions and stresses of psychotherapeutic work: A factor analytic study. *Professional Psychology, 12,* (5), 621–630.

FEIFEL, H. (Ed.) (1959). *The Meaning of Death.* New York: McGraw-Hill.

*FIEDLER, F.E. (1951). A comparison of therapeutic relationships in psychoanalytic, nondirective and Adlerian therapy. *Journal of Consulting Psychology, 14,* 436–445.

FIELDS, M. (1985). The analytic alliance: Pre-empathetic interventions with withdrawn narcissistic patients. *Psychotherapy, 22,* (3), 572–582.

*FINKLE, N.J. (1984). History of psychotherapy. In Corsini, R.J. (Ed.) *Encyclopedia of Psychology,* Vol 2. New York: John Wiley & Sons.

FISHER, L.S. (1986). You are summoned. *APA Monitor,* October, 1986, p. 3.

FLEISCHER, J. & WISSLER, A. (1985). The therapist as patient: Special problems and considerations. *Psychotherapy, 22,* (3), 587–594.

FLETCHER, G.J.O. (1984). Psychology and common sense. *American Psychologist, 39,* (3), 203–213.

*FRANK, J.D. (1961). *Persuasion and Healing.* Baltimore: The Johns Hopkins Press.

*FRANK, J.D. (1979). The present status of outcome studies. *Journal of Consulting and Clinical Psychology, 47,* (2), 310–316.

FRANKL, V.E. (1960). Paradoxical intention: A logotherapeutic technique. *American Journal of Psychotherapy, 14,* 520–535.

FREUD, S. (1906). My views on the part played by sexuality in the aetiology of the neuroses. In Löwenfeld, A. (Ed.) *Sexualleben und Nerven Leiden,* IVte Auflage.

FREUD, S. (1912). The dynamics of the transference. *Zentralblatt* für psychoanalyse, Vienna. In Jones, E. (Ed.) *Collected Papers* (Vol. 2), 1959. New York: Basic Books.

*FREUD, S. (1960). *A General Introduction to Psychoanalysis.* New York: Washington Square Press.

FREUD, S. (1962). Creative writers and daydreaming. In Strachey, J. (Ed.) *The Standard Edition of the Complete Psychological Works of Sigmund Freud* (Vol. 9). London: Hogarth Press.

FREUD, S. (1968/1901). The psychopathology of everyday life. In Strachey, J. (Ed.) *The Standard Edition of the Complete Psychological Works of Sigmund Freud* (Vol. 6). London: Hogarth Press.

FREUDENBERGER, H.J. (1983). Hazards of psychotherapeutic practice. *Psychotherapy in Private Practice, 1,* (1), 83–89.

FREUDENBERGER, H. (1985). Impaired clinicians: Coping with "burnout." In: Keller, P. & Ritt, L. (Eds.) *Innovations in Clinical Practice: A Source Book.* Sarasota, FL: Professional Resource Exchange, Inc.

FRIEDLANDER, S.R., DYE, N.W., COSTELLO, R.M. & KOBOS, J.C. (1984). A developmental model for teaching and learning in psychotherapy supervision. *Psychotherapy, 21,* (2), 189–196.

FROMKIN, V.A. (1973). Slips of the tongue. *Scientific American, 229,* (6), 110–116.

*FROMM-REICHMANN, F. (1950). *Principles of Intensive Psychotherapy.* Chicago: University of Chicago Press.

GARFIELD, S.L. & KURTZ, R. (1976). Clinical psychologists in the 1970's. *American Psychologist, 31,* 1–9.

GELBORT, K.R. & WINER, J.L. (1985). Fear of success and fear of failure: A multi trait-multimethod validation study. *Journal of Personality and Social Psychology, 48,* (4), 1009–1014.

*GENDLIN, E.T. (1971). A theory of personality change. In Mahrer, A.R. & Pearson, L. (Eds.) *Creative Developments in Psychotherapy,* Vol. I. Cleveland: The Press of Case Western University.

GIL-ADI, D. & NEWMAN, F.L. (1984). Patient information and its use by therapists of differing theoretical orientation. *Psychotherapy, 21,* (4), 479–481.

GLASS, G.V. & KIEGL, R.M.V. (1983). An apology for research integration in the study of psychotherapy. *Journal of Consulting and Clinical Psychology, 51,* (1), 28–41.

GOLEMAN, D. (1984a). Analysis: The use and misuse of hidden meanings. *Science Times. The New York Times,* June 5, 1984.

GOLEMAN, D. (1984b). Do dreams really contain important secret meanings? *Science Times, The New York Times,* July 10, pp. 17, 19.

GOLEMAN, D. (1984c). Therapists find many achievers fear they are fakes. *Science Times, The New York Times,* Sept. 11, pp. 17, 19.

GOLEMAN, D. (1985a). Is analysis testable as science after all? *Science Times, The New York Times,* January 22, pp. 19, 22.

GOLEMAN, D. (1985b). Pressure mounts for analysts to prove theory is scientific. *Science Times, The New York Times,* January 15, pp. 15, 18–19.

GOLEMAN, D. (1985c). Social workers vault into a leading role in psychotherapy. *Science Times, The New York Times,* April 20, pp. 17, 20.

GOLEMAN, D. (1985d). Dissatisfied patients urged to consider therapist switch. *Science Times, The New York Times,* July 23, pp. 17, 18.

GREENE, B. (1985). Considerations in the treatment of black patients by white therapists. *Psychotherapy, 22,* (2), 389–393.

GREENSPAN, M. & KULISH, N. M. (1985). Factors in premature termination in long-term psychotherapy. *Psychotherapy, 22,* (1), 83–85.

GUY, J. & SOUDER, J. (1986a). The aging psychotherapist. *The Independent Practitioner, 6,* (4), 26–31.

GUY, J. & SOUDER, J. (1986b). Impact of therapist's illness or accident on psychotherapeutic practice: Review and discussion. *Professional Psychology, 17,* (6), 509–513.

HAAS, L. J., MALOUF, J. L. & MAYERSON, N. H. (1986). Ethical dilemmas in psychological practice: Results of a national survey. *Professional Psychology: Research and Practice, 17,* (4), 316–321.

HADFIELD, J.A. (1954). *Psychological Conflict and Defense.* N.Y.: Harcourt, Brace & Jovanovitch.

*HALL, C.S. (1966). *The Meaning of Dreams.* New York: McGraw-Hill.

*HALL, C.S. (1984). Dreams. In Corsini, R.J. (Ed.) *Encyclopedia of Psychology.* New York: John Wiley & Sons.

HALL, C.S. & VAN DE CASTLE, R.L. (1966). *The Content Analysis of Dreams.* New York: Appleton-Century-Crofts.

HALL, G.G. & MALONEY, H. (1983). Cultural control in psychotherapy with minority clients. *Psychotherapy: Theory, Research, and Practice, 20,* (2), 131–142.

HAMBRECHT, M. (1983). Inappropriate helping behavior and its impact on the identified patient. *Psychotherapy: Theory, Research and Practice, 20,* (4), 494–502.

HARE, R. (1980). A research scale for the assessment of psychopathy in criminal populations. *Personality and Individual Differences, 1,* 111–119.

HARE, R. (1985). Comparison of procedures for the assessment of psychopathy. *Journal of Consulting and Clinical Psychology, 53,* (1), 7–16.

HARITON, E.B. & SINGER, J.L. (1974). Women's fantasies during sexual intercourse. *Journal of Consulting and Clinical Psychology, 21,* 473–478.

*HARPER, R. (1975). *The New Psychotherapies.* Englewood Cliffs, N.J.: Prentice-Hall.

HARVEY, J.H. & PARKS, M.M.V. (Eds.) (1982). *Psychotherapy Research and Behavior Change.* 1981 Master Lectures. Washington D.C.: The American Psychological Association.

HESS, A.K. & HESS K.A. (1983). Psychotherapy supervisor: A survey of internship training practices. *Professional Psychology: Research and Practice, 14,* (4), 504–513.

HOFFMAN, J.J. (1985). Client factors related to premature termination of psychotherapy. *Psychotherapy: Theory, Research, and Practice, 22,* (1), 83–85.

HOLROYD, J. & BOUHOUTSOS, J. (1985). Biased reporting of therapist-patient sexual intimacy. *Professional Psychology: Research and Practice, 16,* (5), 701–709.

HOLROYD, J. & BRODSKY, A. M. (1977). Psychologists' attitudes and practices regarding erotic and non-erotic contact with patients. *American Psychologist, 32,* 843–849.

INMAN, L. (1982). The cost effectiveness of psychotherapy. *The North Carolina Psychologist, 7,* (2), 2–8.

JONES, A. (1985). Psychological functioning in Black Americans: A conceptual guide for use in psychotherapy. *Psychotherapy, 22,* (2), 363–369.

*JONES, E. (1953). *The Life and Work of Sigmund Freud* (Vol. 1). New York: Basic Books.

JONES, E. (1957). *The Life and Work of Sigmund Freud* (Vol. 3). New York: Basic Books, pp. 163–164.

JUNG, C.G. (1964). The state of psychotherapy today. In Jung, C. (Ed.) *Collected Works, 10.* Princeton, NJ: Princeton U. Press.

KARON, B. (1963). The resolution of acute schizophrenia reactions. *Psychotherapy: Theory, Research, and Practice, 1,* 27–43.

KARON, B. (1976). The psychoanalytic treatment of schizophrenia. In Magaro, P. (Ed.) *The Construction of Madness.* New York: Pergamon, 181–212.

KARON, B. (1986). Psychiatrists, psychologists, medication and psychotherapy. *The Psychotherapy Bulletin, 20,* (3), 7–8.

KARON, B. & VANDEN BOS, G. (1970). Experience, medication and the effectiveness of psychotherapy with schizophrenics. *British Journal of Psychiatry, 116,* 427–428.

KARON, B. & VANDEN BOS, G. (1972). The consequences of psychotherapy for schizophrenics. *Psychotherapy: Theory, Research and Practice, 9,* 11–119.

KARON, B. & VANDEN BOS, G. (1974). Thought disorder in schizophrenia, length of hospitalization and clinical status ratings. *Journal of Clinical Psychology, 30,* 264–266.

KARON, B. & VANDEN BOS, G. (1976). Cost analysis for schizophrenic patients treated by psychologist psychotherapists, psychiatric psychotherapists and medication. *Professional Psychology, 7,* 107–111.

*KARON, B. & VANDEN BOS, G. (1981). *Psychotherapy of Schizophrenia: The Treatment of Choice.* New York: Aronson.

KERCHER, G. & SMITH, D. (1985). Reframing paradoxical psychotherapy. *Psychotherapy: Theory, Research and Practice, 22,* (4), 786–792.

*KERNBERG, O. (1975). *Borderline Conditions and Pathological Narcissism.* New York: Jason Aronson.

KNAPP, S. & VANDECREEK, L. (1983). Malpractice risks with suicidal patients. *Psychotherapy: Theory, Research and Practice, 20,* (3), 274–280.

KNIGHT, R. P. (1953). Borderline states. *Bulletin of the Menninger Clinic, 17,* (1), 1–12.

KOBOCOW, B., McGUIRE, J.M. & BLAU, B. (1983). The influence of confidential conditions on self-disclosure of early adolescents. *Professional Psychology: Research and Practice, 14,* (4), 435–443.

*KOHUT, H. (1977). *The Restoration of the Self.* New York: International Universities Press.

KOHUT, H. & WOLF, E. (1978). The disorders of the self and their treatment: An outline. *International Journal of Psychoanalysis, 59,* 413–425.

KÜBLER-ROSS, E. (1969). *On Death and Dying.* New York: Macmillan Co.

LAMB, D. (1985). A time-frame model of termination in psychotherapy. *Psychotherapy, 22,* (3), 604–609.

LAMBERT, M.J., CHRISTENSEN, E.R. & DeJULIO (Eds.) (1983). *The Assessment of Psychotherapy Outcome.* New York: Wiley.

LANSFORD, E. (1986). Weakenings and repairs of the working alliance in short-term psychotherapy. *Professional Psychology: Research and Practice, 17,* (4), 364–366.

LAPKIN, B. (1985). Modifications in the psychoanalytic treatment of adults who "act out." *Psychotherapy, 22,* (3), 655–661.

LARKE, J. (1985). Compulsory treatment: Some practical methods of treating the mandated client. *Psychotherapy, 22,* (2), 262–268.

LAZARUS, L. (1982). Brief psychotherapy of narcissistic disturbances. *Psychotherapy: Theory, Research and Practice, 19,* (21), 228–236.

LEO, J. (1985a). A madness in their method. *Time,* Sept. 30, p. 78.

LEO, J. (1985b). A therapist in every corner. *Time,* Dec. 23, p. 59.

LEVINE, J.L., STOLZ, J.A. & LACKS, P. (1983). Preparing psychotherapy clients: Rationale and suggestions. *Professional Psychology: Research and Practice, 14,* (3), 317–322.

*MAHL, G.F. (1971). *Psychological Conflict and Defense.* N.Y.: Harcourt, Brace & Jovanovitch.

*MARTIN, D.G. (1971). *Introduction to Psychotherapy.* Belmont, CA: Brooks/Cole.

MARTIN, E. & SCHURTMAN (1985). Termination anxiety as it affects the therapist. *Psychotherapy, 22,* (1), 92–96.

MAYS, V. (1985). The Black American and psychotherapy: The dilemma. *Psychotherapy, 22,* (2), 379–388.

MOREAULT, D. & FOLLINGSTAD, D.R. (1978). Sexual fantasies of females as a function of sex guilt and experimental response cues. *Journal of Consulting and Clinical Psychology, 46,* 1385–1393.

MORTIMER, R.L. & SMITH, W.T. (1983). The use of the psychological test report in setting the focus of psychotherapy. *Journal of Personality Assessment, 47,* (2), 134–138.

MOTLEY, M. (1987). What I meant to say. *Psychology Today, 21,* (2), 24–28.

MUEHLEMAN, T., PICKENS, B.K. & ROBINSON, F. (1985). Informing clients about the limits to confidentiality, risks and their rights: Is self-disclosure inhibited? *Professional Psychology: Research and Practice, 16,* (3), 385–397.

MUENSTERBERG, H. (1909). *Psychotherapy.* New York: Moffat, Yard and Co.

NORCROSS, J.C. & PROCHASKA, J.O. (1982). A national survey of clinical psychologists: Characteristics and activities. *The Clinical Psychologist, 35,* (2), 1, 5–8.

NORCROSS, J. C. & PROCHASKA, J. O. (1986a). Psychotherapist heal thyself - I. The psychological distress and self-change of psychologists, counselors and lay persons. *Psychotherapy, 23,* (1), 102–114.

NORCROSS, J. C. & PROCHASKA, J. O. (1986b). Psychotherapist heal thyself - II. The self-initiated and therapy-facilitated change of psychological distress. *Psychotherapy, 23,* (3), 345–356.

*NORCROSS, J.C. & WOGAN, M. (1983). American psychotherapists of diverse persuasions: Characteristics, theories, practices and clients. *Professional Psychology: Research and Practice, 14,* (4), 529–539.

*O'CONNELL, S. (1983). The placebo effect and psychotherapy. *Psychotherapy: Theory, Research and Practice, 20,* (3), 337–345.

OGG, E. (1981). *The Psychotherapies Today.* New York: Public Affairs Pamphlets (381 Park Ave. South, New York, N.Y. 10016).

PAPPO, MARICE (1983). Fear of success: The construction and validation of a measuring instrument. *Journal of Personality Assessment, 47,* (1), 36–41.

PATSIOKAS, A. T. & CLUM, G. (1985). Effects of psychotherapeutic strategies in the treatment of suicide attempters. *Psychotherapy, 22,* (2), 281–290.

PEKARIK, G. (1985). The effects of employing different termination classification criteria in dropout research. *Psychotherapy, 22,* (1), 86–91.

PENNEBAKER, J. & O'HEERON, R. (1984). Confiding in others and illness rate among spouses of suicide and accidental death victims. *Journal of Abnormal Psychology, 93,* (4), 473–476.

PETERSON, A.O.D. (1957). A factor analysis of therapists: An exploratory investigation of therapeutic biases. *Dissertation Abstracts, 17,* (6), 2.

PETRIE, K. & CHAMBERLAIN, K. (1983). Hopelessness and social desirability as moderating variables in predicting suicidal behavior. *Journal of Consulting and Clinical Psychology, 51,* (4), 485–487.

PIPER, W.E., DEBBANE, E.G., BIENVENUE, J.P. & GARRANT, J. (1984). A comparative study of four forms of psychotherapy. *Journal of Consulting and Clinical Psychology, 52,* 268–279.

POPE, K. (1985). The suicidal client: Guidelines for assessment and treatment. *California State Psychologist, 20,* (5), 3–7.

PRINZHORN, H. (1932). *Psychotherapy: Its Nature, Assumptions and Limitations.* London: Jonathan Cape.

PROCHASKA, J.O. & DiCLEMENTE, C.C. (1983). Stages & processes of self-change of smoking. *Journal of Consulting and Clinical Psychology, 51,* (3), 390.

PROCHASKA, J.O. & NORCROSS, J.C. (1983). Contemporary psychotherapists: A national survey of characteristics, practices, orientations, and attitudes. *Psychotherapy: Theory, Research, and Practice, 20,* (2), 161–173.

PROCTOR, E.K. & ROSEN, A. (1983). Structure in therapy: A conceptual analysis. *Psychotherapy: Theory, Research and Practice, 20,* (2), 202–207.

PROCTOR, E.K. & ROSEN, A. (1983). Influence of psychotherapy research on clinical practice: An experimental survey. *Journal of Counseling and Clinical Psychology, 51,* (5), 718–720.

RANDO, T. (1985). Creating therapeutic rituals in the psychotherapy of the bereaved. *Psychotherapy, 22,* (2), 236–240.

RAPPAPORT, P.S. (1982). *Value for Value Psychotherapy.* New York: Praeger.

*REICH, A. (1960). Pathological forms of self-esteem regulation. *Psychoanalytic Study of the Child, 15,* 228–232. New York: International Universities Press.

REICH, W. (1949). *Character Analysis.* 3rd Ed. New York: Orgone Institute Press.

RIESS, B.F. (1967). Changes in patient income comcomitant with psychotherapy. *International Mental Health Research Newsletter, 9,* (3), 1–4.

ROBERTSON, M. (1984). Teaching psychotherapy in an academic setting. *Psychotherapy, 21,* (2), 209–212.

ROGERS, C.R. (1942). *Counseling and Psychotherapy.* Boston: Houghton Mifflin.

ROGERS, C.R. (1951). *Client-Centered Therapy.* Boston: Houghton Mifflin.

*ROGERS, C.R. (1954). Introduction, in Rogers, C.R. & Dymond, R.F. (Eds.) *Psychotherapy and Personality Change.* Chicago: University of Chicago Press.

*ROGERS, C.R. (1961). *On Becoming a Person.* Boston: Houghton Mifflin.

ROOT, M. (1985). Guidelines for facilitating therapy with Asian-American clients. *Psychotherapy, 22,* (2), 349–356.

ROSENBAUM, R.L. & HOROWITZ, M.J. (1983). Motivation for psychotherapy: A factorial and conceptual analysis. *Psychotherapy: Theory, Research and Practice, 20,* (3), 346–354.

ROSSNER, J. (1983). *August.* New York: Warner Books.

ROTH, S. (1985). Psychotherapy with lesbian couples. *Journal of Marital and Family Therapy, 11,* (3), 273–286.

RUBIN, S. (1985). The resolution of bereavement: A clinical focus on the relationship to the deceased. *Psychotherapy, 22,* (2), 231–235.

SALES, B. (Ed.) (1981). *The Trial Process.* New York: Plenum Press.

SCHMITT, J.P. (1985). Client-assumed responsibility: A basis for contingent and noncontingent therapeutic responding. *Professional Psychology: Research and Practice, 16,* (2), 286–295.

SCHROEDER, M., SCHROEDER, K. & HARE, R. (1983). Generalizability of a checklist for assessment of psychopathy. *Journal of Consulting Psychology, 51,* (4), 511–516.

*SCHULMAN, B.H. (1984). Adlerian psychotherapy. In Corsini, R.J. (Ed.) *Encyclopedia of Psychology,* Vol. 1. New York: John Wiley & Sons.

SCHWITZGEBEL, R. L. & SCHWITZGEBEL, R. K. (1980). *Law and Psychological Practice.* New York: John Wiley.

SERGEANT, M & COHEN, L. (1983). Influence of psychotherapy research on clinical practice: An experimental survey. *Journal of Counseling and Clinical Psychology, 51,* (5), 718–720.

SHAPIRO, D. (1984). *Psychological Evaluation and Expert Testimony.* New York: Van Nostrand Reinhold.

*SHERMAN, A.R. (1973). *Behavior Modification: Theory and Practice.* Monterey, CA: Brooks/Cole Publishing Co.

*SHNEIDMAN, E. (1973). *Deaths of Man.* New York: Quadrangle.

SHNEIDMAN, E. (1980). *Voices of Death.* New York: Harper & Row.

*SHNEIDMAN, E. (1985). *Definition of Suicide.* New York: John Wiley & Sons.

SILVERMAN, L.H. & WEINBERGER, J. (1985). Mommy and I are one. *American Psychologist, 40,* (12), 1296–1308.

SLAVSON, S.R. (1943). *An Introduction to Group Psychotherapy.* New York: The Commonwealth Fund.

*SMITH, M.L. & GLASS, G.V. (1977). Meta-analysis of psychotherapy outcome studies. *American Psychologist, 32,* 752–760.

SNYDER, W.U. (1947). *Casebook of Non-Directive Counseling.* Boston: Houghton Mifflin Co.

*SORENSON, R.L., GORSUCH, R.L. & MINTZ, J. (1985). Moving targets: Patients changing complaints during psychotherapy. *Journal of Consulting and Clinical Psychology, 53,* (1), 49–54.

SPITZER, R.L. & KLEIN, D.L. (Eds.) (1977). *Evaluation of Psychological Therapies.* Baltimore: The Johns Hopkins University Press.

*STERN, R.M. & RAY, W.J. (1977). *Biofeedback.* Homewood, IL: Dow-Jones-Irwin Publishers.

STILES, W.B. (1980). Measurement of the impact of psychotherapy sessions. *Journal of Consulting and Clinical Psychology, 48,* (2), 176–185.

*STRUPP, H.H. & HADLEY, S.W. (1977). A model of mental health and therapeutic outcomes. *American Psychologist, 32,* 187–196.

STUART, R.B. (1970). *Trick or Treatment.* Champaign, IL: Research Press.

SUE, D.W. (1981). *Counseling and the Culturally Different: Theory & Practice.* New York: John Wiley.

SURAN, B. & SHERIDAN, E. (1985). Management of burnout: Training psychologists in professional life span perspectives. *Professional Psychology: Research and Practice, 16,* (6), 741–752.

TAYLOR, L., ADELMAN, H.S. & KASER-BOYD, N. (1985). Exploring minors' reluctance and dissatisfaction with psychotherapy. *Professional Psychology: Research and Practice, 16,* (3), 418–425.

TELCH, M.J. (1981). The present status of outcome studies: A reply to Frank. *Journal of Consulting and Clinical Psychology, 49,* 472–475.

TOLSON, E.R. (1984). Psychiatric social work. In Corsini, R.J. *Encyclopedia of Psychology,* Vol. 3. New York: John Wiley & Sons.

TUMA, A. H., MAY, P.R., YALE, C., & FORSYTHE, A. B. (1978). Therapist experience, general clinical ability and treatment outcome in schizophrenia. *Journal of Consulting and Clinical Psychology, 46,* (5), 1120–1126.

TURKINGTON, C. (1986). Impaired psychologists. *APA Monitor, 17,* (11), 10.

UYEDA, M.K. & DELEON, P. (1984). HMO's: Psychologists in medicine. *Public Service Psychology,* Winter 1984, p. 2.

VANDEN BOS, G. (1980). *Psychotherapy: Practice, Research, Policy.* Beverly Hills, CA: Sage Publications.

VANDEN BOS, G.R. & KARON, B.P. (1971). Pathogenesis: A new therapist personality dimension related to therapeutic effectiveness. *Journal of Personality Assessment, 35,* 252–260.

*WALLACH, M.S. & STRUPP, H.H. (1964). Dimensions of psychotherapists' activity. *Journal of Consulting Psychology, 2,* 120–125.

WIDGER, T.A. & RINALDI, M. (1983). An acceptance of suicide. *Psychotherapy: Theory, Research and Practice, 20,* (3), 263–273.